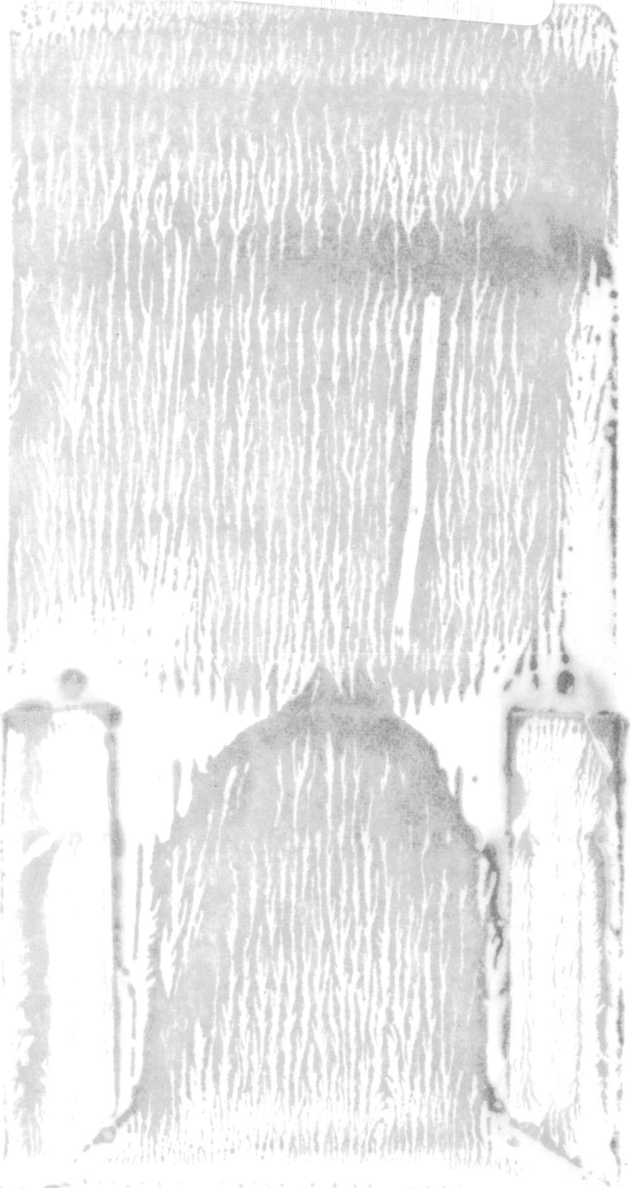

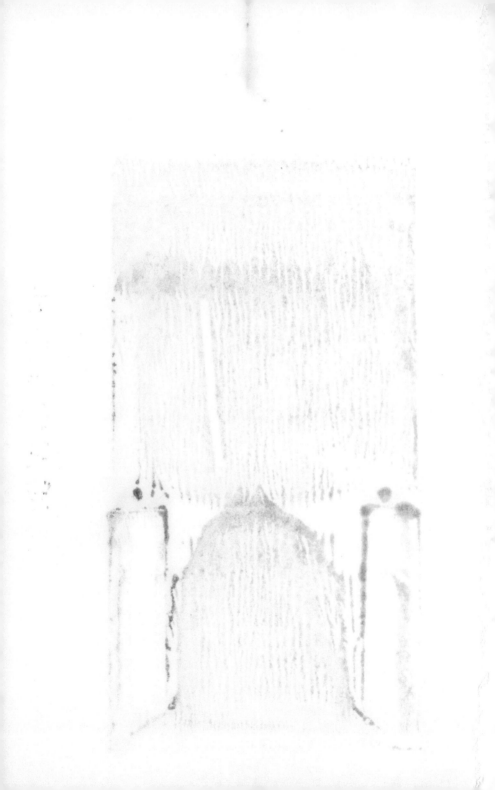

THE
EXPATRIATE PERSPECTIVE

ALSO BY HAROLD T. MCCARTHY

Henry James: The Creative Process

THE EXPATRIATE PERSPECTIVE

American Novelists and the Idea of America

Harold T. McCarthy

Rutherford • Madison • Teaneck
Fairleigh Dickinson University Press
London: Associated University Presses

Associated University Presses, Inc.
Cranbury, New Jersey 08512

Associated University Presses
108 New Bond Street
London W1Y OQX, England

Library of Congress Cataloging in Publication Data

McCarthy, Harold T
The expatriate perspective.

Bibliography: p.
1. American fiction—History and criticism.
2. Americans in Europe. I. Title.
PS362.M3 816′ .03 72–418
ISBN 0–8386–1150–8

First printing February, 1974
Second printing April, 1975

PRINTED IN THE UNITED STATES OF AMERICA

Contents

Acknowledgments

I wish to thank the following editors, publishers, and literary executors for having given me permission to quote from published works:

American Literary Realism, 1870–1910, Clayton L. Eichelberger, Editor, for permission to use, in revised form, "Henry James and the American Aristocracy," *American Literary Realism, 1870–1910* 4 (Winter 1971).

American Literature, Arlin Turner, Editor, for permission to use, in revised form, "Richard Wright: The Expatriate as Native Son," *American Literature* 44, no. 1.

American Quarterly, Murray G. Murphey, Editor, for permission to use, in revised form, "Henry Miller's Democratic Vistas," *American Quarterly* 23, no. 2. Copyright, 1971, Trustees of the University of Pennsylvania.

Arizona Quarterly, Albert F. Gegenheimer, Editor, for permission to use, in revised form, "Mark Twain's Pilgrim's Progress: *The Innocents Abroad,*" *Arizona Quarterly* 26, no. 3 (Autumn 1970). Copyright by *Arizona Quarterly.*

Studi Americani, Agostino Lombardo, Editor, for permission to use, in revised form, "Hawthorne's Dialogue with Rome: *The Marble Faun,* Studi Americani, 14 (Roma, 1968).

Beacon Press, for permission to quote from James Baldwin, *Notes of a Native Son,* 1955. (Rights exclusive of those held by Michael Joseph, Ltd.)

Jonathan Cape, Ltd., on behalf of the Executors of the Ernest Hemingway Estate, for permission to quote from Ernest Hemingway, *Green Hills of Africa,* 1935. (Rights exclusive of those held by Charles Scribner's Sons.)

Dial Press, for permission to quote from James Baldwin, *Nobody Knows My Name,* 1961. (Rights exclusive of those held by Tria French Enterprises, Unltd.)

Grove Press, for permission to quote from Henry Miller, *Black Spring,* 1963. Reprinted by permission of Grove Press, Inc. Copyright © 1963 by Grove Press, Inc. (Rights exclusive of those held by Agence Hoffman.)

Harcourt Brace Jovanovich, Inc., for permission to quote from E.E. Cummings, *Poems 1923–1954,* 1954. (Rights exclusive of those held by MacGibbon & Kee, Ltd.)

Harper & Row, Inc., for permission to quote from Richard Wright, *The Outsider,* 1953, and from Mark Twain, *The Innocents Abroad,* Vols. 1 and 2 in *The Writings of Mark Twain,* The Uniform Edition, Harper & Brothers, 1899–1910.

Agence Hoffman, for permission to quote from Henry Miller, *Black Spring,* 1963. (Rights exclusive of those held by Grove Press.)

Liveright Publishing Corporation, for permission to quote from E. E. Cummings, *The Enormous Room,* 1934.

MacGibbon & Kee, Ltd., for permission to quote from E.E. Cummings, *The Complete Poems of E.E. Cummings,* vol. 1.

The Midwest Quarterly, Rebecca Patterson, Editor-in-Chief, for permission to use, in revised form, "Melville's *Redburn* and the City," *The Midwest Quarterly* 12, no. 4 (July 1971).

October House Inc., for permission to quote from *E.E. Cummings: A Miscellany Revised,* Edited, with an Introduction and Notes, by George J. Firmage, Copyright © 1958, 1965 by George J. Firmage. Reprinted by permission of October House Inc.

Ohio State University Press, for permission to quote from *The Marble Faun,* vol. 4, *The Centenary Edition of the Works of Nathaniel Hawthorne,* 1962.

University of Oklahoma Press, for permission to quote from Daniel Morley McKeithan, ed., *Traveling with the Innocents Abroad: Mark Twain's Original Reports from Europe and the Holy Land,* Copyright 1958 by the University of Oklahoma Press.

G. P. Putnam's Sons, for permission to quote from the Mohawk Edition of *The Works of James Fenimore Cooper,* 1895–1900.

Paul R. Reynolds, Inc., for permission to quote from Richard Wright, *Black Power,* 1954, and *Pagan Spain,* 1956.

Russell & Russell, Inc., for permission to quote from Herman Melville, *Redburn, His First Voyage,* vol. 5 of *The Works of Herman Melville* [1922–1924] (New York: Russell & Russell, 1963).

Charles Scribner's Sons, for permission to quote from Ernest Hemingway, *Green Hills of Africa,* 1935. (Rights exclusive of those held by Jonathan Cape, Ltd.) Also, to Charles Scribner's Sons for permission to quote from the New York Edition of *The Novels and Tales of Henry James,* 1907–1917, and from Percy Lubbock, ed. *The Letters of Henry James,* 1920; permission to quote from these works has also been granted by Alexander R. James, Literary Executor.

Tria French Enterprises, Unltd., for permission to quote from James Baldwin, *Nobody Knows My Name,* 1961. (Rights exclusive of those held by The Dial Press.) Reprinted by courtesy of the author.

Introduction

The Expatriate Perspective is a critical discussion of works by American writers that afford significant perceptions of what it means to be an American. These perceptions came about as a result of the writers' having discovered through living in the countries from which America chiefly derived its cultural heritage the extent to which America had evolved a different culture from that of the parent countries and the ways in which Americans were a distinctively different "social animal." The works discussed are part of the process by which these American writers came to a realization of the nature of their Americanism. In the process of self-discovery, they had to acknowledge the differences, sometimes amounting to direct opposition, between the actualities of life in America and the shaping idea of America that had kept alive for successive generations of Americans the belief in their country as a Promised Land.

While I have relied heavily upon biographical and historical material, my central concern has been with each author as a literary artist and with his revised vision of his American self as it is rendered in imaginative form. All the works dealt with have deep autobiographical elements, even though most of them are novels and a few have been placed by their authors in the category of romance. Indeed, it might be said that these authors have all preferred fiction to autobiography as a means of expressing the more freely and accurately their personal sense of the truth of things. Other American writers than those represented here have of course had their vision of America affected by living in Europe and have used their new perceptions in works of fiction; however, a selection had to be made, and it seems to me that the novelists discussed here are the ones who have used a European perspective to deal most searchingly with the reality and the shaping idea of America.

Viewed purely as forms of the novel, these works attest to the rich variety of the art of fiction in America and to the degree to which the absence of a strong literary tradition fostered the intense individuality of American artists. In the case of James Fenimore Cooper the conventional historical romance is represented—but conceived by Cooper in such a way as to have a realistic purpose thoroughly at odds with the intention of the traditional historical romance. Melville, Cummings, Hemingway, and Baldwin employ a conventional first-person narrative technique. This is done, however, in a characteristically American way in that the deepest interest of the work centers upon the consciousness of the narrator himself in the act not only of perceiving the meaning of his experience but of trying to establish a personal relationship with the universe.

While Hawthorne as "third person" narrates his Roman romance, his personal voice continually breaks through the tissue of the fiction, and the pull and tug of conflicting American values is felt repeatedly as his voice argues with itself from the lips of his characters. Twain's *Innocents* has all the immediacy of a series of firsthand reports dashed off for the American newspaper public; but it is in fact the highly artful result of his personal observations and the reports of his friends, along with facts and descriptions culled from guidebooks, invented characters, burlesque dialogue, and fanciful settings. It is, in short, an epistolary, picaresque tale, dreading perhaps above all else to appear "well-made." Despite the artful artlessness of his persona, however, Twain's voice can at times be heard raising those final questions that are a form of prayer.

James and Miller illustrate well how two authors with similar intentions can produce work that appears to have nothing in common but the language—and not entirely that. Each was concerned to produce his truest personal sense of his experience and to do so in a form that would correspond at all points to his meaning. Each wanted his art to possess the organic interrelations of life. But where James's work conveys the sense of the deep divisions of a culture wholly comprehended in a sensitive, lucid intelligence, Miller's work conveys, as he intended, the sense of a sick, dying culture as witnessed by a self convinced of its individual health and the integrity of its joyful spirit.

In order to place this view of American life in historical perspective, I chose novels relating to the three decades before and the three after the Civil War and to the decades before and after the two World Wars. While all the works have the unifying theme of an American's reassessment of his Americanism as a result of his experience of Europe, it is evident as one proceeds from work to work that, in addition to the variable of the author himself, America and Europe are never the same thing to different authors. Each came to Europe with his own assumptions, had to make his individual revaluations of Europe as a result of actual experience, and turned again home to a rapidly changing America.

On departing for Europe, Cooper thought of himself as fixed as a star in the banner of his Americanism and prepared to spread the gospel of democracy to the heathen of feudalistic Europe. The impetus of his original assumptions carried him a long way, but the political romances he wrote while in Europe disclose his responsiveness to the appeal of some of Europe's oldest traditions and his gradual recognition that America was quite far from being the wholesome democratic republic proclaimed in *Notions of the Americans,* his first effort to convert the heathen. His years in Europe spanned the years of Jackson's presidency with their sweeping social changes as well as years when the forces in several European nations were clearly gathering toward revolution and war. Melville was writing in a New York that was receiving the first tidal wave of Irish refugees from conditions brought about by the murderous system of human exploitation that he had witnessed at firsthand while a young sailor in Liverpool. Hawthorne, after the political brutalities of the Franklin Pierce presidential campaign, thought to escape to the haven of a well-paying consulship in Liverpool only to find American troubles hammering on his door. When he sought his Arcadia, he found there vast dimensions to his narrow Salem past. The bit of transcendentalist sky he could glimpse through the dome of the Pantheon reassured him, but the news from America made him consider an apocalypse as a possible blessing.

Henry James had been to Europe for prolonged periods during his childhood and youth, but the idea of becoming a permanent resident abroad was not seriously considered by him until his efforts to find a place for himself in American society as a writer during the Civil War years and during the period following his first post-Civil War visit to Europe made it crystal clear to him that his future as both man and artist lay in Europe. Even then he did not plan any permanent exile. Only gradually did he settle into the habit of London, and his extensive circle of friends in England and on the Continent always included great numbers of Americans. He was constantly visited by relatives and friends from America; his correspondence with Americans flowed copiously back and forth; and his primary audience and market remained American. James does double duty in this study because he so emphatically dominates his era as a literary artist and because his international theme falls into an early and a late category. The early category includes the works from *Roderick Hudson* through *The Portrait of a Lady*; the late category makes up the novels of his "major phase."

James and Twain have frequently been taken together as the opposed representatives of a European and a native tradition in American life. This opposition, it seems to me, is at best superficial, and just as James saw the strengths and the limitations of the emergent native American character as well as the virtues and evils of the use made of European traditions by Americans, Twain demonstrates in *Innocents* his awakening to a trust in his native self and to the fact that the eastern American culture he had so much esteemed was mostly façade, a mockery of the complex, beautiful, ugly Old World culture with which it presumed to identify itself. Like James, Twain was to turn again and again to Europe for the cultural context that would throw his rendering of American character into meaningful relief. He visited Europe frequently and considered he had found his permanent home in a villa outside Florence until the death of Livy brought his dream to an end. No American writer ever had more intensely ambivalent attitudes toward American culture than Twain, and his knowledge of European life must have played a vital role in his arriving at the capacity to isolate the very essence of Americanness in his writing (it was for the Paleface readers of *The Atlantic* that he was inspired to write the great chapters of *Life on the Mississippi*) and to comprehend in *Huck Finn* the blindly conflicting drives of old authority and new freedom in American life.

Cummings, Hemingway, and Miller represent to a degree three different Americas. Cummings was a patrician of Cambridge, Mass. ("Dear old Cambridge. Dear old 'Mass.,' " as James would say); Hemingway was of the upper-middle-class mid-West; and Miller from working-class Brooklyn. All three found themselves as writers only through their experience of Europe. They found in that land not the grim, iron-walled conventions that made Europe loom like a City of Dis to Cooper and Melville, but a sense of freedom from conformist and bureaucratic pressures in American life, a sense of community in which the way of the artist was held dear, and a society so marked by its hereditary forms that, odd but true, it facilitated original departures. Tradition made it possible to give meaning and direction to change.

All three men found themselves most deeply drawn to those areas of European social life which had least changed through the centuries, to the warm vitality of the artisan and the peasant, the kind of people who in American life would have taken on a sameness and anonymity along with their higher standard of living, and in whom these writers would have found nothing in common and little of interest. Unlike such a man as James, however, who could make his home with the English and live almost as one of them, these writers could experience Europe only as artists and as Americans, using European life to enrich their art and to help define their American culture, but without any real expectation of becoming European themselves.

All of these writers found America changed for the worse upon their return, largely because each had found a way of regarding his country with a critical objectivity and of measuring it and the direction it was taking in terms of what its early promise had been. In titling the sections of this study "Romantic Realists," "American Jacobins," "Neo-Transcendentalists," and "Native Sons," I have sought to indicate certain affinities within each group and significant differences of emphasis from group to group. The titles are also intended to stress a critical interpretation that is in many cases at odds with received opinion.

There are fundamental themes that appear in the work of all these writers and give to their best work a distinctively American quality. I have wished to stress these themes most of all, for they seem to me to constitute a genuine literary tradition. Even though their work may be set in Europe or on the high seas, or be thick with European characters, it is American in its idealistic assumptions: in the freedom from institutional patterns with which it conceives of religion, brotherhood, justice, and individual liberty; in its way of referring all matters to the individual conscience; and in its intuitive confidence that the individual spirit will survive and that civilizations must go to seed. The subdividing stream of American naturalism (to the degree that it is naturalism), however vivid its regionalism or its concern with local and present problems, issues in a superficial literature of theory, of attitudes, even of propaganda, as compared with the literature that issues from the artist as an individual concerned with his personal vision of the reality and myth of America.

Cooper, Melville, and Hawthorne are great romancers; and yet all three in their criticism of America distinguish themselves by their realism. Cooper had a thorough command of American history as well as of the philosophy of American politics, and it was out of this knowledge that he made his assessment of European social systems and then, from his new perspective, of the American democracy. Melville's peculiar excellence was in his ability to probe searchingly into man's metaphysical nature and to express his ontological discoveries in terms of the real, raw life aboard a merchant ship, or a whaler, or a man-of-war. Hawthorne's shadowy allegories prove to have been based on an astute knowledge of psychological processes. I have been concerned with the way in which these romancers, in the light of their European experience, spoke realistically to the subject of the American's society, spirit, and mind. Within the consciousness of each of these men there seems to have existed the image of an ur-American who can never feel himself at ease in any organization, who lives his religion, and who must puzzle out his own *Ethics* in terms of his own experience. The image is "American" because he is the product of ages of civilization and yet is of the wilderness and questions the pressure of any social claim upon his newborn nature.

For many it is still a critical habit to think of Henry James as a Jacobite and not at all as a Jacobin. Yet, far from being in any way an apologist for an old social order *per se* or from wishing to see such an order grafted upon American life, James recognized the vitality of certain traditions in their native context but consistently demonstrated the tragic—or at best the comic—consequences of enclosing the American spirit in European forms. Both James and Twain in their most memorable characters have created anew the ur-American. In their best work they have shown him threatened by what James effectively summed up as "Convention"—form without spirit, cermony lost to its own pomp, money arrogating to itself gentility and grace, society degrading Man. Drawing upon the authority of their personal moral sense, they have sent forth their democratic heroes to battle with the American pseudo-aristocracy, and for both writers Europe has been but an extension of the American battleground. Like Jefferson they could passionately believe that all men are created equal and yet wish to destroy false distinctions as to human worth in order to permit those distinctions to emerge which are true.

The "Pilgrims" in the Holy Land awakened Twain to a sense of reality as dream, a dream that was to darken to the nightmare of *The Mysterious Stranger*. It was the kind of irony reserved for Twain that on his journey to the birthplace of Jesus he should discover the extent to which some of the spiritual leaders of America were without any comprehension of love. Twain moved in his fiction from "the gilded age" of Washington, D.C., to the intimacy of Huck's conscience, searching to give expression to the same theme that occupied James in moving from the "vast, bright Babylon" of Paris to the heart of Maggie Verver—the innocent person silently defying society's massy conventions in an effort to keep love alive at the cost of whatever damnations.

With Cummings, Hemingway, and Miller, it is again a question of the individual. But this time the individual trusts only himself, holds up to the culture an image of its destructiveness, tries to salvage his natural humanity, insists on the meaning of death, and feels himself part of an infinite, eternal Being. For these reasons, I have termed this group the Neo-Transcendentalists. Cummings's *The Enormous Room* and Miller's *Tropic of Cancer* operate as manifestoes in which the "autobiographical-hero" proclaims himself reborn out of a cultural death. He rejoices in his being and in his instinctual life; he discovers civilization to be sick with fear and burdened with its own death. Hemingway, too, felt he had entered upon life for the first time in his first years in Paris, and his stories and novels tell of the death of his "civilized" self and the birth of his transcendental being. He sings his prose-poems to death, is restored continually by immersion in Nature, and yields himself to the great Gulf Stream of being.

Richard Wright and James Baldwin are singularly appropriate as representatives of the post-World War II period, for they speak to our most crucial present dilemma. As native sons they represent an American ethnic stock coeval with the earliest white settlements in America, and they have been accepted as representatives of an indigenous literature. Yet it was only through expatriation that they could feel themselves free of the omnipresent, insidious, coercive myth of the "American Negro" and recover their individual humanity and accept their racial heritage in a true perspective. Only in foreign lands was Wright able to acknowledge the extent to which a culture is vitalized by religious and racial factors for in America his personal experience of these factors had convinced him that they were to be despised and destroyed. For Baldwin it was an amazing discovery to learn that he was, after all, unmistakably an American; that black and white Americans were culturally one people; and that it was the persistence of white Americans in a way of being—a tragically misguided way of being—that continued their neurotic preoccupation with the "American Negro." Baldwin's concepts of the role of the artist and of the relation of the individual to society were far different from Wright's. And yet, by the time of Wright's death, the two were in fact together in their sense of what constituted the permanent values in a culture and of the possibility for changing the deeply rooted metaphors by means of which a nation sought to contain the fear and the love that are ineradicable from man's nature.

Seen in the perspective of all these writers, the facts and forms of America lose their reality, and what remains is America as a creative idea. We circle from the present back to the new, green world of Cooper's Natty Bumppo; to the possibilities of America as imagined by Whitman, Emerson, and Thoreau; to the possible innocence of the protagonists of James and Twain; to the affirmations of man's divinity by writers speaking out of our own bitter, cynical day. And we find ourselves again with the Black and the Young and with all those who believe that they have been dispossessed of a heritage. From their "expatriate" perspective generates anew the idea of America. Those who are lovers, those who have life, will find a tradition from which to nourish their idea in the work of the men who have been the romancers of America.

THE
EXPATRIATE PERSPECTIVE

Part One
THE ROMANTIC REALISTS

Our culture is the predominance of an idea which draws after it this train of cities and institutions. Let us rise into another idea; they will disappear.

—Emerson, "Circles"

1
James Fenimore Cooper: The European Novels

I

When James Fenimore Cooper embarked for Europe with his family in June of 1826, his plans for the European sojourn were far from definite. Perhaps the visit would last a year, perhaps two; mainly he wanted to see something of the European countries and to make those arrangements with the English and French publishers of his writings that would enable him to defeat the literary pirates on both sides of the Atlantic. Far from remaining a detached observer of the European scene and tending to his personal business affairs, Cooper soon found himself actively involved in French politics, a partisan critic of European affairs engaging in print in a public "Finance Controversy," serving as a close advisor to the Marquis de Lafayette, and, as America's prime literary lion, much hunted in the literary salons of London and Paris.

Despite the intense social and political activity, however, he proved himself to be a perceptive and wide-ranging traveler, and he managed all the while to continue his work as a novelist. The contract for *The Prairie* had been assigned before he left the United States, and by the end of the summer he had finished the book in Paris. Within a year he had written *The Red Rover,* and in the summer of 1827 he began *Notions of the Americans Picked up by a Travelling Batchelor,* which was completed about May, 1828. *The Wept of Wish-ton-Wish* was being planned by late October, 1827, and *The Water Witch* was written in Italy in 1829. Sea novels came easily to Cooper, and he might have gone on writing them if only to demonstrate his masterly knowledge of life at sea. They would undoubtedly have continued to demonstrate his sharply realistic grasp of the life about him and his belief that the novel had to blend this pragmatic knowledge with a romantic drama that attached no claim to probability. But his dramatic exposure to European social and political life confronted him at every turn with a realization of how being an American had given him a radically different perspective from that of European political leaders, and so he set about constructing historical romances that would serve as vehicles for the new freight of realistic perceptions he was acquiring daily.

There were more particular incitements. For one, there was the ever-present example and challenge of Sir Walter Scott's romances. Scott's *The Pirate* had first impelled Cooper to demonstrate how a writer who had a thorough, firsthand knowledge of the sea would handle sea-fiction, and so he wrote *The Pilot.* Now he wanted to challenge Scott on a more serious level. He wanted to demonstrate how an American democrat would treat the historical material that Scott had treated as an Old-World aristocrat. The visible evidence of great historic changes was another incitement. The moldering grandeur of the once-splendid Venetian Republic would provide the setting for *The Bravo;* the earth-covered remains of a wall constructed by Roman soldiers to protect their camp from the "heathen" who were dismantling the Roman Republic served as a symbolic image for *The Heidenmauer,* along with the fragments of a medieval castle and abbey; a festival in a Swiss canton, where the visible evidence of archaic, hereditary power and social caste made a travesty of the title of Republic, served as the organizing center of *The Headsman.* In every case the man conditioned by American ideals of what constituted a republic and a democracy chose some episode from Europe's history that afforded the trappings of romance in order to demonstrate not only how false were that period's concepts of republic and democracy but how false were the present age's pretensions—in England, France, Italy, Belgium, Switzerland, and Poland—to provide men with what he took to be their inalienable rights. Over the years when he wrote these novels his European critics drove him again and again to a reexamination of his assumptions about America; his American critics added rancor to the reexamination; the sweeping changes of Jackson's administration gave the reexamination point; and the fact of slavery proved a horror in the path of any apologist for America. All these factors drove Cooper more and more to include America with the reactionary powers under his attack.

As to the historical accuracy of *The Bravo, The Heidenmauer,* and *The Headsman,* Cooper cared very little. For each book he evidently did little historical research and deliberately shuffled his facts about to suit his fictional convenience. Several historical figures are at times merged into one. Actual events are provided with wholly imaginary causes. The handling of doges, barons, and abbots would achieve verisimilitude only on the seacoast of Bohemia. It is not, however, that Cooper was indifferent to history; rather, he would have scorned those readers who expected historical accuracy from historical romance. In his *Recollections of Europe* he described how a French governmental agent spying upon him in the guise of a *littérateur* had asked him if he did not condemn the lack of historical truth in *Ivanhoe,* and how he replied that *Ivanhoe,* as a work of the imagination, had sufficient historical truth to be probable and natural and that was all that was required.[1] What Cooper sought in the historical situation was a metaphor for a universal truth, so that in reading about the past his public would gain insight into the political realities of the day. And he would have agreed with his contemporary Harriet Martineau that "politics are morals," a matter of universal and equal concern.

In a sense, politics was Cooper's business in Europe, since he had sought and obtained a consulship at Lyon from the Adams administration. But he wanted the official appointment solely because it might prove a convenience in traveling and in the handling of correspondence; he hired a Frenchman to handle the duties of the office in Lyon. Still, he was a government official, and this intensified his sense of representing American political ideals and made him a close observer of other American officials whom he frequently encountered. While in Europe he kept up a heavy correspondence with politically well-informed Americans, kept abreast of the newspapers and reviews, and contributed essays on political subjects to publications in France, England, and America. Soon after his arrival in France Cooper sought out the aged Marquis de Lafayette, who was actively engaged in leading the French Republicans, and he rapidly became Lafayette's friend and his advisor on ways of shaping the French political economy to the American pattern. Cooper also associated with leaders of reform movements in other European countries and for a while served as Chairman of The American Committee in Paris to Aid Poland. What is to be noted here is that during his years in Europe Cooper became an exponent of an ideal democracy and republic, in the name of the American example advocating radical changes in European nations, then in time turning on America and its representatives abroad when he found their policies serving to support conservative factions.

The cultural objectives being urged by Cooper upon the French Republicans were not too unlike those sought by such extremists as the followers of Saint-Simon, a founder of the socialist movement. Cooper's political views and actions were such that the French government decided to place him under secret surveillance, and he found himself openly opposing and contradicting United States Embassy officials. In the aftermath of the 1830 July Revolution, with the Doctrinaires working to convert the fruits of the Republican victory into a new aristocracy, Cooper tried to convince French leaders that unless a new Republican ideology were put into effect there was a danger of all being lost that Lafayette had struggled to attain. Anticipating by about fifteen years Karl Marx's argument in *German Ideology* that the rule of a certain class was, in fact, the rule of certain ideas, Cooper tried to persuade the Republicans that they must use their power to secure basic political and economic changes in the nation.

Turning his attention to England, Cooper saw the English aristocracy as terrified by the July Revolution in France because, in his view, the English government was nothing more than a "Monied Corporation," and a popular uprising would cause the bubble of English credit to burst and necessarily bring about the fall of the English form of government.[2] Cooper's use of the term *Monied Corporation* to describe the English government in a letter to Peter Augustus Jay indicates how his mind was equating the action of President Jackson against the bankers who controlled the American treasury with his own attack upon the wealthy aristocrats who controlled European governments. It is in this context of revolutionary fervor that Cooper set about writing his first historical novel, *The Bravo,* which behind its romantic illusion would speak to the exciting political realities of the day.

Along with the romantic interest of Venice itself, the irony of a city-state's being termed a "republic" when in fact it was controlled by a notorious oligarchy determined Cooper's choice of the Venetian Republic at the commencement of the eighteenth century as the time and place of *The Bravo.* The historic situation seemed well adapted to illustrating how, as in England of the 1830s, a privileged group governed the state for its own special interest, believing without question that whatever action was necessary to preserve its private interest was also an action necessary for the welfare of the state. Law, moral principle, human right, all are demonstrated to be of little concern as compared with the rulers securing their special interests—interests that are, of course, identified with the safeguarding of the Republic. Cooper's hero is the common man, the poor and exploited worker. There is, for example, Old Antonio, whose sons have all died in the service of the state and who cannot keep his only grandson from being impressed into the state's galleys. For the son of Senator Gradenigo such service is unthinkable.

To the average American reader of 1831, *The Bravo* must have seemed far closer to gothic romance than to the political realities of his own day—perhaps the more so since "Monk" Lewis had already used the title for one of his own novels. A twentieth-century American reader is in a much better position to appreciate what Cooper was trying to do. Out of his acute perception of the workings of private interests in control of the state, Cooper tried to reproduce the atmosphere of ambiguity, mystery, espionage, and political assassination, which was all a make-believe world to the American innocents of the 1830s. The central character is known as a *bravo,* a hired assassin; he is the one who is suspected by the public of being guilty of various murders. The truth of the matter is that the murders are political assassinations carried out by the state, and the Bravo bears the public suspicion because the state holds his father prisoner. Eventually, at a public trial, the state's judges find the Bravo guilty of a murder that they themselves have carried out. In the terrifying world that Cooper has projected, no one knows how or why the Secret Council will act; governmental agents are everywhere; both day and night, disguises are commonly worn. People mysteriously disappear, yet it is impossible to get a message through to the unknown members of the Council, whose members are masked even to one another. The ultimate *bravo* of the book, the ultimate assassin, is the State.

Americans of Cooper's generation were unfamiliar with the political evil he dramatized in *The Bravo,* that of a strong, central elitist group governing for its own benefit. America's own separation from England had been little more than a sloughing off of the representatives of a foreign power, and there had been no need for any profound rethinking of the premises of government in order to achieve a representative government. By the time Jefferson took office, the political wisdom of a central federation as engineered by Hamilton was taken for granted, although little was done to further it. By the time of Jackson, and especially through Jackson, the government was "by the people" and the era of consecrated individualism was underway. The rising threat to representative government in America was taking the form of private economic groups that sought power and privilege by working through the government rather than by seizing or opposing the federal authority.

The years that Cooper spent in Europe, 1826 to 1833, were years that marked a pronounced change in the direction of American political life. Cooper sensed the change and commented on it before his return, but he did not then imagine the extent to which business organizations (followed in time by farm organizations and labor organizations) would function like the very aristocratic groups he was belaboring, both in their struggle for privileged position and in their alienation from the common interests of the people as a whole. In 1830 Cooper attached to the words *republic, democracy, equality,* and *liberty* meanings defined by a specific political context. Like the Founding Fathers, he assumed that the state was an expression of the moral views of the citizens and that citizenship was a moral, even a divine contract. But for America in the 1830s the center was refusing to hold; Americans were losing the sense of a moral principle binding them politically and of the function of government as an expression of a common ethical relationship. More and more, their ablest leaders took short views. On his return to America Cooper contended to a degree with these matters in *The American Democrat* and in *Homeward Bound* and *Home as Found.* The evil before his eye in 1830 and 1831, however, was the distance of pre-Reform Act England and post-July Revolution France from the American ideal. Still, in attacking European problems through *The Bravo* and *The Heidenmauer* he spoke to problems that were in store for America.

Cooper's basic criticism was of the way in which Europeans conceived of the state. To his American mind, political organization and control were powers to be delegated only by the individual citizens and to be exercised only for their common advantage. The American republic was the great modern example of the triumph of a reasoned approach to government. Even those European states styled "republics" were in fact closed corporations operated for the benefit of a privileged few, albeit the few truly believed that they ruled for the benefit of all. What emerges at once in *The Bravo* is the picture of such an exclusive group ruling for its own benefit but even in its most glaringly selfish acts convinced that it is moved by a concern for the welfare of the Republic.

The Republic, in *The Bravo,* is depicted as not only corrupt but corrupting. The social advantages of the rich and the social deprivations of the poor produce two markedly different classes of men. They look, think, and act so differently that the differences are attributed to nature, to "blood," rather than to social engineering. One is the "natural" ruler-parent, the other the dependent child. "The ignorant and the low are to the state, as children, whose duty it is to obey, and not to cavil," observes a Venetian senator. In his *Notions of the Americans* Cooper thanked God that in America instruction had never been considered dangerous, and he pointed out that "the aggregate of her humanity, intelligence and comfort, compared with her numbers," made America the most civilized nation in the world.[3]

This work was published in 1828, before Cooper had significantly altered his perspective of America, and without doubt he excluded slaves from his calculation. The book's explicit condemnation of slavery, however, leaves no room for doubt as to where Cooper stood on the question of abolishing slavery even before his European experience made him reassess American society and made him painfully aware of how the existence of slavery in America irrefutably compromised in European eyes any claim he might make for the American economy, let alone its democracy and republicanism. A sense of America's great moral fault must have underscored his attack upon the class structure of European nations. To his eyes the bondage of the European peasant, like the bondage of the American slave, was rooted in the economic exploitation of the nation by one limited class, which controlled the government and the forces of production. Slave and peasant could be freed from bondage only by radically altering the economic and political system.

The Bravo shows that the European system of rigid class lines breeds not so much a lack of sympathy as a sense of values in which it is considered natural and inevitable that the poor shall suffer, that the rich must protect themselves from the poor in the interests of both, and that the idea of benefiting the poor at the expense of the rich is an idea both sinful and traitorous, prejudicial to both church and state. The people continue to produce exceptional men, such as Jacopo and Old Antonio, who have all the simple nobility of Cooper's greatest character, Natty Bumppo; and, like Natty, they are hounded by the state. The mass of the people are a manipulated mob. Chapter twenty-two illustrates its epigraph, "We'll follow Cade"; chapter twenty-three shows the rebellious crowd whipped into line and illustrating the epigraph, "A Clifford, a Clifford! We'll follow the king and Clifford." The natural leaders of the people are confined by a cave of ignorance, and their thought is controlled by the grotesque shadows of law and order that their rulers have cast upon the wall. In a direct comment to the reader, Cooper makes it clear that where the governors have an interest in the least separated from that of the governed, justice cannot be pure and the authorities will be biased in their decisions (pp. 384–85).[4]

The rulers of the Venetian Republic see themselves in a context of church and state that they themselves have created. They conceive of themselves as Christian leaders. If enemies of the state must be destroyed, or if the mass of the citizenry must be kept in ignorance, that is how matters are divinely and politically ordered and the interests of the state and church must be served. In other words Cooper was saying that the aristocratic groups in England and France singled out whatever threatened their economic interest as an enemy of the state and then employed the whole machinery of church and state to judge and destroy the threatening force. Under such a system, Cooper pointed out, individual responsibility ceases to exist. Personal conscience is lost to the artifice of the state. "Venice," he wrote, "though ambitious and tenacious of the name of a republic, was, in truth, a narrow, a vulgar, and an exceedingly heartless oligarchy" (p. 144). When one bears in mind Cooper's contemporary target, the judgment is as ruthless as the similar judgment soon to be made on the English and the French governments by Marx and Engels. Hinting broadly at a parallel to be drawn between the powerful financial corporations in America under attack by the Jackson administration and the aristocracy-controlled governments of England and France (the English government was Cooper's primary target), Cooper continued, "It partakes, and it always has partaken, though necessarily tempered by circumstances and the opinions of different ages, of the selfishness of all corporations in which the responsibility of the individual, while his acts are professedly submitted to the temporizing expedients of a collective interest, is lost in the subdivision of numbers" (p. 144).

For Cooper, to label the aristocracy a *corporation* was to identify in a revolutionary manner the true nature of its bond: not blood, but money. To describe Senator Gradenigo, one of the leading rulers and aristocrats of the Venetian Republic, Cooper carefully chose his terms: "he stood in relation to the state as a director of a moneyed institution is proverbially placed in respect to his corporation; an agent of its collective measures, removed from the responsibilities of the man" (p. 82). The name of "Republic" has "been prostituted to the protection and monopolies of privileged classes" (p. 143). The rhetoric of Jacksonian democracy is one of Cooper's more obvious clues to his serious purpose in the novel.

The violence and tragedy of *The Bravo* foreshadow what Cooper felt was immediately in store for Europe. In letters to his friends he left no doubt that revolution and warfare would soon arrive, and he was convinced that aristocrats of several European nations were in league to support one another in crushing the revolts to come. Some seventeen years before the *Communist Manifesto* Cooper wrote, "I have long foreseen that the true contest would be between the Aristocrats and the people, and we are approaching it, in France, rapidly. The people must prevail, but there may be a struggle for it."[5] There was no vision of a workers' paradise in Cooper's, or in Marx's, reflections upon the struggle to come. Rather, in *Recollections,* Cooper described what was to come as a grim and bitter struggle, with one side determined to protect the established order and the other determined to overthrow all that was established "in order to be benefited by the scramble that will follow; and religion, justice, philosophy, and practical good are almost equally remote from the motives of both parties" (p. 312). This was to be the theme of *The Heidenmauer.*

II

As with *The Bravo,* Cooper wanted to treat the historical material of *The Heidenmauer* from a conspicuously democratic point of view, as distinct from the conventional practice, particularly that of Scott, of adopting the point of view of the aristocracy. The democratic point of view sees "society . . . in the act of passing from the influence of one set of governing principles to that of another" (p. 377). While the change is effected with the aid of the peasantry, this class receives no benefit from it; it has merely changed masters. The aristocracy, represented by the Count of Leiningen, joins with the rising middle-class tradesmen, led by Heinrich Frey, to abolish the economic power of the Abbey of Limburg by confiscating its lands and abolishing its right to tax the people. By setting his novel in the period of the Reformation (the story is based upon the destruction of the Abbey of Limburg in 1504), Cooper meant to draw a parallel between that period of upheaval and the ominous unrest of the 1830s. Sweeping and far-from-ominous changes were, he knew, taking place in America, as Jackson's political appointees drove the established bureaucracy out of office, the nomination of the President was about to be democratized, most new states were submitting their constitutions to the people for ratification, and movements were under way to make even some judicial appointments a matter of popular election. Even property qualifications, the hallowed "stake in society," were being rapidly removed or diminished. After some initial misgivings, Cooper had become a strong supporter of Jackson upon reading the new President's first annual message to Congress (8 December 1829), and remained a supporter of Jackson's actions until he returned to America and had an opportunity to observe and experience the results of the great egalitarian change.

From Europe in the early 1830s Cooper could not measure accurately the direction that new economic forces were taking in American life. He had been part of America's landed gentry and, as an up-state New Yorker, had a special disdain for the aggressive commercialism associated with New Englanders. In *Recollections* he could write, with a gentleman-farmer's condescension, "Trade is a good thing in its way, but its agents rarely contribute to the taste, learning, manners, or morals of a nation" (p. 84). As he explained American life to Europeans in *Notions of the Americans,* he pointed out that wealth had no direct influence on American politics (2: 448). It seemed to him that no group had less political power in America than the rich, and for a while in the 1830s this was true. Cooper at this time was among those urging the abolishment of property requirements for voters, and this was to be stressed in *The Monikins.*

In *The Heidenmauer* it is evident that the question of who has the right to property, even the question of what *is* property, was as provoking for Cooper's imagination as the question had been when he wrote *The Pioneers* a decade earlier. The relation of men to the land is central to *The Pioneers*: there is the dispossessed Indian chieftain; the young man who was dispossessed of his heritage because his forebears had been loyal to the Crown; the wealthy Quaker landowner who profited greatly from the Revolution in which he would not bear arms; there are the pioneering settlers; and finally there is Natty Bumppo who, like Thoreau after him, owns nothing and owns everything—if, indeed, men can be said to own anything who are part and parcel of nature.

The "heathen wall" from which Cooper took the title of *The Hei-*

denmauer had been constructed by Roman soldiers to protect their camp from Germanic tribesmen who wanted an active share in determining their own political destinies, as did the men who brought about the destruction of the medieval castle and abbey whose ruins are nearby those of the heathen wall. All this is symbolic, of course, of the futility of any part of the people, however omnipotent its institutions may seem, holding for its own enjoyment what properly belongs to all. Much of the novel is given over to Cooper's dramatization of the earthly splendor of the Catholic church and its deserved destruction as far as its being a "monied corporation" and "vested interest" (p. 109) is concerned; but Cooper is careful to avoid any adverse criticism of the Catholic Church as a form of religion. In *The Heidenmauer* Cooper records his acute observation of religious life in Europe with sympathetic interest and genuine respect. His heroine observes that what matters is not "whether we admit of this or that form of faith,—the fruit of the right tree is charity and self-abasement, and these teach us to think humbly of ourselves and kindly of others" (p. 393).

Cooper's particular criticism of the medieval church was that it practiced discrimination and exclusion on a worldly basis, whereas its very basis for existence was an all-inclusive spirituality. In visiting Europe's cathedrals, the American democrat did not fail to observe the escutcheons and banners of the aristocracy in the House of God, the places reserved for the better-born, and the carefully graduated ceremony with which various civil dignitaries were received in the church. Cooper spoke directly to his American readers as follows, "Here, where all appear in the temple as they must appear in their graves, equals in dependence on divine support as they are equals in frailty, it will not be easy to understand the hardihood of sophistry which thus teaches humility and penitence with the tongue, and invites to pride and presumption in the practice" (p. 107).

But the fact refused to be ignored that in America all did not appear as equals in the temple, and Cooper's prolonged analysis of the corruption of spiritual institutions through their partaking of the material exploitation of the mass of the people led him toward the end of *The Heidenmauer* to an outburst of indignation that must have been directed at American slavery. "At this hour," he wrote, "we see nearly the entire civilized world committing gross and evident wrongs, and justifying its acts, if we look closely into its philosophy, on a plea little better than that of a sickly taste formed by practices which in themselves cannot be plausibly vindicated. The very vicious effects of every system are quoted as arguments in favor of its continuance" (p. 241). The inclusiveness of Cooper's frame of reference makes it unlikely that he intended his American readers to exclude themselves from "nearly the entire civilized world," or that slavery was not to be considered one of the "gross and evident wrongs." If any of his American readers did not at this point grasp his meaning, Cooper made the indictment more specific by his assertion that "men in millions are doomed to continue degraded, ignorant, and brutal, simply because vicious opinions refuse all sympathy with those whose hopeless lot it is to have fallen, by the adventitious chances of life, beneath the ban of society" (p. 241). If Cooper's frame of reference included America, the "men in millions" could only be the American slaves.

The Heidenmauer was to offer "a useful picture" (p. 377) to Cooper's countrymen of how profound changes could take place abruptly and thoroughly in a society. "The reformation, or revolution, or by whatever name these sudden summersets are styled," are a kind of magical awakening in which an entire people finds itself with a new set of values, "much as the eye turns from one scenic representation to that of its successor" (p. 377). And so it might be at this hour, Cooper concluded. If such thoughts were in Cooper's mind at the beginning of the summer of 1832 when he finished *The Heidenmauer,* they were more compellingly present in September, 1832, when he began *The Headsman.*

III

The Bravo, The Heidenmauer, and *The Headsman* are united by a common body of ideas and attitudes, but the underlying force of all three is Cooper's idea of America as a true republic and genuine democracy. The novels disclose his gradual recognition of and response to the gap between his idea of America and the reality of American life. From showing Americans the corruptions of privilege in Europe with *The Bravo,* Cooper had come, with *The Headsman,* to the point of including the Americans themselves in the center of his target. Like its predecessors, *The Headsman* attacked the hereditary bureaucracy, even as the Jackson administration was doing in America, but Cooper's approach is characterized by ridicule rather than by tragedy and satire as in the preceding novels; and the aristocrats, both Swiss Nobleman and Italian Doge, are closer to Cooper's Jeffersonian aristocrats of *Homeward Bound* than to the moral monsters of *The Bravo.* Long, brilliantly written sections are devoted to the evocation of natural settings, for example, the voyage across a lake of a pilgrim-laden ship in the ominous night-silence before a storm (a voyage that might well have influenced Conrad's handling of the *Patna* episode in *Lord Jim*), and a crossing of the St. Bernard Pass based directly upon Cooper's recent personal experience.

For the central focus of the novel, as indicated by its title, Cooper invented the idea of the hereditary office of public executioner: a family has been chosen to supply the canton with its headsmen, and the successive generations cannot evade their hideous task even though it means that they must live scorned and shunned by all others in the canton. No evidence has been found to suggest a historical precedent for the concept of an obligatory heritage of public executioner, and Cooper's critics have been content to assume that the strange device is intended to represent simply another form of his attack upon hereditary class distinctions. But the nature of the persecution and of the particular outrages to which the Headsman and his family (Cooper consistently uses the word *race* for *family,* as conventional usage of the age permitted) are subjected and the impassioned protests of several members of the family should have suggested to readers that what was at issue was slavery; and Cooper planted certain explicit clues to his intention.

American slavery was far worse than any social exclusion practiced in Europe, and without doubt Cooper would have liked to attack it directly; but he knew that such an attack would have been worse than useless. Cooper, widely known as "the American Scott," had made clear in his personal letters his intention that *The Bravo* and *The Heidenmauer* should be compared wth Scott's romances—but as the expression of the democratic, as distinct from the aristocratic, point of view. With *The Headsman* it is reasonable to suppose that he hoped to continue the comparison; but if he wished to take up the cause of enslaved Americans with those very American Southerners who were making Scott's romances a shaping beau ideal of Southern status culture, he had to proceed with the greatest indirection. Any open attack upon slavery would not only have gone unread by the men and women he hoped to reach, but it would have put an end to his career, already under savage attack by American critics, as a writer. In addition, as a spokesman for Cooper in *Homeward Bound* (pp. 100–101) makes clear, Cooper believed with the majority of Americans that the authority to abolish slavery was reserved by the Constitution to the individual States, and this was another essential reason why a veiled appeal had to be made to readers in the slave States, rather than an open appeal to Americans as citizens of the Union.

In *Notions of the Americans* Cooper made it clear that he considered slavery "a prodigious evil" and that the true question "in which the friends of humanity should feel the deepest interest, is that connected with the steps that are taken to lead to the general emancipation, which must sooner or later arrive" (2:353–54). With *The Headsman,* written five years later, he expressed his intent "to delineate some of the wrongs that spring from the abuses of the privileged and powerful "(p. 61. See also *Notions,* 2:367), and to show how privilege and power fail to bring the happiness expected of them when they are premised upon excluding others from the possibility of living in accordance with their God-given nature. The spiritual basis of Cooper's argument on behalf of the "race" of the Headsman is crucially reinforced by the names he gives to two of his principal characters. The three Eastern kings, or magi, associated with the birth of Christ traditionally represent the three races of mankind: Caspar (whom Cooper does not use) represents the children of Shem (Asia); Melchior represents the children of Japhet (Europe); and Balthazar represents the children of Ham (Africa). Melchior is the Swiss Nobleman; Balthazar is the accursed Headsman. Long before "Uncle Tom" was created, Balthazar bore his character: wise, gentle, long-suffering, forgiving all. " 'This is a glorious world for the happy,' " he remarks characteristically, " 'and most might be so, could they summon the courage to be innocent' "(p. 71). Christine, the daughter of Balthazar, is to be given in marriage at a festival for which the whole community has gathered, but in a climax that was to become a ritual pattern in American fiction the bridegroom spurns Christine and breaks off the ceremony when it becomes publicly known that she is of the proscribed "race."

Although Cooper placed his story in the early eighteenth century and carefully rendered the Swiss landscape and local customs, the urgency of his message intruded more than ever before on the element of historical romance. At one point he flatly discarded pretense to direct the reader's attention to his serious purpose: "the task we have allotted to ourselves is less that of sketching pictures of local usages, and of setting before the reader's imagination scenes of real or fancied antiquarian accuracy, than the exposition of a principle, and the wholesome moral which we have always flattered ourselves might, in a greater or a less degree, follow from our labor" (p. 197). Feeling as he did that sweeping changes were at hand, Cooper must have been impatient with the artifice of historical romance. Out of his American past came the conviction that "the world, in its practices, its theories, and its conventional standards of right and wrong, is in a condition of constant change" (p. 197), and the object of wise men should be to give direction and force to what was favorable in the change while taking account of the possibilities in any change of "a reaction for evil" (p. 57). Cooper would have regarded as a tragic reaction for evil the use of America's growth as an opportunity to advance the system of slavery. By the 1830s, however, Southern leaders were defending slavery as necessary and good and in accord with biblical authority; they were making clear their inflexible intention to extend slavery into the states soon to be created.

It was possible for Cooper to see these Southern leaders as they saw themselves. In his European novels Cooper presents his aristocrats, churchmen, and bureaucrats as men defending their traditional privileges because they genuinely believe them to be necessary for the good of all the people. Unless a broadly based and well-directed force for change brings about a change in thought, as illustrated in *The Heidenmauer,* a society will usually accept as its truth the ideas of the ruling caste. Committed to the system that grants them power over the thought and actions of others, rulers are blind to their own possibilities for spiritual development as well as to such possibilities in other men. Balthazar is known to the citizens of the Canton of Berne only in terms of his official status; as a man he is invisible to them. Another character, Maso, is forced to exist as an outlaw because society has cast him in that role despite his persistent acts of heroism. The Burgomaster of Vevey has become wholly absorbed by his official identity, and Cooper casts him as a bachelor who is wedded to the state. He is bound by sacrament to his position; " 'My children,' " he intones, " 'are the public' " (p. 251). Official positions, including his own, are inherited, and they are sacred; the government is an apparatus apart from and above the people. While one sees in this a direct echo of President Jackson's policy of turning the old guard out of long-held public office, the radical quality of Cooper's democratic idea goes deeper. By caricaturing a thoroughly static, artificial conception of a republic, he hopes to refresh his American reader's political idealism —to recreate a sense of the state as an expression of the will of all the people, as an organic concept subject to change and growth, as never restricted in its interest to any segment of the people and premised upon the sacredness of each individual.

The description of the Canton of Berne in the Swiss Republic is strikingly like that being used in America by abolitionists against the rulers in the "slaveocracy": "the government was in itself an usurpation, and founded on the false principle of exclusion, it was quite as usual then, as now, to cry out against the moral throes of violated right, since the same eagerness to possess, the same selfishness in grasping, however unjustly obtained, and the same audacity of assertion with a view to mystify, pervaded the Christian world a century since as exists today" (p. 253). Limiting a man's advancement because he was born into an arbitrarily determined class was simply the opposite side of the false coin that honored a man because he was born into an aristocracy or an oligarchy. " 'This is exalted, because his ancestry is noble; that condemned, for no better reason than that he is born vile . . . our reason is unhinged by subtleties, and our boasted philosophy and right are no more than unblushing mockeries, at which the very devils laugh' " (p. 183). This democratic sentiment is given spiritual weight by issuing from the Doge of Genoa, no less; and it is symptomatic of how Cooper's moral indignation and his concern with present political realities were becoming disproportionate to the mummery of historical romance that was supposed to cloak them.

While Cooper worked on *The Heidenmauer* and *The Headsman,* he had been concerned with the artistic problem of communicating multiple levels of meaning, and occasionally he interrupted his work on these novels to develop the allegory that was to become *The Monikins.* As a novelist he was disgusted with the critical reception accorded his recent work. *The Headsman,* he decided at one point, would be his last novel. Anti-Republican groups controlled most of the European presses, and in America he fell between two hostile camps: on the one hand, reviewers who took their opinions from English periodicals produced for an upper-class market, and, on the other hand, chauvinistic reviewers who denounced Cooper because he was setting his works in Europe and dared, here and there, to criticize American self-idolatry—including that of the sacrosanct American press. When one considers Cooper's passionately republican and democratic intentions in his European novels, the irony of his situation seems bitter indeed. Nor is the bitterness of the irony diminished by the fact that upon his return to the United States his insistence upon intelligence, taste, and respect for the individual was mistaken for habits of aristocracy acquired in Europe.

In *Notions of the Americans* Cooper proposed an American coat-of-arms. "It is a constellation of twenty-four stars, surrounded by a cloud of *nebulae,* with a liberty cap for a crest, and two young negroes as supporters" (1:vii). The same work draws attention to the similarity of condition between the American slave and the European laborer. Both were victims of social systems that thwarted their God-given nature. "God has planted in all our spirits secret but lasting aspirations after a state of existence, higher than that which we enjoy, and no one has a right to say that such are the limits beyond which your reason, and, consequently, your mental being shall not pass. That men, equally degraded, exist under systems that do not openly avow the principle of domestic slavery, is no excuse for the perpetuation of such a scourge, though circumstances and necessity may urge a great deal in extenuation of its present existence" (2:367). In his public debate over the merits of the American system of taxation, Cooper insisted upon the basic role of the American slave in the American economy and on comparing his political situation with that of the French worker. One of his letters published in *Le National* read, in part, "Monsieur Saulnier does not count the slaves in his calculations on the population. Why? Are they not producers? Who produces the cotton, the tobacco, the rice, the sugar of the Southern states? Is it because they do not have the same civil rights as the French workers? But the French worker, has he the same political rights as the white worker in America?"[6] These partisan words, written while Cooper was composing *The Headsman,* suggest his state of mind, and while the situation of the Headsman was no doubt intended to have a bearing upon the condition of European laborers, there are special aspects to the way in which his situation is conceived that make him relevant primarily to the condition of the American slave. And it was principally on religious grounds that Cooper planned to carry out his sneak attack upon the Southern conscience.

From the beginning of the novel, the deeply spiritual nature of Balthazar is repeatedly affirmed as well as that of his "race." In a significant passage Balthazar's wife, herself the daughter of a headsman, protests their treatment in these words:

> "We come of proscribed races, I know, Balthazar, and I, but like thee, proud bailiff, and the privileged at thy side, we come too of God! The judgment and power of men have crushed us from the beginning, and we are used to the world's scorn and to the world's injustice!"

As her plea continues, it is evident that she speaks not for the general class of exploited workers, but for the special class that is at the same time created by the laws of a society and created as inferior and despicable:

> "I know naught of the subtleties of thy laws, but well do I know their cruelty and wrongs, as respects me and mine! All others come into the world with hope, but we have been crushed from the beginning. That surely cannot be just which destroys hope. Even the sinner need not despair, through the mercy of the Son of God! but we, that have come into the world under thy laws, have little before us in life but shame and the scorn of men!"(p. 261).

At the heart of Cooper's argument is his perception that by causing a man to exist in its midst as a slave the slaveholders crippled irreparably that man's identity as a human being and they compromised the spiritual community upon which the concepts of republic and democracy are based. This perception is also at the heart of the social criticism of such twentieth-century novelists as Richard Wright, Ralph Ellison, and James Baldwin. From his Quaker and Deist background Cooper had the conviction of a moral sense, what he described in *The Heidenmauer* as a "moral sentinel," placed by God in each man; it was each man's obligation to use his moral sense and his reason to achieve a better life. Cooper hoped to make clear to his readers who defended slavery that to use reason and the instrument of reason, the law, to frustrate the operation of a man's moral sense of his own nature was to do the work of the devil. For such treasonable use of divine gifts, Dante saw men suffer in the icy, dark, and narrow region of hell.

The chief representative of the law in *The Headsman,* the Bailiff of Vevey, is the chosen spokesman for prejudice. When he learns that the gentle, mild Christine is the daughter of Balthazar, the tenderness he had felt for her is shaded by a cruel contempt. His social conditioning irrationally asserts itself, and it finds expression in words familiar to generations of Americans, " 'The girl is fair and modest and winning in her way; but there is something—I cannot tell thee what—but a certain damnable something—a taint—a color—a hue—a—a—a—that showed her origin the instant I heard who was her parent' "(p.

269). It is not unreasonable to suppose that at least some of Cooper's Southern readers must have supplied from their own experience a prejudice corresponding to that of the Bailiff of Vevey; however, it should be noted that generations of critics of Cooper's European novels have never found in them any concern with the racial issue that was threatening to destroy America as a republic and a democracy. It is worth quoting once more the Bailiff of Vevey. " 'Ignorance is a mask to conceal the little details that are necessary to knowledge. Your Moor might pass for a Christian in a mask, but strip him of his covering and the true shade of the skin is seen' " (p. 269). It should not have been necessary for Cooper to be more explicit than this in order to accomplish his purpose.

Perhaps he did succeed. There is an added irony to the Bailiff's speech in that it is made, unwittingly, to Sigismund, whom the reader believes at this point in the story to be Christine's brother and therefore of the race of Balthazar. But Sigismund's identity is soon scrambled in complications involving Italian twins, a brother assuming a half-brother's identity, a parent of a blond, blue-eyed boy of an accursed race giving his son another name to free him of the racial stigma, and other wondrous devices that are not to be paralleled in American literature until Mark Twain, more student than critic of Cooper, composed his paradox-laden tale of slavery in *Pudd'nhead Wilson,* where a maze of complications strikingly similar to Cooper's reappears. Like Twain, Cooper saw American slaves simply as men debased by manmade laws, and both writers understood the mentality that thought of black men as different in kind from other men. The blacks in Cooper's fiction, like those in Twain's, always bear the stigmata of slavery because both men saw how the black man was coerced to play the part a white society created for him, and both knew what was expected of the black in fiction. Few of Cooper's American readers would have accepted as a human possibility that a family as wise and gentle and well-bred as that of the Headsman could be black. Cooper's Moors had to pass as Christians in a mask. But behind the refined language of Christine one hears the heart of Jim confiding to the heart of Huck Finn in such words as these of Balthazar's daughter,

> "the world believes us to be without feeling and without hope. We are what we seem in the eyes of others, because the law makes it so, but we are in our hearts like all around us . . . with this difference, that, feeling our abasement among men, we lean more closely and more affectionately on God. You may condemn us to do your offices and to bear your dislike, but you cannot rob us of our trust in the justice of Heaven" (p. 384).

Cooper's appeal for truly democratic vistas in America was scarcely heard. Critics used the appearance of *The Headsman* as an occasion to attack Cooper for a variety of reasons—for remaining so long in Europe, for engaging in political controversy in Europe, for publishing views critical of American life. Few at the time seem to have understood what he was trying to do, and the three European novels have remained among the least read of his works. When he returned to a greatly changed America, he proceeded to analyze it in novels that employed a scathing satire while in other novels he gave substance to some of America's most romantic myths. Cooper's European novels offer insights into the reality and the romance of his age. And they bear significantly upon the present day, when Americans are again in need of a persuasion to trust themselves and others, to see the world with a democratic freshness, and "to have the courage to be innocent."

2
Melville's *Redburn* and the City

Both Cooper and Melville were born into the class of New York's natural aristocracy, and in childhood they were assured of the perfection of the young Republic and of the bright promise of their particular future. While Melville was still a boy, however, his family's prospects were sharply reversed by the death of his father; by the time he was twenty he had embarked as a common seaman on a voyage to Liverpool, the first of the voyages that would lead him to see his own civilization in a highly critical perspective; and by the time he was thirty he would be reduced to writing the "beggarly 'Redburn' "[1] "to buy some tobacco with."[2] The early chapters of the novel make plain what he had in mind. It was to be, as the subtitle suggests, a semi-comic adventure story of a gentleman's son serving before the mast, a formula familiar to readers of the day, and in substance it was to be loosely based upon Melville's first sea voyage.

Before the fictional *Highlander* reached its destination, however, Melville's moral commitment to his personal experience broke through the stock formula he had intended. Redburn's response to humanity deepened, the character Jackson was introduced, and Liverpool was observed, not through the eyes of a naïve country boy, but through the eyes of a man who had seen several widely different societies, who had grave doubts as to the direction his own society was taking, and who saw in Liverpool the prototype city of the Anglo-American culture.

The first sight of Liverpool's docks, "long China walls of masonry"

(p. 205),[3] brings to Redburn's mind the memory of New York's waterfront, albeit New York has nothing so impressive to offer. Speculating on the names of the docks, Redburn suggests that they should be named after English heroes. There is a double irony in this remark, for it is an American boy who takes for granted that England's heroes fought to protect the balance of trade and that a dock would be a suitable memorial for the heroic dead, "most fit monuments to perpetuate the names of the heroes, in connection with the commerce they defended" (p. 206). A true hero, Redburn sagely continues, "must still be linked with the living interests of his race": that is, with trade and money.

On several occasions Redburn is brought to remark upon the similarity of Liverpool to New York, the port from which he has sailed, until finally he declares, "I began to think I had been born in Liverpool (p. 193). Immense architectural ghosts of the dead medieval culture rising hauntingly above the commercial metropolis should have made Liverpool seem very different from New York, but in the excitement of his first impressions it is the swirling movement of the two that impresses him and both seem splendid cities. Forgetting the poverty that sent him to sea, Redburn assures his friend Harry Bolton, who despaired of finding a job in New York, "that New York was a civilized and enlightened town; with a large population, fine streets, fine houses, nay, plenty of omnibuses; and that for the most part, he would think himself in England; so similar to England, in essentials, was this outlandish America that haunted him" (p. 362). The essentials in terms of which New York and Liverpool are similar quickly appear in scene after scene before the reader, but few New Yorkers of Melville's day would have recognized the similarities or perceived that Melville was presenting an analysis of New York in terms of Liverpool. Like Redburn, they were too imbued with the promise of America to assess the reality.

"Is Liverpool but a brick-kiln?" asked Redburn, soon bored by his confinement to that city (p. 204). Two years later, bored by his confinement in New York while at work on *Moby Dick,* Melville described himself as "disgusted with the heat and dust of the babylonish brick-kiln of New York."[4] Still later, in *Israel Potter,* he was to build the image of the brick-kiln into an extraordinary metaphor for the nature of the individual life and the structure of society in a great modern city: baked-dry units in a rigid mass—in short, what Bartleby was to see, staring from the office window or across the prison yard. Bartleby would have said of Liverpool as he said of the Tombs in the heart of New York, " 'I know where I am.' "

Sailing to Liverpool, the youthful Redburn has seen almost nothing of the world's cities. He knows something of New York and Boston and Albany (which had about 30,000 inhabitants when Melville moved there in 1830), as did Melville when he made his first voyage, but, like Melville, he was an innocent. The Melville who, ten years later, described Redburn's reaction to Liverpool had seen not only that city but cities on the west coast of South America and tribal cities in the Marquesas. He knew firsthand the possibilities afforded by societies constructed on a fundamentally different basis from those of Western civilization. In addition he had recently completed the writing of *Mardi,* where widely differing nations and cultures are visited as islands, and the habit must have persisted of seeing the local and temporary forms of society in a universal and timeless perspective. In a sense, Liverpool is yet another island visited by Taji, but this time it is an island rising from a sea of property.

Although Melville frequently used natural settings in his fiction, he was always concerned with man in relation to a highly evolved social context. The idyllic countryside of Liverpool is an invitation to Arcadian repose, but, as Redburn finds to his dismay, it is all owned and guarded property. Mantraps, guns, and dogs speed the traveler on his way. And the same would have been true in New York, where the current issue of anti-rent wars, about which Cooper had just completed a trilogy with *The Redskins,* made it clear that the age of the frontier was long gone. City or countryside, Liverpool or New York, all the land encountered in *Redburn,* as later in *Pierre,* is rigidly defined property. A central fact in Redburn's initiatory experience is that property forms the basis of his society. It supplies the definitions of justice, law, and virtue; it proves more powerful than man who conceived it; and it even converts man himself into a category of property.

That such need not be the case was illustrated by Melville's narrator in the valley of Typee, who saw the idea of property as one of the evils of civilization from which the islanders were free, and who summed up all the evils from which they were free in the words "no Money!" Young Redburn, fresh from a country town near Albany, had not thought much about the concept of property until a savage sign warning passersby to keep off the inviting green fields started a dialogue in his mind:

> And who put it there?
> The proprietor, probably.
> And what right had he to do so?
> Why, he owned the soil.
> And where are his title deeds?
> In his strong-box, I suppose.
> Thus I stood wrapt in cogitations.

Title to land? Individual ownership of a piece of creation? It is the same question that had vexed Cooper's Natty Bumppo, and soon Redburn is asking himself, "What right has this man to the soil he thus guards with dragons? What excessive effrontery, to lay sole claim to a solid piece of this planet, right down to the earth's axis, and, perhaps straight through to the antipodes!" (pp. 270–71).

Even more disturbing to the young Redburn was the constant sight of crowds of beggars and cripples, citizens of Liverpool who possessed neither money nor property and hence were themselves without value. Like Melville's Pierre Glendinning, who first encountered the reality of destitution when he saw the whores and drunkards in a New York watch-house, Redburn had nothing in his experience to compare with the sight of the Liverpool poor. With poor and beggarly American blacks, yes; but with native-born white beggars, no. It must be the vote, Redburn patriotically decides, that kept American citizens free of this condition. He conveniently forgets the sense of alienation which being poor and unable to find a job had brought upon him in America. Melville, who knew what it was to be a social outcast in America as a result of his father's bankruptcy, then his brother's bankruptcy, and finally his own privations after the financial Panic of 1837, generously allows Redburn his flurry of patriotic fervor.

Still, despite the recurrent financial panics and cholera epidemics, New York City's ills did not reach the extreme sickness and poverty to be found in Liverpool at the time. Liverpool was among the first of the great cities to rise in the nineteenth century with an ever-swelling mass of inhabitants and an ever-increasing concentration of commerce and industry that made it inevitable that there would be a constant population of men, women, and children who could survive only as beggars or criminals. For Melville's purposes it was necessary that Redburn be young and from the country in order to show how the modern city frustrates all the natural instincts for human community, outrages the moral spirit, and denies humanity any essential distinction.

It might be said that Redburn is aware of several Liverpools: 1) the one that has existed in his imagination, the Liverpool of his father's anecdotes, of his father's guidebook "The Picture of Liverpool," and of his romantic sense of what old European cities ought to be; 2) physical Liverpool with its gigantic maze of concrete docks, masses of ships, sordid slums, crooked streets walled by soot-blackened brick buildings, and the "Old Church" based upon the "Dead-House"; and 3) the human Liverpool. What had guided the father in dealing with the city soon proves worse than useless as a guide for the son. Redburn must try to make some meaning of a city in which there is a continual contradiction and confusion between the values of the past, which insist upon their vitality even when experience proves them to be hopelessly dead—the world of churches, social clubs, and the titles and statues that have a reference to a social or political order and the real power of the society which rests in the concrete docks.

The buildings that pretend to be emblematic of the city's culture are all derelicts to Redburn. The spaces of the city that had possessed spiritual and aesthetic value for his father have shifted in such a way as to crowd out these values in order to provide for the vastly increased commerce. The city that had begun in history as an organic process of nature has been replaced by the city as a mechanical artifice of mind. The very survival, let alone the comfort, of great numbers of Liverpool's inhabitants had been ignored in adapting the city to its all but exclusive function as a trading center. Goods and men are shipped in and shipped out; trade is the one thing that counts. The only meaningful structures in the city are those which serve trade, and except for the human litter of beggars and thieves, almost all human life is adapted to processing the endless circulation of goods and men.

About the docks and in the central mercantile areas the crowd swarms continually. Each morning Redburn joins the flow. How does a young man establish community with this ever-changing movement? A disillusioned Redburn observes that "upon the whole, and barring the poverty and beggary, Liverpool, away from the docks, was very much such a place as New York . . . the same elbowing, heartless-looking crowd as ever" (p. 260). If at this point Melville had New York uppermost in mind because he was living there while he wrote *Redburn,* the balance would be redressed shortly when he revisited England upon finishing *Redburn.* Of one dreary day (Friday, November 9, 1849) he recorded in his journal, "While on the Bridges, the thought struck me again that a fine thing might be written about a Blue Monday in November London—a city of Dis (Dante's)—clouds of smoke—the damned &c.—coal barges—coaly waters, cast-iron Duke &c.—its marks are left upon you."[5]

Melville used this image in *Israel Potter,* adding to it a comment upon the crowd, "that hereditary crowd—gulf-stream of humanity—which, for continuous centuries, has never ceased pouring, like an endless shoal of herring, over London Bridge" (p. 210). Israel Potter had fled to London, "for solitudes befriend the endangered wild beast, but crowds are the security, because the true desert, of persecuted man" (p. 203). Redburn walks through the cities of the plain, through the cities of Dickens, of Balzac, of Dostoievski, past "scores of tattered wretches" picking over rubbish, past "multitudes of beggars" whose petitions are scrawled on the paving stones "in an hour's time destined to be obliterated by the feet of thousands and thousands of wayfarers," past a "lane of beggars" who thronged the docks in neighborhoods where "the sooty and begrimed bricks of the very houses have a reeking, Sodomlike, and murderous look" (p. 245).

In the center of this unreal, *fourmillante* city Redburn comes across a statue that was not in his father's guidebook, which haunts him so that he must return repeatedly to stare at it. The statue is of Nelson, with Victory and Death, and with the figures of four captives, supposedly representing Nelson's victories, at its base. Again Redburn thinks of how England's heroes are linked with her trading empire, and this leads to thoughts of slavery in his own country and to the reflection "that the African slave-trade once constituted the principal commerce of Liverpool; and that the prosperity of the town was once supposed to have been indissolubly linked to its prosecution" (p. 198). Touching deftly upon the issue of abolition, Melville has Redburn recall that his father had often spoken to gentlemen visiting their house "of the unhappiness that the discussion of the abolition of this trade had occasioned in Liverpool." Thus Melville brings the image of New York and its problems more clearly through the Liverpool palimpsest.

In *Mardi* he had already used a city's monuments to comment ironically upon its pretensions. The red stripes on the flag over the capital of Vivenza (America) are compared to the bloody stripes on the back of the man employed to raise it, and at the base of the statue to liberty are pasted the rewards for runaway slaves (2:226). There is an echo in this of Cooper's suggestion in *Notions of the Americans* for an American coat-of-arms that would have had Negro slaves as its supporters. Statues of war heroes seem to have summoned up a lively iconoclastic impulse in Melville, and his contemptuous treatment of Nelson was to be paralleled in *Israel Potter* by reference to John Paul Jones as a barbarian in broadcloth, an embodiment of the primeval savageness ever latent in man and ever present in "the heart of the metropolis of modern civilization" (p. 81).

Melville had remarked in *Typee* upon the ease with which a native could bring up a numerous family of children, while civilized man, "the most ferocious animal on the face of the earth," was often at his wits' end to provide for his starving offspring (p. 150). A counterpart to the public statue of the warrior Nelson is the secluded, sculpturesque group of a mother and her children resignedly starving to death in a cellar off Launcelott's-Hey. Redburn makes the appalling discovery that the baby at the mother's breast is actually dead. No passerby interferes; and when Redburn summons a policeman, he is rebuffed by the startlingly modern idiom, " 'It's none of my business, Jack . . . I don't belong to that street' " (p. 233). Officialdom has only a mechanical and arbitrary connection with mankind; and, like death, it has its own dominion. The waters of the docks and the alleys of the city provide a daily harvest of corpses for the nearly dead scavengers who collect them for the bounty which for a short, miserable while secures their own survival. "There seems to be no calamity overtaking man, that can not be rendered merchantable" (p. 230), muses Redburn, but with rather different implications to the thought from those associated with an earlier American folk-hero, "Poor Richard."

The old city had been a living shell continually renewed by the ways in which it responded to the needs of the people of Liverpool. The immense commercial pressures of the nineteenth century had hardened and shattered the old shell, leaving the dead shards to provide a cityscape that expresses the relationship of the new social power to its victims. The corpses that accumulate overnight in the docks and alleys are collected in the Death-House, and there each day a crowd can be found gazing speculatively upon the nameless dead. Because the Death-House is the foundation of the church, the area surrounding it is a graveyard; and each day "swarms of Laborers" cross and recross it, erasing with their boots the death's heads and crossbones carved on the horizontal stones. The value of death, along with the value of life, is lost to the unending stream of men hurrying on their commercial errands. The dead are merely the waste-product of the society. Once their utility, even as corpses, has ceased, they are not so much forgotten as disposed of.

Melville's technique of ironic association, which links the figure of dying Nelson and his slave-like captives with the figures of the dying mother and children, and associates this group with the bodies collected for public inspection in the Death-House communicates the idea that the city itself is a house of the dead. The people have no real life, but like the dead in some modern *Inferno* are driven through the harsh, grimy spaces of the city by mysterious, vindictive forces. Like Hawthorne, for whom the church as a symbol of institutionalized religion is associated with an absence of the spirit that breathes life and hope, Melville has the church rise above the Death-House to typify the corpselike nature of the established church in the modern city. The mummery of Christianity had exasperated the blind guide in *Mardi* to plead, " 'Off masks, mankind, that I may know what warranty of fellowship with others, my own thoughts possess' " (2:-20–21). In his first two novels Melville had indicated how the Christian missionaries brought with them a way of life that was destructive to many genuinely Christian elements in the pagan societies. Just as their concept of religious practice was wholly unsuited to the way of life of the primitive islanders, so the religious practice of the Protestant sects in Liverpool (and New York) was wholly irrelevant to a people for whom death and suffering had become a meaningless fresco on the concrete walls of the docks and the sooty brick walls of their dwellings. The language and gestures of official religion alienated them all the more from the possibility of recognizing any divinity in their own nature. Melville considered the usual sermon to be, in a real sense, anti-religious; and at one time he wrote to Hawthorne, "Take God out of the dictionary, and you would have Him in the street."[6]

By means of Liverpool, Melville was depicting the modern secular city. Religious services were, of course, held at the usual times and places, and Redburn attended them as a well-bred American boy. But what Melville conveys is how the church responds mainly to class traditions that are themselves archaic survivals, and how it is wholly irrelevant to the society as a whole. The church is not in the least persecuted; far worse, it is ignored, or, at best, exploited as a social convenience. Although Redburn's unusual clothing raised some eyebrows, he was always admitted to the Sunday services and seated inconspicuously behind a pillar. The sailor lad was welcome to listen to the service. But love? hospitality? "But, alas! there was no dinner for me except at the sign of the Baltimore Clipper" (p. 263). Melville was to remark in *Pierre* that "by all odds the most Mammonish parts of this world—Europe and America—are owned by none but professed Christian nations, who glory in the owning, and seem to have some reason therefor" (pp. 288–89). In *Redburn* he anticipated this comment in many ways, but especially in Redburn's sense of how money and money in the form of property make the laboring class invisible as persons to those whose sense of human values has been transmuted by the world of commerce. No longer was it a question of serving God or Mammon, but one of making God serve Mammon.

The monopoly of the established church upon matters of divinity was its prime economic holding. Man is not merely invisible; as Redburn cries out to his readers, "We are blind to the real sights of this world; deaf to its voice; and dead to its death" (p. 379).

Such a note, Melville realized, might compromise the success of his adventure story, and, besides, he had explicitly promised his publisher that the novel would contain none of the mind-troubling matter that had characterized *Mardi.* Thus, he kept his pot boiling with an account of an adventure in an Arabian Nights London, of Carlo, the singer, and of Harry Bolton's mishaps. The moral springs of Melville's creative process would not let him dally for long, however, with Harry's fanciful escapades. The character Jackson was much more compelling to Melville's imagination, for he would serve to tell Americans some truths about themselves even as Liverpool served to tell them about their greatest commercial city. While much of the American reading public regarded criticism of America as a form of treason and preferred to believe that evil was located abroad, Melville wished to insist upon the truth that evil existed everywhere. In *Mardi* he had expressed the idea this way: " 'The grand error of this age, sovereign-kings! is the general supposition, that the very special Diabolus is abroad; whereas, the very special Diabolus has been abroad ever since *Mardi* began' " (2:238). Like a character of Hawthorne's fiction whose eyes have been fixed so long and so relentlessly upon evil that he can see only the evil in the world, it is Jackson who is appointed to guide the young American to the Diabolus who is in Liverpool and who is everywhere.

If Jackson has nothing of the dynamism of Ahab, of whom he cast such a strong foreshadow, he has also nothing of the sneaking malevolence of Claggart, with whom he shares an intolerance of innocence. Whether flinging the beeves' hearts in the face of the cheating innkeeper, or claiming his right to the most perilous position on the ship in the violence of a storm, Jackson is the acknowledged leader of the crew. He knows from experience on pirate ships, slave ships, and emigrant ships the evil of which human beings are capable; and he himself demonstrates man's capacity for suffering. If he has been an assailant, he has also been a victim. He will not allow his shipmates the luxury of a God.

Like Teiresias accusing Oedipus of his guilt, Jackson tries to force upon Redburn a knowledge of the evil of which Redburn is product and part. In so doing he bears Melville's message to the self-righteous readers who have allowed themselves to feel an affinity with the "Son of a Gentleman in the Merchant Service" of the novel's subtitle. Jackson has seen and acknowledged the truth of a part of human experience, a part that, in time, will be seen by Zola and subsequent practitioners of naturalism as the whole of life. But it was a part of their experience that Americans, especially in their fiction, wished to deny; and Melville wants to smash the corrupt luxury of American innocence, the innocence he projected through Captain Delano in his story *Benito Cereno,* that mocks the truth. Melville sees Jackson in terms of the defiant rebels and sinners, Cain, Tiberius, and Satan, for Jackson is the best seaman aboard, he is the natural leader of the crew, and his death has a heroic dimension. As with so many of Hawthorne's characters, sin was the necessary condition for Jackson's vision of human evil, of its disguises and its pervasiveness and its outrageous depths. The cliché attached by Redburn to Jackson's death, "the wages of sin," is an ironic sop by Melville to a public conditioned to associate evil with sickness, poverty, and social exclusion, as well as with other races and other nations. Jackson is one of those who, to the optimistic gospel of social progress and human perfectibility, "says NO! in thunder."

At the time Melville wrote *Redburn* the pressures upon both Liverpool and New York were radically altering the physical and cultural structures of both cities. A crucial event for both was the total failure of the potato crop in Ireland in 1846 and the resultant Irish exodus. Liverpool was the major port of departure for the sailing-ships that transported the emigrants in the years immediately following the famine and New York was the major port of arrival. The emigrants swarmed into Liverpool, which did its best to cram them aboard ships and send them to New York, where those who survived the voyage could struggle for survival in the city. Melville's voyage to Liverpool, on which the novel was partly based, took place in 1839, but he was writing the novel in New York in 1849 and basing much of it—especially the emigrant chapters—on the accounts of emigration that appeared frequently in newspapers and magazines in 1847 and 1848, on reports of proceedings in both Congress and Parliament attempting to regulate conditions aboard the ships transporting emigrants, as well as on his observation of the arrival of these ships and their passengers in New York. His account of the hardships of the steerage passengers aboard the *Highlander* suggests that the year he had most in mind was 1847, "the black year of emigration," as it was described by the London *Times* (Sept. 17, 1847), when the "ship fever" Melville describes was epidemic.

The treatment in *Redburn* of the Irish migrant workers in Liverpool and of the Irish emigrants as steerage passengers on the return voyage of the *Highlander* dramatizes the social dislocations produced by the economic power concentrated in the city. It is the truth upon which Jackson insists, his vision of human exploitation. Now the crowd is made up of herded Irish laborers, "penned in just like cattle," sounding "like a drove of buffaloes," passing "vast quantities of produce, imported from starving Ireland," and on their way "to help harvest English crops" (pp. 255–56). Redburn comments upon the striking fact that the poor are all whites—the Negroes he saw in Liverpool were all sailors: "In Liverpool indeed the negro steps with a prouder pace, and lifts his head like a man; for here, no such exaggerated feeling exists in respect to him as in America" (p. 259). Melville's point is akin to Cooper's, namely, that in Europe the exploited workers and farm laborers had the status of slaves. Denied not only any ownership of the earth on which they had lived for generations but denied also any share in the food they produced, the potato blight presented millions of Irish with the brutal alternatives of starving to death at home or, if money could be found for the passage, emigrating to America. Hawthorne's English notebooks records a conversation he held while he was the American Consul in Liverpool with a quiet, decent Irish family whose money could get them no further than Liverpool and who faced the prospect of returning to Ireland and death by starvation.

Along with the Irish, Melville's Redburn holds the point of view of the dispossessed. An Irishman at the head of a troop of laborers shouts, "*Sing Langolee, and the Lakes of Killarney,*" and communicates immediately Melville's perception of the individual person, the homely bundle of habits, beliefs, landscapes, and dreams gathered there. This never-dimished capacity for divining the person beneath society's extrinsic categories comes through in Redburn's conversations with the most varied characters—a Lascar from the Indian ship *Irrawaddy,* or a sailor ballad-singer, or the skipper of a salt-drogher. What is prized is the unique identity, the remoteness from familiar categories, the perspective on life of a man who might be a racial curiosity (the Lascar), a beggar (the ballad-singer), or a man who is captain and crew of his snug vessel (the skipper of the salt-drogher). The handling of these casual encounters and their significant placement are remarkable technical achievements in the novel.

Melville alters drastically the persona of Redburn when he deals with the emigrants, as though his own commitment to the subject matter was too intense to be contained in such a young, healthy, and cheerful youth. Melville saw a terrible history summed up in the ignorant, bewildered Irishman who replaced the cargo of lumber in the dark holds of the sailing ships. The compassion he felt for the laborer was a world removed from the human basis upon which Thoreau drove his shrewd bargain for the boards of the Irishman's shanty or gave his advice on diet to another Irish laborer and his family. There is an awesome indictment of America in the art itself of Cooper and Melville, namely, in the subtle, devious ways that they had to take to bring their message home. The horrors of the emigrant's journey come through almost casually, touching chiefly those aspects of the voyage in which the emigrant was most subject to being dehumanized and where legislation had proved ineffective in curbing the exploiters' greed. Some of these are the overcrowding of passengers into a cargo hold crudely converted to steerage accommodations; false or inadequate advice about food and clothing necessary for the voyage; barbarous sanitary conditions; no provision against shipwreck; practically nothing in the way of medical care; and an insistence upon their status as inferior creatures, which was characteristic of the vicious traffic in human beings.

Shortly after the *Highlander* left Liverpool it was discovered that a "crimp" had put aboard a corpse under the pretense that he was delivering a drunken sailor. This grim epsiode is an omen for the whole emigrant shipment. Over twenty of the passengers die under horrible conditions before the ship reaches New York. Like the corpse of the unknown sailor, the corpses of the emigrants are cast with little ceremony into the sea. There is something of the ghastly quality of Poe's *Narrative of A. Gordon Pym* about the voyage, an unreality of hallucination, but if anything Melville was gentling the truth. He is not precise as to the number of passengers on his fictional *Highlander,* but the number of deaths in proportion to the "four or five hundred" steerage passengers was possibly understated as concession to his readers' ignorance of what was actually happening on the tragic crossings. In *The Great Migrations* Edwin C. Guillet records that "on three vessels alone in 1847 there were 313 burials at sea, apart altogether from subsequent deaths among the 322 who were sick on arrival, and it may be assumed that sea-burials in such numbers were marked by no ceremonies whatever." He adds, "Of slightly more than 100,000 persons who left the British Isles for America in 1847 a total of 17,445, or 16.33%, died during the passage, in quarantine, or in hospital."[7] In *The Uprooted* Oscar Handlin places the normal mortality on the emigrant sailing-ships at about 10%, "although in the great year, 1847, it was closer to 20."[8] Melville could not have known that the two years immediately preceding his writing about the emigrants in *Redburn* were to prove to be two highly exceptional years for death and sickness, but he could see that the horror of these voyages was but part of a greater horror.

Early in the voyage to Liverpool, self-centered Redburn found himself "a sort of Ishmael" (p. 79) in the ship, resented by the sailors because of his somewhat fastidious manner. In the course of the novel Redburn's early self-concern swiftly enlarges to lose itself in the widening circle of his concern for others, especially the morally desperate and socially stricken men; he takes on the understanding, compassion, and inclusive love characteristic of the Ishmael of *Moby Dick.* His sympathy is deep for the emigrants who are themselves "Ishmaels," driven out from their homelands, friendless, and even harried into antagonism for one another by their desperate living conditions aboard ship. In a familiar Melville metaphor, the ship becomes a social microcosm. The rigid, cruelly unfair division of its spaces is determined by the power of an abstraction—money—without regard to human need, or, for that matter, human life. The mass of the population (the emigrants) is jammed into a filthy steerage slum; the cabin-passengers in private quarters with ample deck space live in fear and contempt of the inhabitants of the steerage, and all the more so when the latter are suffering from the diseases brought on by their wretched quarters; the crew operates as a police force to see that the outrageous distribution of space and material goods is enforced. Against this metaphor, which locks assailant and victim together in a vivid economy of violence, Melville poses the metaphor of the Great Wall of China, wherein each man may own a stone and share equally in the ownership of the world—"for the whole world is the patrimony of the whole world" (p. 378).

In part *Redburn* was a plea for legislation that would improve the working conditions of sailors and the treatment of emigrants. Yet, even as he made his plea, Melville knew that any legislation that might pass in Parliament or Congress would only treat superficially the social structure that resulted in so much suffering for the great mass of men who, in Melville's metaphor, were the wheels supporting and moving the coach, which is society, above the dust and mire. Can the wheels of this world be lifted up from the mire? "There seems not much chance for it in the old systems and programmes of the future, however well-intentioned and sincere; for with such systems, the thought of lifting them up seems almost as hopeless as that of growing the grape in Nova Zembla" (p. 178). The old systems and the new programmes merely offered variations on how to divide and possess individually what Melville believed to be the patrimony of all. His most passionate exhortation in *Redburn* comes at the center of the book, when he fuses this belief with the related belief that all men are one. The two beliefs are unified in his idea of America: "We are not a nation, so much as a world" (p. 216); and, again, "We are the heirs of all time, and with all nations we divide our inheritance" (p. 217). What was needed was not reform of the social machinery but a transformation of cultural values. To work toward that great end, Melville had to speak from the belly of the whale. *Redburn,* however, bears the promise of revelation, and it may be that Melville intended not disparagement but a special praise in referring to it, in a letter to a friend, as "a little nursery tale of mine."[9]

3
Hawthorne's Dialogue with Rome

In the summer of 1858, when Hawthorne began planning and sketching out the romance that was to mature into *The Marble Faun,* he had written no fiction for five years, and it was over six years since he had completed work on *The Blithedale Romance.* He had not intended that there should be such a break in his work as a novelist. In the autumn of 1852 he started work on a novel, but he had to set it aside in order to write the campaign biography of his close friend from Bowdoin College days, Franklin Pierce. When he sailed for England in July, 1853, to assume the post of American Consul in Liverpool with which Pierce had rewarded him, his intention was to give little time to official duties and to begin work soon on a novel that would make use of his experiences in England. His official duties, however, proved far more demanding than he had anticipated. Although he compiled voluminous notebooks about his English experiences, it was April of 1858, when he was settled in Rome, before he produced his sketch for an English novel, and he promptly and permanently set it aside.

In late October of 1858, when he began the actual writing of *The Marble Faun,* his fanciful ideas for the romance promised to resume the treatment of themes that had been characteristic of his finest work. The four years spent in England and the year and a half spent in Italy, however, had produced a great change in the forces that fed Hawthorne's creative imagination. As a result, when he had finished *The Marble Faun* it proved to be a work that was almost indifferent to the moral and psychological tensions he had created in his earlier novels and stories. His Italian notebooks and the novel disclose that his mind recognized as surely as ever the evidence of psychological and moral paradox, but there was no longer the same concern with such matters. His experience of Rome was the culmination of his European experience, of years of attentively observing strange persons and places and customs, of making subtle distinctions, of discovering what it meant to be an American, or to be an Englishman, or to be an Italian, or a Catholic. He and his wife had kept daily notes of their observations and with the assiduity characteristic of New England's pilgrims to Europe—an assiduity that was to prove amusing material for Henry James—the daily jottings were dutifully explored and developed at length in notebooks. The rich tapestry of romance was there before him and all his impressions were gathered together; it was quite the opposite of the condition in America, where the writer had to exercise what Henry James termed a "grasping imagination." Instead of lending itself to the support of his drama, however, the Roman setting came to dominate the novel with its own rich significance and as the eternal city to become "the interest behind the interest."

Rome gave a physical immediacy to Hawthorne's acute sense of the past, which had so belatedly had its total immersion. It provided a concept of a city that showed him at least the possibility of an earthly community's being organized as a city of God. Despite its layers of dirt and corruption, Rome seemed to Hawthorne to provide for the individual's spiritual life and at the same time to join the individual to a community that extended to past generations as well as to those to come. Yet, while they were strikingly alive as individuals, the Romans were part of an insistently visible history that mocked any pretense of one individual's significance. E. M. Forster's novel *A Passage to India,* like the Whitman poem to which it owes its title, describes the movement from one plane of consciousness to another. But whereas Whitman describes the passage with exuberance, Forster's novel communicates rather the irritation with which the newly liberated character turns in distaste from the outgrown chrysalis of national attitudes and parochial religious discriminations. It is this latter attitude that is communicated by *The Marble Faun.* It is not so much that European life had taught Hawthorne anything new about the spiritual conditions of man's existence, as that the human spirit caught in the peculiar tensions of an American Protestant culture no longer seemed to him a unique and urgent drama.

Far from catering to American chauvinism, which was particularly virulent at this period, Hawthorne's novel issues from a mind that has come to regard nationality with boredom; feels, in fact, a weary exasperation with most human institutions; and sadly considers guilt and sorrow in at least some measure as inevitable to the human condition. It is clear that when Hawthorne sketched out his novel, he must have operated much as he had when he designed his earlier novels. He had his contrasting characters with their heavily representative natures, symbolic towers, denials and affirmations in public places, God's nature and man's city, a framework of carnivals, and broken fountains; in short, all the ritual devices of his creative process were in place. The elaborate structure, however, served only to bear the weight of the author's dialogue with Rome. In *The Marble Faun* Hawthorne's divided and subdivided mind finds expression in the ambiguities and ambivalences of his characters while at the same time, in a way that carries his habitual detachment to an extreme, it seems to regard the various human voices as one syllable, meaningless and profound, echoing from the stones of the eternal city.

Given the fact that his family's history extended back two centuries into the history of Massachusetts, it is remarkable how little attachment Hawthorne felt for his native land. So far as the country was concerned, he had seen little of it, and he wondered in his notebooks how one could be expected to feel patriotism for such a geographical expanse. While he believed in the principles of a republic and of a democracy, he felt scarcely any attachment to the political entity The United States of America. The "Customs House" section of *The Scarlet Letter* had made him unwelcome in Salem, and his writing a campaign biography for the anti-abolitionist presidential candidate had caused his friends in the Boston-Cambridge-Concord area to drop off from him, as he remarked, like autumn leaves. It had been with a great sense of relief that he had left America, and he had gone to England with an anticipation of peace and contentment, as though he were a long-exiled colonial returning home.

Ironically, his office in Liverpool proved to be a concentration of America. If he had had any illusions about American innocence, his encounters with Americans during his four years as American Consul to Liverpool would have dispelled them. "I first got acquainted with my own countrymen there," he wrote to his publisher Fields,[1] and in *Our Old Home* he recorded that he grew better acquainted with many of the American characteristics during those four years than in all his preceding life.[2] His customs jobs in Salem and Boston had been peaceful sinecures, but in Liverpool he was in almost daily contact with officers and men of the merchant marine who were involved in murders, beatings, robbery, and other violent crimes. He had to deal with Americans who demanded his assistance in their fanciful claims to English titles and estates, or who, free from hometown restraints, became involved in sordid debauches. And the news from America was grim. He wrote in March, 1854, to his friend Horatio Bridge that it sickened him to look back to America;[3] and he wrote in September, 1856, to his friend W. D. Ticknor that America looked like "an infernally disagreeable country this side of the water."[4] By contrast there was the growth of his feeling for England, which he was later to assign to the character Redclyffe in *Doctor Grimshawe's Secret*: "he began to feel the deep yearning which a sensitive American—his mind full of English thoughts, his imagination of English poetry, his heart of English character and sentiment—cannot fail to be influenced by, —the yearning of the blood within his veins for that from which it has been estranged."[5]

What emerges in Hawthorne's European notebooks as his basic objection to American life is its formlessness and rootlessness, the centrifugal movement that seemed to grow ever more intense. Religion in America, as he had known it, typified the dispersion. In "The Celestial Railroad" he had made plain his contempt for the direction that American Puritanism had taken by way of Unitarianism to transcendentalism. In "Earth's Holocaust" all churches, from cathedrals to white, wooden New England chapels, are consumed to ashes by reformers, and Hawthorne was willing to acknowledge that they were all made of corruptible stuff. Although the need for spiritual communion is a central theme in his work, Hawthorne could never find such community in American churches. In Hawthorne's fiction organized religion, especially as it draws its strength from Puritanism, is a force destructive of the individual personality and operates as a socially binding force principally through its exploitation of sexual guilt and of the mystery of death. American Protestantism's concept of sin is the greatest sin in his fiction because it created an ineradicable dissatisfaction with the human condition—with man's moral imperfection and his mortality. Hawthorne was never baptized into any church, never sought to identify himself with any formal religious organization. In such impressive structures as Rome's Pantheon and the Vatican's St. Peter's, he found that for him the only religious element was the opening that enabled him to see the sky. Hawthorne sensed the hopelessness of his case: he required his individual relationship with God, an individualism fostered by the conditions of the religious situation in America; yet he also required a sense of spiritual community, a sense that would have been transmitted through precisely that ancient ceremony and tradition which seemed most alien to American life.

His social difficulties paralleled his religious difficulties. While he had joined the Brook Farm experiment mainly for practical reasons connected with his finances and his marriage plans, there had undoubtedly been a fugitive hope of community in his action. The hope did not survive the actual experience, and Hawthorne's letters to his beloved Sophia during this period reflect much of the detachment and alienation he would later reproduce as aspects of his character Miles Coverdale. His hope of finding social community grew particularly warm in England. English country houses gave Hawthorne a deep sense of what was meant by such words as "family" and "home," and of what it meant to have a sense of belonging to the land. For him, of course, again the knowledge came to late. He commented ironically on the fact that an American democrat should feel such an attraction to the product of England's caste system. Furthermore, he found a basic imperfection in the coexistence of almshouses and country estates. In *Our Old Home* he wrote, "There may come a time, even in this world, when we shall all understand that our tendency to the individual appropriation of gold and broad acres, fine houses, and such good and beautiful things as are equally enjoyable by a multitude, is but a trait of imperfectly developed intelligence, like the simpleton's cupidity of a penny" (p. 306).

After his first six months in Rome, Hawthorne knew what it was he had been searching for in order to find spiritual peace. But, again, the knowledge was incompatible with his deep-rooted American idealism. The Catholic Church was superbly adapted to human needs, he acknowledged; nevertheless, priests were only men and he could not place his spiritual trust in such corruptible vessels as the Italian priests seemed to be. The visible forms of Roman Catholicism impressed Hawthorne strongly and he was struck by the manifold ways in which its spiritual solace was available to the Roman people. In America, conversely, religion itself was a kind of priest in the service of regional views, or the ideas of reformers, or the personality of such charismatic leaders as his character Hollingsworth of *The Blithedale Romance.* American religious groups were dedicated to a patriotic optimism, and their emphasis upon political dogmas of industry and opportunity were quite at odds with Hawthorne's personal sense of the proper concern of religion—as well as with the theological premises of the historic Christian disciplines. Growing and changing with the nation, Protestantism assumed forms that were at times a travesty of Christian doctrine. In the decade prior to his leaving America, for example, Hawthorne could observe most of the major Protestant denominations split apart over the issue of slavery.

The friends who fell away from Hawthorne because, in his support of Franklin Pierce, he appeared to oppose abolition greatly misunderstood him; and Hawthorne was in no position to attempt to make clear where he stood on the issue of slavery. Had he done so publicly, his friends might have been startled by the trenchant sweep of his dissatisfaction with American life. In 1861 he could write to his friend Bridge, on the subject of the black regiments then being formed in Massachusetts, "we should see the expediency of preparing our black brethren for future citizenship, by allowing them to fight for their own liberties and educating them through heroic influences. Whatever happens next, I must say that I rejoice that the old Union is smashed. We never were one people, and never really had a country since the Constitution was formed."[6] Despite the fact that he was the product of generations of Americans and that his writings were felt to have a uniquely American tone, Hawthorne had come to feel almost no attachment to his country, geographically or politically, and he judged it to have been a failure as a society. His notebooks provide evidence that he considered several times the possibility of making his home in Europe. When he eventually returned to America, an American's return to his ancestral home in England was to be the obsessive idea in his pathetic struggle to create a final romance.

Only after he had lived a while in England did Hawthorne realize the extent to which America had made him. Like Cooper a quarter of a century before, he discovered the radical nature of his democratic thinking, and he found himself in a culture that seemed to him positively medieval—a kind of Massachusetts yankee at King Arthur's court. It was a direct confrontation with man's cultural history that formed a counterpart to the direct involvement with man's depraved nature necessitated by his consular duties. Hawthorne had soon abandoned the idea of writing any fiction while he served as consul. In whatever time could be wrested from official duties, he dedicated himself to studying the life about him. The usual tourist spots were covered, and there werc repeated, painful visits to art galleries. But on the evidence of his notebooks, what moved Hawthorne most and told him most about European life was architecture—the castles, cathedrals, and historic strongholds, but also humbler forms, stone cottages, country churches, and above all the ancient cities themselves.

In America the individual had seemed of supreme importance, and the Emersonian "Now" rang with assurance. In England Hawthorne reaffirmed his faith in the individual and in the present, but with diffidence. In Rome he had to confess that the individual seemed an infinitely small thing and the present but a moment in time. It was not merely the aesthetic presence of so much shaped stone that moved Hawthorne, but the consciousness of the intensely realized forms of human life, the traditions and ceremonies, that it embodied. The organic theory of architecture about which Horatio Greenough wrote, as did Emerson and Thoreau, found expression on many occasions in Hawthorne's English notebooks. He preferred his philosophy and his history, as well as his sermons, in stone. America, by contrast, was still the wilderness. American land, comments Middleton, the American protagonist of *The Ancestral Footstep,* " 'is but so much grass; so much dirt, where a succession of people have dwelt too little to make it really their own.' "[7]

Part of the fascination of the European cities was their horror. Hawthorne's walks took him everywhere, into the Liverpool slums and the filthy byways of London's City, where he discovered what poverty could mean. In Rome the beggars swarmed everywhere, even in the gates and courtyards of the most splendid churches and palaces. Like Melville on his first voyage to Liverpool, Hawthorne found the degree of poverty to be something unimagined in America. When he first encountered the poor children of England's great cities, Hawthorne wondered what it signified to be human. In "Glimpses of English Poverty," he asked how such little wretches, deformed, diseased, starved, and filthy could be informed with an immortal principle—and if they had none, what claim could he assert for his own? The same question was being asked in America by the Abolitionists about the slaves.

Race had made the slaves invisible as men to many Americans, and class distinctions had made the poor invisible as men to many Europeans; but for Americans such as Cooper, Melville, and Hawthorne, shocked by the frightful suffering of the poor whites they saw in Europe's cities, there could be only one response: either all humanity shared equally in the hope of heaven and equally in the possibility of fulfillment of their human potentiality, or there was no salvation possible for anyone. The exposure to English poverty impressed Hawthorne with the ways in which "the flow and reflux of a common humanity pervade us all," and he concluded "Glimpses of English Poverty" with the demand, "Is, or is not, the system wrong that gives one married pair so immense a superfluity of luxurious home, and shuts out a million others from any home whatever?" (p. 309). In what is possibly the most powerful metaphor in all his account of England, Hawthorne describes his response after a personal encounter with the children of the English poor: "Slowly, slowly, as after groping at the bottom of a deep, noisome, stagnant pool, my hope struggles upward to the surface, bearing the half-drowned body of a child along with it and heaving it aloft for its life, and my own life, and all our lives. Unless these slime-clogged nostrils can be made capable of inhaling celestial air, I know not how the purest and most intellectual of us can reasonably expect ever to taste a breath of it. The whole question of eternity is staked there. If a single one of those helpless little ones be lost, the world is lost!" (p. 282). He saw elsewhere in England "countless multitudes of little girls" who had been taken from workhouses, educated at charity-schools, and by and by were to be apprenticed as servants. They looked stupid, animal, and soulless. Such encounters stirred Hawthorne profoundly and held before him the question of what significance attached to an individual life, or, for that matter, to the universe. In *The Marble Faun* this question glides ironically into the story in many ways, as when the central characters find their contemplation of churches and shrines interrupted by beggars, or when extremes of wealth and poverty are juxtaposed, or when old stone buildings evoke the sense of endless human generations pursuing more or less the same mortal errands in their dark rooms and stairways.

All the factors that had contributed to puzzling and challenging Hawthorne in England were to be intensified and prolonged in Rome. In England the superb cathedrals seemed anciently rooted, but in Rome there were churches centuries older. In many instances the churches were composed visibly of parts of pre-Christian temples, and some of these rested upon the altars raised by vanished peoples to gods unknown. Churches were everywhere in the city. Their bells were continually to be heard, and priests and monks were everywhere to be seen. The people went in and out of the churches at their individual need, partaking, as it seemed to Hawthorne, of the sacraments of the church with a casual familiarity. It was utterly unlike New England with its Protestant Sundays. The Roman poor were thoroughly at ease in churches that Hawthorne compared to gigantic jewel cases. Furthermore, there was through high and low, sinner and saint, a sense of religious community that made sense neither to the democratic nor to the puritan biases of his mind. More than ever Hawthorne felt himself in a kind of existential world where none of the absurd values about him had meaning and where his own interior values were being drained away. In the flux of Roman experience, all judgments were apt to find themselves reversed the following day.

In April, 1858, Hawthorne sketched out the story of an American who returns to his ancestral English home (published posthumously as *The Ancestral Footstep).* While he worked on it, he got the idea of doing a fanciful piece about a faun who finds himself among the human race. The story of the American had to be set aside, and no doubt Hawthorne intended to resume work on it that summer. But the faun idea took over his creative imagination. The idea lent itself to certain obvious developments, and when Hawthorne sketched it out at Florence in the summer, he must have thought of the projected work in terms of his previous fiction—innocence corrupted by passion, the progress from a guilty despair to penitence and responsibility, and happiness regained but tinged with sorrow. It may well be that Hawthorne's symbolic formulations had always involved some degree of compromise and his own metaphysical uncertainties fed the artfulness of his ambiguities. But as he wrote *The Marble Faun,* transferring many of his notebook entries almost directly to its pages, the actuality of his life in Rome broke through the romance he was planning.

When the family returned to Rome in October after the summer in Florence, he could not resume work on the book chiefly because of his daughter Una's severe, recurrent attacks of malaria. Rome, with its omnipresent reminders of man's mortality, took on a tragic cast, which intensified his already highly ambivalent feelings for the city. At times it was a "loathsome corpse"; at times he confessed a deeper attachment to it than to any other place he had ever known: "we are astonished by the discovery, by and by, that our heart-strings have mysteriously attached themselves to the Eternal City, and are drawing us thitherward again, as if it were more familiar, more intimately our home, than even the spot where we were born" (p. 326).[8] Everything about the city, as well as the campagna and Florence, seemed to contribute to the development of his sketch for the novel. When he set about the final writing in the summer of 1859, at Redcar in Yorkshire, the themes of the novel and the characters served repeatedly to introduce the Roman setting and to provide Hawthorne with a chance to express the shifting and conflicting reactions that had made up his life in Italy and most particularly in Rome.

What had promised to be the central theme, Donatello's fortunate fall, was taken up only occasionally. It was as though man's fall, too, had taken on a different value for Hawthorne, and was being seen in a perspective that blurred religious distinctions and viewed morality as capable of being modified in the organic process of history. The drama of Donatello and his friends was to have taken place chiefly against the background of Rome, that ancient, monstrous, beautiful, complex expression of human life. As it turned out, the setting overpowered the original, fanciful idea, and the novel became the record of the dramatic struggle between the author and the ancient city, between a personal idealism and brutal realities, between an American and history.

The first third of *The Marble Faun,* while it brings in the major characters and advances to the murder, is chiefly intent on the setting. All of the tourist's Rome is there: the sculpture gallery of the Capitol, the catacombs, painters' studios, the Borghese Villa and its gardens, a sculptor's studio, and Rome by day and by night. The observations in the notebooks are methodically used. As the action of the work follows Hawthorne's movements and his major moods—the first spring in Rome, the summer at Villa Montauto, the sad winter of 1858–59, and the final Carnival—the author's voice is continually heard.

In all of Hawthorne's novels there is a sense of his presence, and with each successive one it becomes more marked. There is, however, in all the American novels a sense of his detachment from the experience he is rendering. If he was passionately involved in the creation of *The Scarlet Letter,* the characters nevertheless have each an integrity of conception that gives a quality of Greek tragedy to their encounters. Hawthorne's very personal sense of alienation broods over *The House of Seven Gables,* but the characters have a distinct life. In *The Blithedale Romance* he consciously wears the mask of Miles Coverdale, even though at times the mask is his own face. No character in *The Marble Faun,* however, has a consistent identity. Each one, at times, is speaking the author's thoughts as he recorded them in his notebooks, and this is true even when they contradict one another. Hawthorne is always, somehow, "there."

In much of the novel Hawthorne speaks directly to the reader, even when it would have been a simple matter to transfer his remarks to a character; and, when a character expresses an opinion that Hawthorne does not want to be taken as his own, the opinion is cautiously qualified. Hawthorne had projected aspects of his own personality into such disparate characters as Chillingsworth, Aylmer, Clifford, and Coverdale; but in *The Marble Faun* he communicated contradictory aspects of his own personality in single characters. Kenyon, the "man of marble," inadvertently repulses Miriam even as Hawthorne felt that his own reserve inadvertently chilled others. The warm sympathy Kenyon has for Donatello at Monte Beni was like the warm sympathy Hawthorne knew he had sometimes communicated to such a friend as Pierce or Melville. Donatello's joy in nature is Hawthorne's, and even more, the joy he had observed in his son Julian. Donatello's estrangement from nature was Hawthorne's, as when Una was believed to be dying, and all the fountains seemed broken.

It is almost comic to see how Hawthorne uses Hilda with her sorrow to express his own sense of agonized weariness at dutifully treading for the hundredth time the cold marble floors of the art galleries of Roman palazzi. And Kenyon's baffled efforts to make the clay express the quality of Donatello's personality he feels to be true is Hawthorne's sardonic comment on his own struggle to make words capture the same elusive quality. No doubt with his first sketch for the novel Hawthorne had different intentions for his characters, but in the course of writing it he transformed his fanciful idea to his felt reality. The narrow but certain moral oppositions that had served him in the past had become disoriented by a variety of Roman experiences.

Few characters are more objectionable to the modern reader than Hawthorne's Hilda, the daughter of the Puritans. She is accused of being egotistic and frigid, and her rejection of Miriam is considered inexcusable. The principle that Hilda represents, however, was one that Hawthorne had always believed valid and central to religious conduct. That a mortal's first duty is to his own salvation was sound

Puritan teaching; and in the pursuit of his salvation he was to shut out all possible access of evil, whether it came from family, friends, or others.

If virtue was thereby "fugitive and cloistered," unpraiseworthy, as Milton maintained, it nevertheless had its eye on the sole prize worth striving for—salvation. Bunyan's Christian, when he saw the way to save himself, put his fingers in his ears so as not to hear the cries of his wife and children "and ran crying, 'Life, life, eternal life.'" It is this purest Puritan strain that makes of Hilda a lodestar for the Unitarian Kenyon. He depends upon a reasoned morality, but he believes that Hilda's heart instinctively knows truth. Like the steel blade to which she is twice compared, she slices a clear distinction between good and evil. Furthermore, Hawthorne intends to suggest that the principle Hilda represents, unswerving virtue in pursuit of salvation, is the one that serves the ideal of womanhood. It is with this idea that the daughter of the Puritans keeps a lamp burning at the loftiest shrine in Rome to the Blessed Virgin.

Perhaps the pre-Rome Hawthorne would have left the matter of Hilda there. But the Italian way of treating abstract ideas would give him no peace. The Italian painters' practice of infusing a warm humanity into their works, and especially into their Madonnas, outraged him at times. For that matter, the very human qualities of the Italian priesthood and aristocracy broke in continually upon his sense of propriety. And the earthy Romans seemed always to have befouled with a token of their humanity precisely the spots chosen by Sophia for an access of the sublime. The Italian painters' use of the same model for mistress, for Venus in glowing nudity, and for Madonna in heavenly robes confounded him: "And who can trust the religious sentiment of Raphael, or receive any of his Virgins as heaven-descended likenesses, after seeing, for example, the Fornarina of the Barberini Palace, and feeling how sensual the artist must have been to paint such a brazen trollop of his own accord, and lovingly? Would the Blessed Mary reveal herself to his spiritual vision, and favor him with sittings alternately with that type of glowing earthliness, the Fornarina?" (p. 337). Apparently she would, for Hawthorne proceeded to praise Raphael's cherubs and madonnas "and withdraw all that we have said." Both he and Sophia denounced the Roman clergy in their notebooks, and Sophia wrote that her sense of the corruptions of the priests, and some, she recorded, were "said to be peculiarly corrupt," made her sensible of a hollowness and emptiness in every ceremony she saw.[9]

As the novel proceeds, the Hilda principle is made more flexible. The daughter of the Puritans is placed in a position similar to that in which she had found Miriam; she has an overwhelming burden and needs to confide in someone. She tries prayer to saints, who were once human beings and keep "within their heavenly memories, the tender humility of a human experience." But she finds the human element is necessary, and so she confesses to a priest. How far Hawthorne has gone in compromising the Puritan principle can be seen in Hilda's response to Kenyon's question, " 'Then you are not a Catholic?' "

" 'Really, I do not quite know what I am . . . I have a great deal of faith, and Catholicism seems to have a great deal of good. Why should not I be a Catholic, if I find there what I need, and what I cannot find elsewhere?' "

She echoes a direct comment of Hawthorne to the reader (on page 346) as she continues: " 'The more I see of this worship, the more I wonder at the exuberance with which it adapts itself to all the demands of human infirmity. If its ministers were but a little more than human, above all error, pure from all iniquity, what a religion would it be!' " (p. 368). Hawthorne's disclaimers about Catholicism are now given to Kenyon, but it is clear that Hilda has changed. No longer the perfect copyist, she sees as profoundly as before the intention of the artist, but her new knowledge of reality enables her to see the limitations of every work of art—and of every mortal. She still affirms that there is "only one right and one wrong," but her point of view is expressed in the context of a discussion of the way in which "a mixture of good . . . may be in things evil," so that Kenyon's description of her position as "unworldly and impracticable theory" seems to be Hawthorne's last word on the subject.

In contrast with the care Hawthorne took to soften the rigidities of Hilda, almost nothing was done to restore the sorrow-stricken Miriam. Except for the scene at Perugia, Miriam makes but a few brief appearances in the second half of the novel. After her vivid moments leading up to the murder and shortly thereafter, Hawthorne reduces his dark heroine almost to the status of a voice offstage. Her conduct at Perugia, however, is striking. While waiting for Donatello to recognize her at the base of the statue of Pope Julius III, she uses language that should be used in relation to Donatello's penitence. Unlike Hawthorne's tortured sinners in the American novels, Donatello merely placed himself beneath the statue and felt the blessing upon his spirit. Without prompting from anyone, Miriam tells Kenyon, "his heart must be left freely to its own decision whether to recognize me, because on his voluntary choice depends the whole question whether my devotion will do him good or harm. Except he feel an infinite need of me, I am a burden and fatal obstruction to him!' " (p. 317).

In these words, Kenyon, who had been reading an old copy of Dante's *Divine Comedy* at Monte Beni, might have recognized, albeit oddly adapted to a lover, the conditions of voluntary choice and infinite need that lead Dante's sinners to God. It was Miriam, too, who proposed that Donatello's election should be made in a public spot, at high noon, and where the statue of Pope Julius extends its hand in blessing. In assisting the sinner, through his love for her, to find salvation, Hawthorne's dark heroine is functioning like the Madonna.

Hawthorne's handling of Donatello is even more extraordinary. After the crime, Hawthorne applies the Puritan psychology of conversion to his sinner. There is conviction of sin and with it the awakening of the soul, the humanizing of the faun. Donatello leaves Rome as a City of Destruction, and goes through his period of despondency leading to despair and thoughts of suicide. Then Kenyon (Reason, Instruction) persuades him to take up his burden. At this point, Hawthorne drops the matter of sin and guilt, precisely where, in the light of his earlier works, it should have proved most suitable to his genius. What might have been a pilgrim's progress to Rome loses its penitential aspect. There are crosses along the way and shrines to the Madonna. "Beholding these consecrated stations, the idea seemed to strike Donatello of converting the otherwise aimless journey into a penitential pilgrimage" (p. 296). Whether he actually did so or not, Hawthorne does not let us know.

For his struggle-of-the-burdened-conscience, Hawthorne turns awkwardly to Hilda, and her burden is relieved by a New England priest. Although Hawthorne had always believed that sin and suffering, not crime and punishment, were important, Donatello plans to turn himself over to the law. It is not that Hawthorne believed the Roman judges to be less corrupt than the Roman priests. As he causes Miriam to remark, " 'I have assured him that there is no such thing as earthly justice, and especially none here, under the head of Christendom' " (p. 433). In his transformation, Donatello takes on nothing of the tragic dignity of Adam, penitent for having sinned against his God. Donatello has become a modern man in wrong with the law, who is "bound to submit himself to whatsoever tribunal takes cognizance of such things, and abide its judgment."

Kenyon, who so far as the reader can discover never knows exactly what has caused the fearful change in his friends, is the self-appointed spiritual guide to Donatello. His advice, however, is for a kind of muscular Christianity, "effort! crowd it out with good . . ." (p. 273); at best his advice is moralistic, and when he prescribes travel to Donatello, "The little adventures and vicissitudes of travel will do him infinite good" (p. 284), he sounds precisely like the conductor on "The Celestial Railroad."

Hawthorne makes Kenyon representative of a broad strain of American moral thinking. That such thinking was not to Hawthorne's taste is evident from such an author-to-reader passage as this, shortly before Kenyon takes over his ministry to Donatello, in which "the iron rule in our day to require an object and a purpose in life" is Hawthorne's subject: "It makes us all parts of a complicated scheme of progress, which can only result in our arrival at a colder and drearier region than we were born in. It insists upon everybody's adding somewhat (a mite, perhaps, but earned by incessant effort) to an accumulated pile of usefulness, of which the only use will be to burden our posterity with even heavier thoughts and more inordinate labor than our own. No life now wanders like an unfettered stream; there is a mill-wheel for the tiniest rivulet to turn. We go all wrong, by too strenuous a resolution to go all right" (p. 239). In the light of such a view, Kenyon's counsel to Donatello to make the wide world his cell was scarcely intended to be an endorsement of the American Protestant ethic.

Kenyon seems quite incapable of taking his own advice when, on returning to Rome, the discovery that Hilda has disappeared crushes his spirits. In one of the finest passages in the novel, Hawthorne describes Kenyon's state of mind, which might very well have been his own state of mind during his second winter in Rome when Una was gravely ill. The ponderous gloom of the past bore down irresistibly upon the individual sorrow. "Your own life is as nothing" when compared with the immeasurable distances stretching through triumphal arches, past obelisks to the brilliant sky. You ask for "a gleam of sunshine, instead of a speck of shadow, on the step or two that will bring you to your quiet rest. How exceedingly absurd!" (p. 410). Thus Hawthorne measured his individual significance against the Eternal City.

If the doctrine of work and effort seemed all wrong, and the hope of happiness absurd in the face of the Roman record of ancient cultures and man's continuous, futile adaptations, it was like whistling in the dark to repeat the idea so popular in Concord that "all towns should be made capable of purification by fire, or of decay, within each half century," or to boast that in America each generation had only its own sins and sorrows to bear. For Hawthorne, the damage had been done; placed against the evidence of time, the tensions he had posited in *The Marble Faun* dissolved away. The image of the faun was to have given way to the image of an American Adam, with the archangel Kenyon prating of redemption. But the image of man that pervades the work is that which came to Kenyon as he mused over the statue of the Laocoön in the Vatican sculpture gallery: man and his generation forever in the coil of evil, an image that had always been part of Hawthorne's creative imagination. Now, however, Hawthorne felt it differently, and he wrote: "What he most admired was the strange calmness diffused through this bitter strife; so that it resembled the rage of the sea made calm by its intensity, or the tumult of Niagara which ceases to be tumult because it lasts forever. Thus in the Laocoön, the horror of a moment grew to be the fate of interminable ages" (p. 391). This was the vision of man's condition that informed the work Hawthorne constructed from the stones of Rome.

Part Two
THE AMERICAN JACOBINS

A foreign country is a point of comparison wherefrom to judge your own. One use of travel is to recommend the books and works of home—we go to Europe to be Americanized; and another, to find men.

—Emerson, "Culture"

4
Henry James and the American Aristocracy

When Henry James was seventeen the news of the raid on Harpers Ferry and the capture of John Brown reached him in Europe, and he remembered the occasion "as the very first reminder that reached me of our living, on our side, in a political order."[1] The James family had spent three years in Europe, returned to America for a year, and were back in Europe for one more year. In 1860 the family returned to America and settled first in Newport, R.I., then in Cambridge, Mass. The European experience had made James highly conscious of political and social order, and during this period of the 1860s, as his autobiographical writings show, he was impressed by the ability he had acquired to analyze American life objectively, as though he were observing a foreign country. He had seen a wide variety of forms and ceremonies that expressed conceptions of church and state and social order, and he was able to compare. There was no question of his not feeling himself American; but at the same time, he was "detached." As he expressed it, "the effect of detachment was the fact of the experience of Europe."[2]

Soon after his return in 1860, however, he found himself involved in a recognition scene very much like the kind that was to play so crucial a part in his fiction. In *Notes of a Son and Brother* he describes how, during the Newport period, "like dear old Walt," he visited a hospital for invalided soldiers. Like Whitman he moved from patient to patient, drawing from each "his troubled tale," and offering each some solace. Like Whitman, he felt a deep communion with the men;

but unlike Whitman, he perceived that as an American he was radically apart from them: "our common Americanism carried with it, to my imagination, such a disclosed freshness and strangeness, working, as I might say, over such gulfs of dissociation, that I reached across to *their,* these hospital friends' side of the matter."[3]

This was the starting point for James's realization, quite opposed to the popular view, that Americans were only superficially one people. Certain sectional differences had always been taken for granted; but the popular view held Americans to be a distinct nationality, holding a common ethical point of view, and devoted to the same political ideals. Very shortly after James's return from Europe most young American men whom he knew were engaged in a war on behalf of "union," but his personal discovery was "of the point where our national theory of absorption, assimilation and conversion appallingly breaks down."[4]

Quite inevitably this led to his wondering what it meant to be an American. He had grown up with the belief that American community was a "*consecrated* association,"[5] but he found that in fact such community did not exist. Americans could be many things. Like the Europeans whom he had recently studied, they could have concepts of political and social life radically different from one another and be quite incapable of comprehending one another's view. These were realizations that came painfully to one who knew "in the old, the comparatively brothering, conditions what an American at least *was.*"[6]

During the 1860s and early 1870s James was examining his American environment with the greatest care, searching always to discover how he might convert his experience to fiction. His personal sense of what experience he might use and of the literary effects he might create was directed, however, by his overriding concept of fiction as a criticism of manners. James could watch his brother Wilky march off to battle as Adjutant of the 54th Massachusetts out of Boston, "the first body of coloured soldiers raised in the North," and then in search of literary material set about scrutinizing his genteel Harvard boarding table, presided over by Professor Child, for resemblances to Balzac's grim Maison Vauquer in *Le Père Goriot.* Many decades after the event, reminiscing autobiographically about his early efforts to become a writer, James indicates only by indirection how much America meant to him as a social and political ideal and he describes with an element of caricature his involvement with a class of Americans who were, as he speaks of "*our* Newport," incurably cosmopolite.

If James was detached from American life, he was also detached from the cosmopolite American elite even though that was the class of Americans with which he was destined to be associated not only in Newport, Boston, and New York, but also in London, Paris, and in the great Italian cities. Members of this elite class furnished much of the material for his fiction. James stayed in their palazzi, villas, and country houses; he enjoyed and admired much of their life; but he also, with a disinterested detachment, saw the many ways in which these Americans were essentially opposed to what was traditionally valued as distinctive in the American spirit. This observation formed an important part of the "international theme" in the novels beginning with *Roderick Hudson* and ending with *The Portrait of a Lady* wherein James used Americans within a European setting to express his reactions to American life. Some of the more immediate and obvious criticisms had to do with American conformist and commercial pressures as opposed to the needs of the artist, the American dedication to work and duty as opposed to an appreciation of leisure and enjoyment, the American male's absorption in making money, and the American female's absorption in affirming a frigid morality. As the writing of these early novels progressed, James concentrated more on a basic confrontation: the menacing threat of the forces of wealth, exclusiveness, and convention to a society that had prided itself on being open, generous, and dedicated to an ideal of human community: not a union of political convenience, but a "*consecrated* association."

When James returned to Europe for good, he began *Roderick Hudson* with a sketch of Northampton as he felt Balzac would have drawn a provincial town. He etched in the dedication to business, the hostility to leisure, the conscious morality, and the misconception of art that he felt to be true of provincial America. Shifting the scene to Rome, he presented his American readers with a lesson in the nature of creative activity. Several of his characters illustrate different types of the artist, and the title character is an extreme example of the romantic artist. Part of James's intention was to indicate the vital role played by the irrational in such a personality. Great art, Roderick argues, cannot come out of humdrum experience and a deference to commonplace morality. While almost all the characters are American, and the action is largely contained within the American moral perspective of Rowland Mallett, the novel lives in a Roman atmosphere of artistic values, spontaneous and independent behavior, and cultural variety that constituted a direct challenge to the American scene.

The criticism of American life both explicit and implicit in James's novels seemed to many critics then and later to align James with the European critics who had had so many harsh things to say about America's great experiment. James knew, however, that while his European experience had helped him to understand American life, his insights would have been impossible had he not been an American; and the insights were his own. Nor was he put off by paradox—such as the demand for conformity existing in American life along with the harsh resistance to absorption, assimilation, and conversion. He had accepted an even more ironic paradox, namely, the clamor for democratic equality existing along with the struggle of individual Americans to secure for themselves the privileges of aristocracy. Unlike the majority of Americans of his time, James was aware of the moral principles implicit in the political nature of a state and of how these principles should be manifest in the behavior of the influential members of the state. What he observed in the "best" circles of American cities was the operation of the principle of social exclusion, and he repeatedly demonstrated it in operation with the added ironic dimension of placing the Americans in a European framework.

America had, with its Revolution, rejected the aristocratic idea, and there was nothing in the way of ancient castles and cathedrals to act as a reminder of the hostile authority that had been cast off, nor was there an articulate Tory Party that required a corresponding articulation of liberal principles. But while the political structure of class rule disappeared, capitalism soon recaptured for itself the aristocratic privileges, and all of James's international novels include some treatment of representatives of this new American aristocracy engaged in an effort to consolidate their exclusive position. The *absence* of the old feudal forms was certainly felt in American life, and Cooper, Hawthorne, and Melville commented on this as well as James. All of these writers recognized the continued operation of the old forces of privilege in American life despite the absence of visible forms. It was against these powerful, if invisible, forces that Whitman made his strongest protest in *Democratic Vistas*: "For feudalism, caste, and the ecclesiastic traditions, though palpably retreating from political institutions, still hold essentially, by their spirit, even in this country, entire possession of the more important fields, indeed the very subsoil, of education, and of social standards and literature."[7]

Repeatedly James's novels present for critical analysis representative Americans who are the product of what Whitman termed a "theory of character grown of feudal aristocracies," and the novels show, in the consequences of such a theory of character and principle of exclusion, the need, again to quote Whitman, for a new standard: "yet old enough, and accepting the old, the perennial elements, and combining them into groups, unities, appropriate to the modern, the democratic, the west."[8] With this statement, James would have been in full agreement.

Pre-Civil War fiction in America had been strongly affected by the aristocratic idea. Irving's sketches of English life in *Bracebridge Hall* and his Knickerbocker patroons, Cooper's Littlepage trilogy and Temples and Effinghams, Hawthorne's evocation of Colonial America, and the hierarchic structure in most of Melville's work suggest the variety of forms the idea could take. Sir Walter Scott's aristocratic romances had a powerful influence, especially upon Southern plantation novels; and the work of the South's most important novelists influenced that society through their marked aristocratic slant. That this literary idea was false or distorted or alien to American ideals did not alter the fact of its extensive effect upon the lives of the genteel in the cities of the eastern seaboard.

The story of Roderick Hudson offers one of the few instances in which James's mind was "violated by an idea," for that character is designed to illustrate a type of the artist. The force of James's creative imagination is much more evident in the treatment of Rowland Mallett and, particularly, of Christina Light. Christina is the victim of her American mother's desperate efforts to marry her to wealth and nobility. What James thought of this emergent American Dream is evident from his treatment of Mrs. Light, the dreamer. The vehicle for James's social criticism is Christina, even more than Rowland. Her candor is ruthless. Knowing what it is to be one with the rich and fashionable in "the great world," and knowing, too, that she has been *made* for that life, she nevertheless has taken the full measure of its hollowness. Her appraisal is partly rooted in what James observed of Americans in European social circles, and partly, and more deeply, on what he had observed, while preparing his early American travel sketches, on the verandas of Newport, Saratoga, and Lake George.

Other criticisms of American life emerge in *Roderick Hudson* through the satirical treatment of Mr. Leavenworth, a man who strenuously proclaims his Americanism while, with an equally intense conviction, he holds all Europeans (indeed all non-Americans) to be socially inferior. Mr. Leavenworth objected to Christina's marriage to a Neapolitan prince, averring " 'If she wanted a fine bright fellow—a specimen of clean comfortable *white* humanity—I would have undertaken to find him for her without going out of my native State.' " (p. 302).[9] Color apart, such an American as Leavenworth would be in full accord with Mrs. Light's effort to marry her daughter for the highest price her beauty could fetch in the international market, and in accord with the destruction of Christina's—or Roderick's—individual spirit. James's treatment of the wealthy American art collector attacks the provincial ambition of creating an American art—the term "American" having reference to vague, pompous concepts of the patron. Mr. Leavenworth would not have recognized the Negro head sculpted by Roderick in Northampton, Mass., as art at all; he wanted statues of "Intellectual Refinement" and "Conscious Temperance." Mr. Leavenworth as a type lingered long in James's imagination and reappeared in *The Golden Bowl* as Adam Verver. Like other of James's collectors (Newman, Acton, Osmond, Rosier, Verver) he confounds human with material values, and collects the statuesque Miss Blanchard as his bride and something to crown his accumulations.

The Mr. Leavenworths, James implies, are the product of a narrow, specialized way of life that had become dissociated from its own cultural history. At one point in *Roderick Hudson,* in response to Rowland Mallett's urging that she enjoy life, Mary Garland, the product of generations of Unitarian ministers, asks, " 'Is this what you call life? . . . all this splendour, all Rome; pictures, ruins, statues, beggars, monks.' " Rowland replies, " 'It's not all of it, but it's a large part of it. All these things are impregnated with life; they're the results of an immemorial, a complex and accumulated, civilisation' " (p. 334).[10] Given great economic power and no anchoring traditions, Mr. Leavenworth and the class of which he is the type tried to order a visible tradition that reflected their estimate of themselves and to call it "America." As James demonstrates, Leavenworth knows nothing of art or of America. James was not arguing against an indigenous art or that European cultural artifacts should do service in America; he was demonstrating how important such visible symbols were as an expression of human experience, as well as in maintaining an idea or belief. Mr. Leavenworth's proprietary Americanism was intended as irony, but the point of James's irony was not always taken by his American readers.

James's problem as a critic of American life was to make Americans see themselves. His most effective method was to employ "Europe." "Europe" may bear only a superficial resemblance to the actual Europe, but it serves in James's fiction to throw into relief the cultural deficiencies of America as James felt them. The setting in his fiction is always functional, an extension of character and theme. In the international novels the European settings—room, apartment, house, church, city, countryside, and even human fixtures—are all used with artistic deliberation to draw attention to what is American in the American characters.

These American characters, including those who have spent most of their lives in Europe, are not conceived by James as innocent or evil; they are, in one form or another, provincial. Further, the association of America with moral purity and Europe with corrupt experience is unwarranted. Such Jamesian Americans as Mary Garland, Daisy Miller, Isabel Archer, and Milly Theale are neither more innocent nor morally finer than such Jamesian Europeans as Fleda Vetch, Hyacinth Robinson, Nick Dormer, and a number of the "super-subtle-fry" in shorter works. Or, from another viewpoint, Isabel Archer's innocence is no more "American" than that of one of her progenitors, Dorothea Brooke of George Eliot's *Middlemarch.* Eugenia and Felix, as their names suggest, bring good breeding and a joy in life to their moralistic American cousins and calculating Robert Acton of *The Europeans.* No Europeans receive quite the acid treatment that James meted out to the representative Americans of *The Bostonians.* If many of James's Europeanized Americans are warped in spirit, many (especially the *ficelles*) have weathered the European years with a moral fibre that stems straight from their American heritage.

While James believed that American culture was provincial, he recognized that it could still produce people with moral spontaneity and intellectual grace; and venerable, decaying European establishments could often express an accumulation of values among the finest of which the human spirit is capable. In order to recognize and preserve what was best in their own culture, and to broaden and enrich that culture, Americans had to go the main cultural stream from which they broke away. James's international novels served to assist Americans with what he called their "complex fate."

Christopher Newman is an example of an American belatedly coming to terms with his cultural inadequacies. First he is seen in the Louvre ordering copies of great masterpieces from an attractive girl. Newman is unable to judge her lack of talent and is insensitive to her physical charms, which will in time command the life of one aristocrat and the fortune of another. James is suggesting that Newman's ignorance of aesthetic values in paintings and persons is related; the American aristocrat searches for art as he searches for love—in ignorance and on the basis of fatuous abstractions. He wants a woman whom he can perch on the pile of his fortune, as Newman characteristically puts it, like a statue on a monument. " 'I want, in a word, the best article in the market,' " he declares (p. 49), and is led by another aristocratic American to pay court to a tall, pale, ascetic widow whose chief value in her own *monde*—but a value that presumably has no meaning for Newman—is in her Bellegarde blood.

James makes the Bellegardes an example of an old noble family clinging to an anachronistic estimate of the value of their name. Although living in cosmopolitan Paris, they are as provincial in their understanding of what constitutes human value as the American who has given most of his adult life to accumulating a fortune. Newman knows that the Bellegardes consider him only because of his fortune, but he does not appreciate how utterly he is disregarded as a person until he drops the word that he is very rich, and the old Marquise asks him flatly, " 'How rich?' " Newman himself weighs nothing in her balance. The Bellegardes are used by James to demonstrate the American's ignorance of painting, literature, architecture, music, religion, history—in short, of the whole cultural process out of which his own nation emerged. Newman cannot see any use in Valentine Bellegarde's mode of life and feels that a man's mind is wasted if not at work making money—Valentine, he suggests, might put his to use manipulating railroad stock—and his most distinctive virtue is his moral sense, itself the result of a complex historical process of which he is ignorant. James presents America's new man as a latter-day Natty Bumppo.

For all their picturesqueness, James's European aristocrats are usually shown as being of questionable morals and badly in need of money. The most notable exception is Lord Warburton of *The Portrait of a Lady,* but even he is made to argue his own obsolescence. In addition, Lord Warburton, who had traveled through the United States and knew much more about the country than Isabel, pointed out to her that, "of all the people in the world, the Americans were the most grossly superstitious. They were rank Tories and bigots, every one of them; there were no conservatives like American conservatives. Her uncle and her cousin were there to prove it; nothing could be more mediaeval than many of their views" (1:95).

While their order was defunctive, the Bellegardes and the Warburtons could offer to the Duke of California and to the American heiress the historic idea of family. In *The American,* by way of emphasizing the separateness of the individual in the American community and in contrast with the quick dispersion of American families such as Newman's, James stresses the Bellegarde family as a unit that had endured through time despite great political and social upheaval, that extended beyond national borders, that had its own standard of loyalty, and relegated questions of taste, morals, and law to an extrinsic category. Claire de Cintré has a need to obey her mother that has a primal quality in it; it is, she says, "like a religion." Compared with those bound in this ancient bond of blood, the individual American, a creature of vast, gilded, rented salons, shuttling across continents and seas, seems very much an "Ishmael," an "isolato," a "victim." Like the great American novelists who preceded him, Cooper, Hawthorne, and Melville, James felt keenly the absence of the tradition of family in American life, and like those earlier writers his imagination often projects the solitary person aching to escape from his freedom into those ceremonies of belonging prefigured in the ancestral home.

Daisy Miller provides a concise example of how James used "Europe" to depict the nature of the American aristocrats, their exclusiveness, *a priori* standards, and essential hostility to traditional American values. Vevey is described as being practically an American watering place, and the Roman settings are all familiar backdrops for American tourists and Americano-Europeans. Mrs. Costello, the aunt of Winterbourne and an American noblewoman of high degree, imparts some of her social wisdom to her nephew: "She admitted that she was very exclusive; but, if he were acquainted with New York, he would see that one had to be. And her picture of the minutely hierarchical constitution of the society of that city, which she presented to him in many different lights, was, to Winterbourne's imagination, almost oppressively striking" (p. 23).

Like their counterparts in a European novel of manners, the American aristocrats demonstrate the principle of exclusion and the pressure of conformism. Their judgments are based on highly parochial standards, a dread of sex, a distrust of foreigners (nonaristocratic Europeans), and an assumed title to superiority and leadership. Unlike her counterpart in a European novel of manners, who challenges a recognized system, Daisy Miller is as ignorant of the social forces that reject her as she is of the historic culture of Switzerland or Italy. Symbolically, Daisy dies in the Coliseum; it is a martyrdom of love; and it is also James's witness to the death of something spontaneous, open, and instinct with community in American life. In contrast to Daisy, the character Winterbourne suggests another element in American life that had been there from the beginning and that the new aristocracy had taken as its own; it is the element that Hawthorne symbolized as the imprisoned heart.

Seen in a context of national destiny, *Daisy Miller* is tragic; but the heroine herself, uncomprehended and uncomprehending, is pathetic. Her mind is little more developed than the minds of the workers in Melville's rural "Tartarus of Maids," or those of the young men and women living in the mill towns of New England at the time James wrote his novel, whose dwelling units were designed to "reflect sharp social and class divisions: the unskilled operatives lived in late colonial cubes, for instance, while the agent-executive occupied a high-Georgian block with a Greek facade."[11] For his portrait in depth of an American lady, James required a heroine whose mind, while it would bear the limitations, would eminently possess the virtues of its time and place and history.

Isabel Archer is discovered by her aunt pursuing the new learning, "German Thought," in a rambling old house in Albany that belonged to her grandmother. The house and the evocation of the life lived there is created out of James's memory of his childhood visits to his relatives. It might also have come out of Melville's memories of childhood or Cooper's. Isabel first appears in the novel on the grounds of Gardencourt, the English country estate owned by her relatives, the Touchetts. Archers, Touchetts, and Gardencourt are part of an agrarian ideal of natural aristocracy. The Touchetts would be thoroughly satisfied by the marriage of Isabel to Lord Warburton, who lives nearby in an estate comparable to their own; it would be a joining of the old American spirit (albeit agitated by the new "German Thought") to solid, responsible traditions. They would also have approved of her marriage to Caspar Goodwood, whose harsh American frontier quality is part of their own stock. But they view only as a fatal error the joining of the free, young American idealist to Osmond, who is Convention.

In the days when Isabel and Osmond loved one another he stated to her candidly, " 'No, I'm not conventional; I'm convention itself' " (2:21). He offered to explain what this meant, but Isabel did not have time to listen. He meant that he believed in authority, and in a completely disciplined, ordered, hieratic society. In his imagination he saw himself as one of those exclusive few at the top of the social pyramid who would set the example and give the law for others. James had first seen Rome in the days when Pio Nono still ruled the Papal States, and in *Roderick Hudson* wrote of how Roderick was delighted by the old imperial and papal city, "the sufficient negation of his native scene. And indeed Rome is the natural home of those spirits with a deep relish for the element of accumulation in the human picture and for the infinite superpositions of history. It is the immemorial city of convention; and in that still recent day the most impressive convention in all history was visible to men's eyes in the reverberating streets, erect in a gilded coach drawn by four black horses" (p. 92). Until he acquired Isabel's fortune, Osmond had renounced ambition; but he once confessed to her that as a young man there were two or three men he envied—the Emperor of Russia, the Sultan of Turkey, and, at moments, the Pope of Rome (1:382).

Osmond believes he does represent a genuine concept of society, a concept that is in direct opposition to that of which, as Osmond discovers too late, Isabel is unalterably representative. Omond is actually devoted, however, to the appearances associated with an authoritative system, to the forms, expensive elegance, and display of privilege. James had recognized all that went into Osmond in the lives of his wealthy Americo-European friends, some of whom were closer to Isabel in their personality, while some, like the expatriate Mr. Luce in Paris "wished to know what one had crossed that odious Atlantic for but to get away from republics" (1:305). Isabel is to move in the circle of such Americans, whose counterparts at home were building Venetian Gothic townhouses in Boston, or the château on Fifth Avenue, New York, into which the Vanderbilts moved the year *The Portrait of a Lady* was published, and "Biltmore," the château near Ashville, N.C., of George Washington Vanderbilt, which James described as "a thing of the high Rothschild manner."[12]

In the gilded age immense fortunes were being acquired in America by men whose idea of themselves and of their relation to society required a costly medieval style of architecture, suggestive of nobility, and far different from the classical Greek structures popular in the early years of the Republic, which were intended to evoke ideals of republicanism and democracy. The heroine of an English novel would have recognized in Osmond's aristocratic ambitions a social norm; Isabel is never more American than when she sees her husband's mind as a "house of darkness," unless it is when she sums up his irrelevance to any fundamental structure in the remark, "He has a genius for upholstery" (2:131).

The story does not seem to end, and the abyss across which the disenchanted couple stare at one another is one that continues to widen and to extend divisive branches in American life. In Isabel's profoundest moment, part of a passage that James considered the finest thing in the book, she reflects: "His ideal was a conception of high prosperity and propriety, of the aristocratic life . . . but they attached such different ideas, such different associations and desires, to the same formulas. Her notion of the aristocratic life was simply the union of great knowledge with great liberty; the knowledge would give one a sense of duty and the liberty a sense of enjoyment. But for Omond it was altogether a thing of forms, a conscious, calculated attitude" (2:198). The Preface that James wrote to accompany *The Portrait of a Lady* ends on as inconclusive a note as the novel itself. He speaks of the "international" light as "the light in which so much of the picture hung. But that *is* another matter. There is really too much to say."

5
Mark Twain's Pilgrim's Progress

The title of Mark Twain's book *The Innocents Abroad,* its subtitle, *The New Pilgrims' Progress,* and the Preface, which begins "This book is a record of a pleasure trip," all illustrate the irony, even the bitterness, that underlies the humor of the work. For Twain had come to believe that the innocence of the Pilgrims on the *Quaker City,* chartered for a cruise to Europe and the Holy Land, was a form of their guilt, that their pilgrimage had produced no spiritual progress, and, as he wrote his first night back in New York (19 November 1867) after the ship's return, while the expedition "was advertised as a 'pleasure excursion' . . . it did not look like one; certainly it did not act like one" (1:144).[1]

For Twain himself, however, there had been a decided pilgrim's progress. The letters about the voyage that he published in the *Alta California,* the New York *Herald,* and the New York *Tribune,* and the full treatment of the voyage prepared as *The Innocents Abroad* disclose a seriousness on Twain's part that abruptly deepened as he journeyed through the Holy Land, even though it continued to find expression in a caustic humor.[2] For Twain the pilgrimage brought successive revelations about his own religious conceptions and about those of his fellow pilgrims; and it gave him a thorough awareness of some of the unique varieties of religious experience that were involved in one's being American. By the end of the voyage of the *Quaker City,* Twain's religious assumptions had been radically changed and were in the process of being further modified by reflections upon the nature of man and of society, and upon man's place in a spiritual cosmos, reflections that were to play a decisive role in his later writing.

That Mark Twain should have embarked as a traveling journalist on the *Quaker City* was ironic to begin with. The pilgrimage had been designed to suit a group of men and women who were from the most conservative end of America's broad social and religious spectrum. They represented the oldest Christian tradition in American life in its derivative-Calvinist form, extensively modified to accommodate secular values. The separation of church and state that these American Pilgrims acknowledged was extended to include a distinction between the ethical commitments of secular and of religious life. They were to have been shepherded by the famous Reverend Henry Ward Beecher; some of the Pilgrims were members of his fashionable Plymouth Church; C. C. Duncan, Captain of the *Quaker City,* was a superintendent of the Plymouth Church; and a special selection board screened applicants for the cruise to insure that the passenger list would be made up only of the financially and spiritually elect. The shipboard "pleasures" of the cruise were to consist largely of Bible readings and religious discussions, of group study of Bible commentaries and of guidebooks to the Holy Land. For gladder moments the *Plymouth Collection of Hymns* was to be used.

How "The Wild Humorist of the Pacific Slope" was accepted into this company of the chosen is hard to understand (especially as, according to Captain Duncan, he reeked of cheap whiskey at the time of his interview).[3] It may have been that the small celebrity Twain had acquired as author of the recently published *The Celebrated Jumping Frog of Calaveras County and Other Sketches* and as a man who had recently delivered a successful lecture at the Cooper Union made partial amends for the failure of such promised celebrities as the Reverend Henry Ward Beecher and General Sherman to join the cruise. Twain's basic purpose was simply to travel and to pay for his travels by sending letters to the *Alta California* as he had recently done in Hawaii. At the outset he had no real knowledge of the social or religious nature of the Pilgrims or of the kind of pilgrimage they had in mind.

The vast difference beteeen Twain's sense of religion and that of the

Pilgrims is indicative of the broad range of religious thinking included under "Protestantism" in post-Civil War America. Twain's father had been a freethinker or agnostic who practiced a stern morality. Twain's mother was a Presbyterian–renowned in her youth for her dancing. Her legacy to her son Samuel was more in terms of wit, high spirits, and a joyous response to life than in any Calvinistic discipline. Sam Clemens had attended Hannibal's Old Ship of Zion Sunday School, had been required to attend church services, and, according to his friend and biographer Paine, had read the Bible through before he was fifteen years old.[4] Once Twain left Hannibal, however, there seems to be little evidence that he gave much attention to attending church or to Bible reading; nevertheless, all the available evidence suggests that his moral character was especially fine—remarkably so, given the steamboat, mining camp, frontier town, and roving journalist circumstances under which he lived prior to boarding what amounted to a floating Sunday School, the *Quaker City*.

Although Twain was at first somewhat cowed by the social and religious credentials of the Pilgrims, this condition did not last long. His trust in his own moral sense and his distrust of the official guardians of morality had already been proven by his criticisms of the moral shortcomings of the Nevada Territorial Legislature;[5] by his attacks on the corrupt police force of San Francisco and its Chief, Martin A. Burke;[6] and by his highly qualified praise of the Sandwich Island missionaries and his derisive comments upon the American minister to those islands.[7] One letter observed that, while dedicated and hardworking, the missionaries were "ignorant of all white human nature and natural ways of men, except the remnant of these things that are left in their own class or profession."[8] As with Melville, Twain's first sense of drastic limitations in American churchmen came through observing them in the context of a non-Christian culture.

Back in San Francisco after his stay in Hawaii, Twain wrote about religion in a carefree, comic way. "Reflections on the Sabbath" treated with ridicule the very fundamentalism that was soon to surround him. His father, his uncle John Quarles, his boarding-house friend Macfarlane, his friends in Virginia City, Carson City, San Francisco, and on Jackass Hill had done their work well in shaking Twain's mind loose from religious orthodoxy. Yet he was not a "free-thinker." As he described himself in a letter of 1864, while not "a very duty Christian," he took "an absorbing interest in church affairs."[9] Possibly the expression "absorbing interest" might best have been appreciated by Twain's companions Dan DeQuille and "The Incompetent," but there would seem to be no doubt but that his childhood training had left him with a felt certainty of the divinity of Jesus; and while his articles in the *Enterprise* made humorous use of the Bible, he had the same felt certainty that the Scriptures were sacred. These certainties are clear from his letters as the *Quaker City* proceeded toward the Holy Land. Equally clear is his increasing doubt of the sincerity of the Pilgrims, who took Jesus and the Bible with melancholy earnestness and whose faith required rigorous daily exercises.

The extreme difference between Twain and the Pilgrims in regard to the practice of religion and the conduct of life illustrates well a central conflict in the experience that made up American life. Twain with his imagination and moral spontaneity and with his thirst for fresh experience is akin to the summation of a type of American character that Henry James intended in creating his heroine Isabel Archer. The Pilgrims, who were mostly conservative, wealthy, socially established Easterners (some were described in the brochure as "Prominent Booklynites"), are akin to those congealing, stratifying forces in American life which James summed up as "Convention" and which he typified in his character Gilbert Osmond. The abyss that opens between Twain and the Pilgrims in *Innocents* is essentially the same as that which divides Isabel and Osmond in *The Portrait of a Lady*. Both works express conflicting ideals in American life. The costliness of the *Quaker City* cruise, the type of dignitary sought as passenger, and the Holy Land destination all testified to rigid cultural attitudes and a high, fixed social station.

Twain, on the other hand, from the time he left Hannibal, had been in almost perpetual motion and in a constant search for the meaning of his experience. His adventures on the Mississippi, and in Nevada, California, and Hawaii had brought him into direct involvement with some of the more brutal facts of American life. None of these had been exempt from his moral questioning. For the Pilgrims, religion was a thing apart from daily affairs despite the fact that for many of them religion was a trade. Twain quickly discovered that they were capable of a ruthless aggression, savage selfishness, and blind indifference to human suffering in their pursuit of Jerusalem. The utter disconnectedness between their preaching and their practice was made-to-order for Twain's sense of comic contradiction.

As a social critic, by 1867 Twain had labored only at the fringes of American society. The Pilgrims of the *Quaker City* were to bring him close to its center; and his experience immediately following his return, in Washington, D.C., in New York, and in Connecticut, while he was writing *Innocents,* was to place him where the rhetoric of trust in God, equality, justice, and unity were most eloquent, and where the conspiracies for power, for exploitation of the country, and for social exclusion were most intense.

As the cruise of the *Quaker City* proceeded, Twain came to the conclusion that the pietistic behavior of the Pilgrims was not a simple hypocrisy. They had, he decided, lost early in life their capacity for spontaneous joy and carefree leisure. They had a driving sense of duty and purpose. In their understanding of the Bible and in what they expected of the Holy Land there was a grim literalness. Pervading all was a self-righteous sense of themselves as a separate, chosen people. It was their version of what it meant to be an American.

Twain must have reasoned to himself about the Pilgrims much as in time to come his character Huck would reason with Jim about the King and the Duke. They were frauds and humbugs, but they could not help being what they were, and it was hopeless to try to change them. In his final letter written at the end of the voyage, Twain insisted that he even liked the Pilgrims. He had come to regard them as he would regard a peculiar creature in a zoo; in fact, a bird in the Marseilles Zoological Gardens seemed the perfect embodiment of a Pilgrim. Among its sad attributes were "tranquil stupidity, supernatural gravity, self-righteousness, serene, unspeakably satisfied, stately piety of demeanor, tremendous seriousness, and a way of seeming to say, 'Defile not Heaven's anointed with unsanctified hands' " (1:144). This is an excellent description, also, of James's representative wealthy American art-collector, Mr. Leavenworth of *Roderick Hudson.*

When Twain was traveling from Baalbec to Damascus on horseback with a small group that included three uncompromising Pilgrims, a dispute arose because the trip to Damascus should take a full three days—but the third day was a Sunday and the Pilgrims refused to violate the Sabbath by traveling on that day. Their solution was to cover the distance in two days despite the intense heat of the desert that made the journey agonizing for their companions and a torture for the horses. The insight that such a typical experience provided Twain into the mentality of the Pilgrims helped him to understand encounters he had had with a similar mentality in his early years, and it enabled him to understand and to cope successfully with that same mentality in the years immediately ahead of him.

In *Innocents* he treats the religious behavior of the Pilgrims as though it were some odd quirk of nature that reasonable men could not be expected to credit: "I am talking now about personal friends; men whom I like; men who are good citizens; who are honorable, upright, conscientious; but whose idea of the Saviour's religion seems to me distorted" (2:194). They are men who, in citing the Bible, speak "of gentleness, of charity, and of tender mercy," but who, in their actual conduct of life, are concerned exclusively with securing their personal salvation in accordance with their reading of the letter of the Biblical law.

During the passage through Italy, Twain's own Protestant biases had remained unexamined. Anticipating the Marat-mood that came with his later readings of Carlyle's *French Revolution,* he "grew savage" and said to the Florentine beggars, " 'Curse your indolent worthlessness, why don't you rob your church?' "(1:330). It was an indignation characteristic of American travelers in Italy, and one that was shared by another foreign correspondent for the New York *Tribune,* Karl Marx, whose first volume of *Kapital* was appearing that year. "I fell down and worshipped it," Twain says of Florence's Duomo in the same letter, "but I had it in me to burn it down if I had a chance." When he learned that the Medici Chapel was built to house together Christ's Holy Sepulchre and the sepulchres of the Medicis, he waxed even more furious. In Rome he devised skillful, comic juxtapositions to equate and denigrate the Basilica of St. Peter and the Coliseum, and the same flamboyant assurance carried over into his attacks upon

Mohammedanism in the Holy Land. The cathedrals, shrines, and relics of Italy were all a swindle; but by the time Twain had finished his visit to the Holy Land he had come to the sobering conclusion that without such works of the Catholic Church, there would have been nothing to remember. By identifying specific grottoes with specific episodes in the Bible, for example, and erecting a church around them, the Catholics knew how "to drive a stake through a pleasant tradition that will hold it to its place forever" (L.253). Like Hawthorne, Twain became more and more aware of a provinciality in his ideas as to what forms the religious impulse should and should not take. The hospitality of the Convent Fathers of Palestine at Mars Saba led him to admit that he had been trained to prejudice and to hate, as when he wrote, "I have been educated to enmity towards everything that is Catholic, and sometimes, in consequence of this, I find it much easier to discover Catholic faults than Catholic merits" (2:382). Twain's pilgrimage to the Holy Land had become a voyage of discovery into his own past.

By 1867 Twain had established for southwestern readers a certain persona, and when he engaged to send letters to the *Alta California* from the *Quaker City* it was taken for granted that this persona would be maintained. Readers familiar with his satires, burlesques, and hoaxes, with his irreverence, originality, and individuality were eager for the fireworks that would come when Mark Twain took on the Europeans. For a considerable while—and especially from France and Italy—they got what they had expected; but the Holy Land was another matter. Here Twain's persona came dangerously close to a destructive attack upon the mythopoeic conception of Biblical lands that was an intrinsic part of religious teaching in America and, of course, was part of his own romanticized and sentimentalized religious thinking. European roads, railroads, railway stations, art galleries, palaces, and cathedrals had revised sharply upwards Twain's concept of the quality of European life; in his attacks upon Catholicism in Italy he had catered deliberately to the prejudices of his Protestant readers. When he felt compelled to report truthfully the bizarre discrepancy between America's image of the Holy Land and the desolate reality, however, he found himself involved in the painful task of destroying his own cherished dreamland, of telling his public truths that were not at all amusing, and of debunking even the Bible itself.

Although he could permit himself occasionally a minor rhapsody upon the beauty of a Holy Land scene when viewed by moonlight or from a great distance, he felt compelled to report to his readers how barren the countryside was, how overcrowded and filthy and small the renowned "cities" were, and how diseased, ragged, and ignorant the natives were. If there had not been an obligation to send back the agreed-upon letters, Twain would have had time to assimilate his bewilderment at the incredible discrepancy between the myth and the reality of the Holy Land and to communicate his truth in the shape of some grotesquely comic lie. As it was, he had time only for the rough honesty he had once demanded of the editor of the Carson City *Independent,* "Any editor in the world will say it is *your* duty to ferret out these abuses, and *your* duty to correct them. What are you paid for? What use are you to the community? What are you fit for as a conductor of a newspaper, if you cannot do these things?"[10] The Pilgrims saw only what they had been prepared to see and recited the word-pictures painted in their guidebooks. Twain tried to convey his truth gently. He praised what he could find to praise and invited the counsel of some of the Pilgrims, notably "Mother" Fairbanks, to smooth over rough spots in his writing and in his approach to his subject; but he held tight to his own sense of the truth of the matter.

Part of the subtitle that he affixed to the first edition of *The Innocents Abroad* was the qualifier that countries, nations, incidents, and adventures would be described *as They Appeared to the Author.* His Preface further stressed that the author was reporting what he had seen with his own eyes. Yet, while he told most of his truth—it took time for Twain to believe all of his own truth—he also managed to revise, excise, decorate, borrow, and devise material so as to produce a book that did not directly challenge the mythical Holy Land of Protestant America. Twain faced the split that Henry James was frequently to dwell upon in his criticism and in his stories of writers and artists between what the culture knew to be true and what it would admit to be true. Twain also faced the divorce between Protestant Biblical mythology and the Biblical land of historical fact that was emerging as part of a larger pattern of scientific, scholarly investigation of the background of Christianity, an investigation that was to have a dramatic impact upon every aspect of American intellectual life. Boylike, Twain could not lie to himself as to what he had seen in the Holy Land, and he could not keep that truth out of his letters to America; but not the least of his discoveries in the Holy Land was that of how the Pilgrims could repeatedly and convincingly lie to themselves.

Like the many Americans who were now beginning the great pilgrimage back to Europe, these Pilgrims were, to some degree, not merely in search of self-definition, but in search of an understanding of the history out of which their nation had emerged and of some acquaintance with the many cultures out of which Americans had tried to form one people. What made the task difficult was their innocence of their own deeply ingrained cultural conditioning. Twain was repeatedly surprised by revelations of his own ignorance, and much later he was to make this comment upon himself: "Ignorance, intolerance, egotism, self-assertion, opaque perception, dense and pitiful chuckle-headedness—and an almost pathetic unconsciousness of it all. That is what I was at 19 and 20, and it is what the average Southerner is at 60 today."[11] In his lecture, "The American Vandal Abroad," which was based in part on *Innocents,* Twain took as his moral that travel liberalized the Vandal and made a better man of him. Still, it was a novelty for Americans to hear themselves described as brutish in relation to the culture of Europe. Writing to his mother in the year *Innocents* was published, Henry James anticipated Twain's judgment in his remark, "It's the absolute and incredible lack of *culture* that strikes you in common travelling Americans."[12] From James's point of view even cultivated Americans were provincial because the conditions of American life had to a large extent isolated them from the main currents of Western civilization. Twain's comments on the culture of Americans in *Innocents* and in subsequent writings indicate that he fully shared James's view. At the start of his voyage to the Holy Land, Twain had proudly affirmed his provinciality, but the process of finding himself in history and of locating his ethics in a supra-national context began quickly.

Speculation upon how the Biblical legends must have grown and upon the definite forms they had assumed in the minds of the Pilgrims quickened Twain's own creative awareness. His first lessons in the art of story-telling from the lips of such slaves as his father's "Uncle Ned" and his uncle John Quarles's "Uncle Dan'l" must have included versions of Biblical episodes similar to that recounted by Jim to Huck about "King Solermon." Accounts he read in the Pilgrims' guidebooks to the Holy Land must have struck Twain as being marvelously fanciful. He wrote, "A man may rave like a very lunatic, and yet escape criticism. I expect that it is as much as I had better say. I have been taught to revere the Scriptures, and that reverence is pretty firmly grounded. Perhaps it would have been well to teach me to revere the commentators. Some of them don't. I am very sure of that" (L.166. Cf. *Innocents,* 2:145). The slave versions of Biblical matters and the Holy Land guidebook versions might well have kindled the sense of the incongruous and grotesque that he had practiced as part of the art of the southwestern narrative. Soon his own versions of Biblical and Holy Land guidebook subjects began to appear in the letters he sent to America.

The closer Twain approached to Jerusalem, the more he raged against the misleading descriptions of the land given by the guidebook writers. Eventually he was referring to the Bible as a misleading guidebook. On the torrid journey from Baalbec to Damascus he noted that his personal pack included "a guide-book (the same being a Bible)" (L.180); for *Innocents* the expression was altered to read, "a guide-book, and a Bible" (2:174). The sight of the miserable horses on which they were to undertake the journey provoked the bitter comment, "The display was exactly according to the guide-book, and were we not travelling by the guide-book?" (L. 181. Also in *Innocents* 2:175). The freedom he took in his letters with Biblical characters and stories became more and more extravagant. A burlesque retelling of the story of Joseph and his brothers included a recognition scene with Joseph exclaiming over Benjamin, " 'Ha! the strawberry on your left arm!—it is! it is my long lost brother!' (Slow music)" (L.223). The whole story was greatly revised for *Innocents* and the recognition motif omitted. Twain gives a detailed account of the barrenness of the country, of the small, isolated, primitive "cities," and of their wretched inhabitants. He came to the conclusion that the conditions he saw were those which prevailed in the time of the patriarchs and during the lifetime of Jesus. The fabled Biblical lands and the kings who had talked with God retained a validity only as a part of his memory of the Hannibal years.

The actual Holy Land reminded Twain more than anything else of the desert lands of the Nevada Territory and of Arizona. The country from Cesarea [*sic*] Philippi to the Sea of Galilee "they say is a most favorable specimen of Palestine. If it is a favorable specimen of Palestine, surely Palestine is Washoe's born mate" (L.227). Significantly, he followed a grim description of the land and its people with a terse account of some of the miracles performed by "the Saviour" in that region, concluding, "But the most notable event happened yonder close to Bethsaida. There were fed the five thousand with five loaves and two little fishes. Only five and two for five thousand" (L.229). Twain was working in his truth edgewise. The letter was followed by a "Note by the Editors" remarking upon the "strange conduct" of their correspondent in offering such information to the public "with such a confident air of furnishing news"; but Twain offered no explanation. Twain's western readers needed no prompting at the end of his straight-faced recital of Christ's miracles to supply his habitual remark at the end of a "stretcher": "I pass."

"Washoe," he marveled, "is six times as large as Palestine." "The longest journey our Saviour ever performed was . . . about as far as from Sacramento to Carson City. . . . He spent his life, preached his gospel and performed his miracles within a compass no larger than an ordinary county in the United States. It is as much as I can do to get this stupefying fact through my head" (L.227–29. Omitting local references, Twain included these remarks in *Innocents,* 2:258). As Twain's group proceeded on horseback toward Palestine, Twain discovered himself to be increasingly at home in the terrain—and far more competent to judge it and its inhabitants and their probable history than his Pilgrim companions, to whom the country and its inhabitants seemed utterly strange.

Of the natives of Cesarea Philippi, Twain wrote, "They reminded me much of Indians, did these people" (2:222). A letter from Palestine comments laconically, "we met half a dozen Digger Indians (Bedouins)" (2:312). About the only sight in this Arizona-Nevada Holy Land to strike Twain as wholly out of place, and wholly absurd, was the sight of the Pilgrims jolting awkwardly in their saddles, elbows flapping wildly, their eyes shielded by colored glasses, their heads swathed in yards of protective cloth, and each holding aloft a bobbing, green-lined umbrella. "Here, you feel all the time just as if you were living about the year 1200 before Christ—or back to the patriarchs—or forward to the New Era . . . and behold, intruding upon a scene like this, comes this fantastic gang of green-spectacled Yanks" (L. 205–6. With slight changes the passage was used in *Innocents*, 2:214).

The Biblical phrase "all these Kings" had once suggested to Twain the monarchs of powerful European countries, but now the mighty were indeed fallen. "It suggests only a parcel of petty chiefs—ill-clad and ill-conditioned savages much like our Indians, who lived in full sight of each other and whose 'kingdoms' were large when they were five miles square and contained two thousand souls. The combined monarchies of the thirty 'kings' destroyed by Joshua on one of his famous campaigns, only covered an area about equal to four of our counties of ordinary size" (2:239–40). In an image that is eloquent of his disillusionment (and one he felt obliged to omit from *Innocents),* Twain speaks of the attractions of Palestine gradually but surely passing away as though they were the trappings of an abandoned opera house in a western ghost town: "The paint and the gilding are peeling from its cheap theatrical scenery and exposing the unsightly boards beneath" (L.259). His first reaction to Jersualem was, "So small! Why, it was no larger than an American village of four thousand inhabitants . . ." (2:325), roughly, that is, about the size of Hannibal when Twain left it. He concluded his first letter from Jerusalem with the statement that although he had been trying to comprehend that this was the city where Solomon dwelt and Jesus was crucified, he had not succeeded—"and never shall. I know that well enough" (L.264). This meaningful, personal avowal was dropped from *Innocents* and replaced by concealing platitudes.

The Church of the Holy Sepulchre, the ultimate goal of the pilgrimage, was the ultimate disappointment for Twain. There, the sacred evidence so miraculously recovered by St. Helena annihilated all capacity for religious response in Twain. His ironic wit touched upon almost every facet of the scene. It was as though he were seeing once again one of the roadshows he had seen a hundred times in the southwest, with their tricks and wonders. The lively devotions of some Italian monks were "some kind of a circus performance" (L.212); the vain, invidious distinctions between Christian sects were glaringly evident; and Twain produced a gesture of piety with difficulty: "With all its claptrap side-shows and unseemly humbuggery of every kind, it is still grand, reverend, venerable—a God died there" (L.280–81). The God who died there was, for Twain, the dogmatic Christ of the Church, and the death divided Christ for him into two creative forces: the historical Jesus and what he termed for the first time a "mysterious stranger" (2:257).

In the primitive village of Nazareth, Twain's "creative memory" was stirred by his sense of the daily village life and what it must have been like years, or even centuries ago, to be a boy growing up there. He could not bring himself to comprehend that a *God* had lived there, "the gods of my understanding have been always hidden in clouds and very far away" (2:222). There is a strong suggestion that Twain was remembering his own childhood and his brothers, especially the saintly Henry, when he speculates on what the brothers of Jesus thought of Him. A decade later Twain was to write to his brother Orion, "Neither Howells nor I believe in hell or the divinity of the Savior, but no matter, the Savior is none the less a sacred Personage, and a man should have no desire or disposition to refer to him lightly, profanely, or otherwise than with the profoundest reverence."[13] It was a truthful paradox, and Twain's way of saying, "Oh, Lord, I believe, help Thou my unbelief."

Despite his denials, despite his study of Lecky and his assertions of Man's determined fate, the incredible, cosmic Person was ever there in Twain's mind, tyrannizing his conscience, always more and more the mysterious stranger. All his irreverence in *Innocents* and in subsequent books was an act of reverence, an expression of his will to believe. In the attacks he felt driven to make upon the Pilgrims' conception of Bible, Holy Land, and Christ, he was anticipating the criticism that John Dewey was to launch at William James, wherein Dewey would insist that in America the will to believe, in its preoccupation with metaphysics, had resulted in a blindness to the actualities of life, and in a self-righteousness that is anti-democratic and inhumane.

Through writing *Innocents* Twain began to realize the imaginative possibilities of his Washoe days and moved closer to the seminal memories of his childhood days, the world of Hannibal and the river, that was to prove the richest source of his creative process. With the realization of how he differed in his conception of religion from the Pilgrims, and with his imaginative recovery, through the personality of Jesus, of the childhood promise of liberation, Twain had arrived at what was most vital in the relationship of Protestantism to democracy in American life—its existence as a movement, rather than as an authority and organization, and its concept of the authority of the Bible as being in the spirit of the prophet rather than in that of the lawgiver. But the paradox of belief and unbelief remained, and the final god of *Innocents* is the Sphinx, "MEMORY—RETROSPECTION," a mysterious stranger brooding over the realities of history and the endless changes in human life with a terrible indifference to man's fate, indifferent as the moon to the American pilgrims hacking at its face for souvenirs.

6
Henry James: Love in an Anglo-Saxon World

I

With his last three completed novels, *The Ambassadors, The Wings of the Dove,* and *The Golden Bowl,* Henry James took up again on a major scale the method of analyzing society by placing Americans in a European context. In doing so, however, his approach was markedly different from that used in his last major "international" effort, *The Portrait of a Lady.* That work, and the preceding novels involving Americans in Europe, shed James's critical light on several specific aspects of American life—the neglect of art, the obsession with business, the cultural split between men and women, the pressures for conformism, the violation of individual privacy—and evolved a fundamental criticism of the way in which America's traditional idealism and generosity of mind were being taken over by a new, economic aristocracy that was avid for all the perquisites of the old aristocracy of blood.

With the last three novels James thought in more inclusive terms than in the earlier ones. His mind had always managed to evade programmatic ways of thinking, especially as such ways might find themselves organized into national, or religious, or class points of view. What he had to say in the novels of the major phase was not directed to one society as against another, but to the English-speaking whole, "to what interests me: which is human Anglo-Saxonism, with the American extension, or opportunity for it, so far as it may be given me still to work the same."[1] The evil in this society, as it is rendered in the novels, is its mind, which has become alienated from sensuous experience. The mind of the society has come to operate in terms of arid formulations—cold local customs and arbitrary laws—and has coerced its imagination to the primary objective of accumulating wealth. It is opposed to leisure, to the genial uses of the imagination, to art as a creative process, and, most destructive of all, to the nature of love.

A treatment of conflicting American and European manners was what the reading public had come to expect from James as an international theme, but the novelist was growing more and more to feel that a literature that insisted upon national differences was beside the point. He had written to his brother William in 1888: "For myself, at any rate, I am deadly weary of the whole 'international' state of mind—so that I *ache,* at times, with fatigue at the way it is constantly forced upon me as a sort of virtue or obligation. I can't look at the English-American world, or feel about them, any more, save as a big Anglo-Saxon total, destined to such an amount of melting together that an insistence on their differences becomes more and more idle and pedantic."[2] In addition, James felt he could no longer trust his sense of the American scene; if he dealt with Americans, they would have to be in Europe. Howells's fiction conveyed to James the extent to which America had altered since his last visit in the early 1880s. A volume of Howells's tales brought him "stray echoes and scents as from another, the American, the prehistoric existence."[3]

The *données* for *The Ambassadors* and *The Wings of the Dove* came to him without any sense of necessarily involving a specifically American element. When he first speculated on the character who was to become Strether, a character and situation suggested by an anecdote concerning W. D. Howells, James noted, "He may be an American —he might be an Englishman."[4] The *donnée* of *The Wings of the Dove* he referred to as "the little idea of the situation of some young creature (it seems to me preferably a woman, but of this I'm not sure)."[5] While the father and daughter of the *donnée* for "a little tale" that was to become *The Golden Bowl* were first seen as "intensely American," the Americanness seems to have had reference to an innocent intimateness, which James evidently believed would not occur between a European parent and child. In each case the *donnée* crystallized a theme latent in James's imagination, some felt conviction about the way life should be lived as distinct from the way in which society caused it to be lived. In the subsequent development of each novel he arranged the sex, nationality, age, and relationship of characters to suit his Anglo-Saxon concept. Given popular superstitions, it was more suitable for the American to be ascetic and for the Parisian to be voluptuous; but James knew very well, and had demonstrated previously in his fiction, that the roles could be reversed.

While the characters in James's earlier novels who have a highly developed moral sense undergo experiences that modify their understanding of life, their habit of judging life from a special moral point of view remains unchanged. They are like those Americans whom James described in his biography of William Wetmore Story as clinging the more tightly to their clue of duty the more they tried to lose themselves in the labyrinth of Europe. As might be expected, James's American readers have been slow to recognize any implication of provincialism in the highly developed moral sense of such characters as Rowland Mallett, Winterbourne, and Isabel Archer. On the other hand, they have been quick to perceive as moral lapses the preference of European or Americano-European characters for a privileged class, arranged marriages, and a mistress or lover.

In the later novels James made a fundamental change. The highly moral central character (Strether, Densher, Maggie) begins the experience with an untroubled moral sense. When the novel's web of experience has been completed, the character has been transformed by a discovery of love, of the nature and strength of love, and of his own capacity for love. The moralistic reader of the earlier novels (*Roderick Hudson, The American, Daisy Miller, The Portrait of a Lady*) can find no inconsistency in the moral behavior of the character who clings to the clue of duty; but in the later novels such a reader has to come to terms with Strether's insistence upon Chad's maintaining an adulterous liaison with Madame de Vionnet, with Densher's willingness to marry Kate Croy (albeit without the legacy), and with Maggie's adroit handling of her husband's adultery with her step-mother in order to secure his love. The reader for *Harper's* who handled James's project for *The Ambassadors* reported, "I do not advise acceptance. We ought to do better."[6] He was disturbed by the element of adultery, and, as the editors of the *Notebooks* observe, his summary of the "Project" is "a masterpiece of miscomprehension"; but the nature of his miscomprehension only proved him to be a representative American reader.

In contemplating his possible treatment of the *donnée* for *The Ambassadors,* James was aware that there was a great danger of being taken for banal and that the possibility was increased by setting his story in Paris. He *did* want to tell the old story of Paris, but this time he wanted his Anglo-Saxon readers to come out on the other side—where one's loyalty was to love, and where leisure and enjoyment were esteemed in preference to conventional morality and the ethic of work, duty, and success. "I'm afraid it *must* be Paris; if he's an American," James reasoned in his notebook.[7] As the novel became a reality, Woollett, Mass., and Paris became symbolic poles for two opposite ways of being. Each has its goddess, the matriarch Mrs. Newsome, all "fine cold thought," and Mme. de Vionnet, a deeply passionate woman.

Dark, brooding Waymarsh is the shadow of Strether's American history. Waymarsh's sense of duty never deserts him, and it is a duty *not* to enjoy, not to drop his moral guard, and to be aware continually of the money (and Mrs. Newsome is also money) that his friend risks losing. His American reasons are clear: Chad must be brought back for the sake of the business; if the business makes more money, Strether "will marry more money." His views on Europe are equally clear: "The Catholic Church for Waymarsh—that was to say the enemy, the monster of bulging eyes and far-reaching quivering groping tentacles—was exactly society, exactly the multiplication of shibboleths, exactly the discrimination of types and tones, exactly the wicked old Rows of Chester, rank with feudalism; exactly in short Europe."[8] Echoing in this statement are rankling undertones of the dispute that James began with American critics by his comments in his *Hawthorne* upon the features of European life that an artist missed in his effort to render the relatively plain features of American life.[9]

The "Europe" of the major phase is more a staging, more deliberately an extension of the novel's theme and characters, than ever before in James's work. He turned completely from the element of naturalism that had entered into the composition of *The Bostonians, The Princess Casamassima* and *The Tragic Muse.* The novels of the major phase demonstrate how James could use "Europe," the features of its "accumulated life," to give visible dimensions to human greed, power, suffering, and loss. James's sense of everything was what mattered, and thereby the whole novel took the form of an aesthetic idea.

In *The Middle Years* James wrote of how, once he was settled in London, he expected the meanings of the city to come to him "in the air of the passions of the intelligence."[10] This Keatsian "negative capability" is evoked in *The Ambassadors* when, with the gaunt duty-ridden Waymarsh before her, Maria Gostrey says that she wants to see continued in carefree Little Bilham "the happy attitude itself, the state of faith and . . . the sense of beauty." He is not one of the Americans who "have all wanted so dreadfully to do something." She asks apropos of the "good American": " 'What *is* it, to begin with, to *be* one, and what's the extraordinary hurry? Surely nothing that's so pressing was ever so little defined.' " When Strether has finally seen the necessary lovers drifting by on the river and the landscape is complete, he knows at last that he is part of the human city, the "vast, bright Babylon." In positively forbidding Chad to leave Mme. de Vionnet, he believes he is acting for Chad's welfare as well as out of love and compassion for Mme. de Vionnet. Although Strether insists he must, personally, gain nothing, he cannot help but be aware of what he himself has gained. Even more, he is aware of what he will have avoided becoming even though he does return to Woollett. While he continues to have the highest respect for Mrs. Newsome, she no longer has the same meaning for him. He has not been merely "liberated"; he has been profoundly changed. As he says of Mrs. Newsome, " 'She's the same. She's more than ever the same. But I do what I didn't before—I *see* her.' "[12]

II

The *donnée* of *The Ambassadors* and that of *The Wings of the Dove* acted upon the same spring in James's mind—a person's desolate sense of having missed something, perhaps the most important thing, in life. What turns out to have been missed is love. Mme. de Vionnet, especially in the depth and helplessness of her passion, gives Strether the recognition and the measure of what is missing in his relationship with Mrs. Newsome. *The Wings of the Dove* culminates in related recognitions, but there are differences, and the international bearing is different also.

James meant that *The Wings of the Dove* should be thoroughly Anglo-Saxon; that a reader should be unable to tell whether an American or an English author wrote the book; and that it should have the same significance for an English as for an American reader. The obsession with money, the drive for empire, the heaping up of the world's loot: these were as much a part of New York as of London. Both countries had their economically based aristocracies and their dispossessed classes. In both countries the old idea of Christian community—"the *consecrated* association"—[13] had broken apart. The economic aristocracy was international; its bond, as Cooper had long since observed, was money not blood; and it regarded marriage principally as a property contract. This is the world of Aunt Maud and Lord Mark and of the many American heiresses who linked Europe to America in the late decades of the nineteenth century.

In novels of the 1880s James had given his view of the English government as an instrument of a privileged class. In his letters he had deplored the ferocious greed and brutal imperialism of both England and America. He saw the English government and class structure, "this great precarious, artificial empire,"[14] as engaged in a struggle that would probably end in collapse. At the height of the American newspaper campaign for an invasion of Cuba he wrote to his brother William: "I confess that the blaze about to come leaves me woefully cold, thrilling with no glorious thrill or holy blood-thirst whatever. I see nothing but the madness, the passion, the hideous clumsiness of rage, of mechanical reverberation; and I echo with all my heart your denouncement of the foul criminality of the screeching newspapers."[15] James was completely aware of the savage exploitation at home and abroad that made possible the palatial elegance at Lancaster Gate. As one who moved freely in such realms as Aunt Maud's, he knew, too, how extremely difficult it was for anyone born within its special world of values to think of changing it for another. As early as *Roderick Hudson* he had shown this awareness in connection with Christina Light. Yet *The Wings of the Dove* undertakes to persuade the reader that its central characters desire such a change, and, acting in the world's way, find themselves overtaken and all their values changed by love.

While it is true that both the novel and the Preface emphasize Milly Theale's being an American, her nationality is dictated more by the needs of the action than by the thematic meanings of the novel. Principally, James wanted the character unattached. It is as the presence of someone who wants desperately to live, who needs love, who is exquisitely responsive to love, and, finally, as one whose love broods over the others after death that Milly functions thematically. She is in the foreground of Books 3, 4, and 5; in the other seven Merton Densher and Kate Croy are central, and Milly is absent from the last two. While James drew upon his early recollections of the very American Minnie Temple in creating the character, he also drew upon his recollections of the highly Europeanized Lizzie Boott.[16] The association of Milly with the princess in the Bronzino portrait brings a chilling sense of her doom, but it also evokes the sense that Milly's essential spirit belongs to no one time or place.

Since James was writing an Anglo-Saxon novel in *The Wings of the Dove,* the forces that were conveniently polarized between Woollett and Paris in *The Ambassadors* were here contained within one society. Where Strether had been shown in the process of moving from one way of being to another, *The Wings of the Dove* shows Kate and Merton trying, at first, to have a life apart from that society, but so involved in pressures of Aunt Maud's world that they are led to the deceit practiced on Milly, hoping always that some avenue of escape will appear. The source of corruption in the novel is the materialistic society dedicated to its "awful game of grab," as James was to describe it in *The Ivory Tower.* Aunt Maud is emblematic of the rapacious society, and Kate and Merton are led to violate Milly's love not because they want her fortune for themselves, but because her fortune will free them from the talons of Aunt Maud and Kate's other rapacious relatives. Criticism of the novel has persistently seen Kate Croy as evil, even "demoniac," and of course as the personification of wicked old Europe. Kate and Merton are both, in fact, victims, and it is their struggle that provides the drama. In life and in death, Milly is a principle the eventual recognition of which enables Merton (and possibly Kate and James's reader) to make a judgment upon the society that has driven them to their betrayal. Kate's final comment to Merton, that they can never be again as they were, carries a suggestion of Adam and Eve recognizing their fallen condition; but it also carries the suggestion that, thanks to Milly, they have been saved from the terrible world they might have won.

III

"Can wisdom be kept in a silver rod,
Or love in a golden bowl?"

The subject matter of *The Wings of the Dove* and that of *The Golden Bowl* had been maturing together for about a dozen years in James's mind, and with both novels he elaborately answered *no* to Blake's question. A late-Victorian ormolu tone of empire encrusts *The Golden Bowl.* It opens with the Prince, himself a recently purchased treasure, musing over the piles of treasure gathered in London shop windows and comparing what he sees to the staggering opulence achieved by his Roman ancestors. The marvel is that the present empire has not yet fallen. In *The Middle Years* James was to recall that it struck him as a miracle that such a fool's paradise as that of the English upper class continued to exist.[17] He frankly enjoyed the amenities of the fool's paradise and even at the tender age of forty-three had sighed that "the gilded bondage of the country house becomes onerous as one grows older";[18] yet it was a marvel to see how unconcernedly the lords and ladies danced at the edge of the abyss: "It was as if they had come up to the very edge of the ground that was going to begin to fail them; yet looking over it, looking on and on always, with a confidence still unalarmed."[19] Americans and Italians could never quite attain the dedicated frivolity of those English aristocrats of whom Henry Adams was to relate in his *Education* that the highest compliment you could pay a person was to say that he was utterly mad. *The Golden Bowl* sets its town and country houses in this unsubstantial pageant of the Anglo-American Gilded Age, and only Maggie's human needs link it to our common humanity.

Unlike the earlier Jamesian heroine, such as Catherine Sloper and Isabel Archer, who found it insupportable that, though she might have been loved, her lover primarily required her fortune, Maggie Verver in her initial innocence not only can accept the situation, but she can joke about it with her purchased Prince. He, in turn, is satisfied in knowing that he has been thoroughly inspected by experts and that his extemely high price has been met. The marriage was carried out by lawyers on both sides. Adam Verver's purchase of the Prince coincides with his purchase of paintings by Luini, even as his later purchase of a wife, Charlotte, will coincide with his purchase of some tiles of a particularly fine finish. Everyone in this special world knows each other's value; each is an object of great price.

In *The Ambassadors* Maria Gostrey had left Paris rather than find herself in a position of having to lie for Mme. de Vionnet; and in *The Wings of the Dove* Susan Stringham's concern for the truth led her to search out Densher in his rooms in Venice. Directly in contrast to these scrupulously honest *ficelles,* Fanny Assingham of *The Golden Bowl* is involved in continuous lies and deceits. An immense flaw is concealed by the gilt of this small enclosed world. Charlotte Stant is the principal deceiver in the first half of the novel, and in the late stages, when she is led away on a leash by Adam to American City, she seems to have deceived herself into believing in a future of disseminating culture in the necropolis of her husband's accumulated plunder. With her lover's letter in her hand, she accepts Adam for her husband; and Charlotte's most memorable confrontation with Maggie comes on the terrace at Fawns when both women lie to one another, are conscious of each other's deceit, and seal the deception with a kiss.

Although the relationship between Maggie and Adam is extremely close in the first half of the novel, James was careful to avoid any implications of incest, and, in fact, the two figures seem to have no relation to sex. Maggie, despite the bambino, remains virginal; and Adam throughout the novel presides over his domain like an impotent

Fisher-King. Indeed, the references to America in the novel suggest a waste land, as when Fanny says to Maggie, " 'I see the long miles of ocean and the dreadful great country, State after State—which have never seemed to me so big or so terrible,' "[20] or as Maggie understands Charlotte's sense of mission "—that of representing the arts and the graces to a people languishing, afar off, in ignorance."[21] Maggie last sees Charlotte as dehumanized, led away by Adam and his lasso.[22]

Like Mrs. Newsome of *The Ambassadors* and, in part, like Milly Theale of *The Wings of the Dove,* Adam is mainly a force in the novel. The reader is never taken into his consciousness. Adam never indicates what he knows of the behavior of the others. The slight, silent figure, always dressed the same plain way, is like the simple figures on a bank statement that represent tremendous power. Mrs. Newsome is described as having no imagination, and if Adam Verver has imagination, it is all for accumulating economic values (money, a Prince, paintings, tiles, Charlotte). "Variety of imagination—" James wrote in reference to Adam, "what is that but fatal, in the world of affairs, unless so disciplined as not to be distinguished from monotony."[23] The asexual, impersonal colorlessness of Adam Verver, joined to his great economic power, makes him, for the purposes of social criticism in the novel, emblematic of the force in American life that Henry Adams imaged as the dynamo.

Unlike the American characters in the novel, Prince Amerigo does no wrong. He does not lie, and when he has sexual intercourse with Charlotte it is with the assumption that this is the way he is expected to behave. His wife has turned him over to Charlotte, preferring to be with her father, and since Charlotte is made of the same "moral paste" as the Ververs, he is willing to follow her cue to adultery. He always felt his ethical and even his ontological separateness from the Americans. They had acquired him for his historic values and knew nothing of what he termed his "single self, the unknown, unimportant . . . personal quality."[24] He reflects on the Americans as follows: "Those people—and his free synthesis lumped together capitalists and bankers, retired men of business, illustrious collectors, American fathers-in-law, American fathers, little American daughters, little American wives—those people were of the same large lucky group."[25]

He could never be one of them, and he saw his own moral nature as "a tortuous stone staircase—half-ruined into the bargain!" The mechanized, modern, lofty moral sense of the Americans took them up, in his image, like an elevator in a skyscraper.[26] In the second half of the novel, he observes the elevator's efficient descent.

Maggie's discovery of the split crystal under the gilt of the bowl, like most of James's revelation scenes, is a discovery of sexual betrayal. At that moment, Maggie becomes sexually aware, and all the other characters take on a sexual reality for her. The peculiarly American sexlessness of the intimate father-daughter relationship was James's first inspiration for the story; to this he immediately added immense wealth, as though it were a kind of Thanatos that would preclude Eros. Until Maggie has her recognition, she is seen by the Prince as having a "rather neutral and negative propriety,"[27] and does not really exist for him as a person. With Adam, whose impotence James implies as clearly as he can, the two compose a parody of a family, dandling the bambino, "adoring" one another, "adoring" their bartered spouses and their acquired world.[28] The persons are selfless and their emotions are mechanized; but Maggie's discovery propels her into the jungle of immediate personal relationships, the tangled growth of sexual realities beneath the cultural gilt and glaze. Her love for the Prince asserts its terrible, compulsive power and drives her to discover solutions to her difficulties utterly at variance with the polite formulae of her narrow experience. In 1887 James had written in a letter to a friend, "it is rather a melancholy mistake, in this uncertain life of ours, to have founded oneself on so many rigidities and rules—so many siftings and sortings. . . . Let us be flexible . . . let us be flexible! and even if we don't reach the sun we shall have been up in a balloon."[29] Faced by the fact of her husband's adultery with Charlotte, Maggie gives no thought to the rigidities and principles that control social ethics in the Anglo-Saxon world. She sets out to regain her lover, using the very weapons that had been used against her—patience, cunning, and deceit.

More than anywhere else in his fiction (unless one accepts this as the basis of the attraction of Verena Tarrant for Olive Chancellor in *The Bostonians*) James stresses the power of the sexual need that one person can have for another. James describes Prince Amerigo as having a genius, among other things, for intercourse; the polite meaning is clear, but James is also stating that the Prince is a highly gifted lover. By winning him back Maggie may be said to reassert the moral order of the family, but her overriding need is for love. She is willing to endure the knowledge of his adultery, and to see the adulterous Charlotte depart with Adam and without punishment—unless her destiny in the American waste land is seen as punishment enough.

The element of uncertainty and possible tragedy that clouds the endings of *The Ambassadors* and *The Wings of the Dove* is present here for Maggie. At the close, when the Prince puts his hands on Maggie's shoulders "his whole act enclosing her," and says, "I see nothing but *you,*" the force of what he says kindles a strange light in his eyes, "so that for pity and dread of them she buried her own in his breast." Maggie needs pity of his eyes because she realizes how inadequate she is to sustain his love; and she is in dread of his eyes because she reads in their strange light the prospect of her possible failure. There is small consolation for the American bride in her husband's philosophy, " 'Everything is terrible, *cara*—in the heart of man.' "

By the time he had completed *The Golden Bowl* James realized that America had become almost as remote and romantic a concept for him as Europe had been in his youth. He determined to visit America for one last time in the hope of finding a truly new America that would be the promise of the old America he had known in his youth and not at all like the Anglo-Saxon world of his late fiction. It was his turn to light out for the territory, "intensely the Middle and Far West and California and the South" and "scarcely a bit New York and Boston" —[30] he had been there before.

Part Three

THE NEO-TRANSCENDENTALISTS

"My servant Death, with solving rite,
Pours finite into infinite.
Wilt thou freeze love's tidal flow,
Whose streams through Nature circling go?
Nail the wild star to its track
On the half-climbed zodiac?
Light is light which radiates,
Blood is blood which circulates
Life is life which generates,
And many-seeming life is one—
Wilt thou transfix and make it none?"

—Emerson, from "*Threnody*"

7
E. E. Cummings: Eros and Cambridge, Mass.

Edward Estlin Cummings's *The Enormous Room* has been recognized from its first appearance as a work of extraordinary power and originality. Its power, however, has been seen as lodged in its indictment of the kind of social brutality consequent upon war; and its originality has been viewed in terms of the technical innovations that subsequently became associated with Cummings's unique poetic style. The treatment to which Cummings was subjected in the French detention camp at Ferté Macé was so utterly alien to anything known at firsthand by Cummings's American reading public, and the writing was made up of so many disconcerting innovations, that Americans of his generation could not respond to the detention camp as a metaphor of their own society, to the "Delectable Mountain" inmates as an image of their own imprisoned selves, and to the "enormous room" as a joyous metaphor of being. Yet these metaphors bear the real significance of the work, a significance that places it in the tradition of those works of American literature whose most distinctive vision is of the human spirit transcending a cultural apocalypse.

The Cambridge-Harvard environment in which Cummings passed almost his entire life prior to the swift series of moves that culminated in his detention in the French concentration camp represented one of the most secure fortresses of ruling-class culture that had ever existed in American life. In his autobiographical *i: six non-lectures* Cummings wrote that in the Cambridge of his youth "social stratification not merely existed but luxuriated."[1] The Cummings family, with

Cummings's father as distinguished university professor and Unitarian minister, was at a command post within the cultural fortress. Yet, in the year 1917, Cummings underwent a succession of experiences that resulted in his discovering himself to be profoundly opposed to all the values presumably guarded by Cambridge, Mass., committed to a judgment of that culture as destructive of the most precious elements of human personality, and dedicated to rescuing his being from the nonbeing of that culture.

Cummings's sense of the provincial, restrictive nature of the Cambridge culture began well before his decision to volunteer as an ambulance driver in the Norton-Hartjes Ambulance Corps. As a Harvard undergraduate he had made a study of the directions being taken in French literature, music, and painting. He summed up his view in a Harvard Commencement address, entitled "New Art," delivered in June, 1915.[2] It seemed to him that French artists had produced art that was in supple response to fundamental drives of their individual personalities, whereas in America the artist was still forced to adjust himself to outworn nineteenth-century forms. A derivative, academic taste and an overripe Victorian authority stifled creative impulse in America. Such new art as was being produced was relegated to the margin of community tolerance along with burlesque.

To Cummings's mind, the linkage of the new art with burlesque was significant. Both were genuine forms of art, it seemed to him, and both were celebrations of the sexual impulse. Early in his undergraduate days Cummings took up his study of burlesque at the Old Howard Theatre (originally a church) in Boston's Scollay Square. It is a measure of his departure from Cambridge cultural standards that he could seriously maintain that the burlesque was in a direct relation "to the whole fundamental structure of uncivilized and civilized theatre from prehistoric Then to scientific Now."[3] There should be, it seemed to him, a wholesome, spontaneous play of sex in art, and the treatment of sex degenerated into the obscene and vulgar in proportion to the suppression exercised by Mr. Sumner and the Watch and Ward Society of Boston. More generally, there was a direct relation between the repressive measures exercised by society and the frustation of the creative impulse in all the arts.

Upon leaving Harvard Cummings found work answering letters for a New York magazine publisher, a job that was supposed to support him while he found his way as an artist. The possibility, however, of joining the Ambulance Corps presented him with the opportunity, as he saw it, of becoming acquainted with Europe without becoming a soldier. Like many other young Americans who were to become the literary exiles of the twenties, Cummings responded not to President Wilson's patriotic rhetoric but to the rare opportunity for experiencing an aesthetic liberation similar in kind to that which Henry James arranged for Lambert Strether. On the voyage to Europe Cummings met Slater Brown, who shared his enthusiasm for art and his indifference to the war. Brown was to be Cummings's constant companion until the former was transferred from the camp at Ferté Macé to the prison at Précigné. An official mix-up allowed the two to spend most of the month of May, 1917, on their own in Paris, where Cummings discovered many marvelous differences from the culture he had known. These included, "last but most," the "beautiful givers of illimitable gladness."[4]

This brief stay in Paris startled Cummings into a realization that levels of being that had seemed irreconcilable in everyday life as he had known it in America could not only coexist in everyday life but each level might be more alive for the presence of the other. It was the same discovery that Henry Miller was to make in Paris in the early thirties. The surging physical growth of New York had diminished mankind to a tribe of pygmies, but Paris "(in each shape and gesture and avenue and cranny of her being) was continuously expressing the humanness of humanity."[5] Cummings's evaluation of Paris might be worth little as sociological analysis, but it undeniably indicates his conviction that the city was organized about human physical and spiritual needs that were stifled in the American cities he had known. The American metropolis seemed to take for granted the submission of the human spirit to immense material presence and to social combinations that lost their humanity in their great size and complexity. The European city gave first consideration always to the human spirit—what Cummings termed an "accepting transcendence."[6] The American city clamped the human spirit to its economic geometry like a saint fastened to a gridiron.

When he joined the Ambulance Corps at its base near Noyon,

Cummings found himself subject to much the same kind of authority as that from which he had felt himself finally freed in Paris. The men in charge of the Corps, judging from Cummings's comments, were intent upon projecting the image of American manhood as disciplined, efficient, neat, and of a superior class. Cummings's intent was the reverse. "I was, in contrast to *les américains*, not bent upon making France discover America but rather upon discovering France and *les français* myself."[7] Cummings and Brown, to the consternation of their superior officers, allowed themselves to go as ungroomed as the common workingmen and, worse yet, to fraternize with these workingmen. In America they had accepted unthinkingly their status in an elite class. When the fact of caste was insisted upon, however, they rebelled against it as bigotry. A conscious class attitude and deliberate class distinctions seemed irreconcilable with their sense of themselves as Americans. They emphasized their attitude by associating exclusively with the common workingmen and soldiers, by acquiring the workers' patois, and, in Cummings's case, by actually moving in with the workingmen. Brown's letters to America, letters which, as evidence of treasonable attitudes, eventually brought about his and Cummings's imprisonment showed hostility toward the American and French officials rather than toward the German forces and asserted that the common soldiers of both armies wanted peace but were driven to war in a climate of fear and hate artificially manufactured by military and civilian authorities.[8]

The attitudes expressed in Brown's letters were considered sufficient to warrant his arrest, but Cummings was to be detained merely for investigation as an associate of Brown. Cummings could have been released from detention both before and after he was taken from the American Ambulance Corps base simply by assuring the investigating officers of his patriotism and by disassociating himself from the conventional iconoclasm in Brown's letters. At first Cummings's insistence upon sharing Brown's views and fate was largely the product of his desire to pursue what promised to be a comic adventure. Later, before the investigating commission at the Ferté Macé camp, his refusal to respond in a way that would win his captors' approval and his own liberation was the result of a considered rejection of the society of which the commission seemed an excellent representative. Cummings had come to recognize a relationship between the war and the brutally repressive nature of the concentration camp and the more generalized brutality and violence that maintained the repression that was so essential a part of his culture.

At first, because the experience of being a prisoner was amusing, Cummings maintained full self-control and enjoyed the sense of toying with his stupid captors. His assurance was that of a member of the privileged class who knows that he has encountered an official blunder and condescendingly waits for the officials to recognize their error and withdraw with apologies and regrets. He is "being yanked from the putrescent banalities of an official non-existence into a high and clear adventure" (p. 7). When first shut in a cell, he feels "an uncontrollable joy" because of being "myself and my own master"(p. 23). When the train journey is resumed, Cummings thinks of the gendarmes who are escorting him as "the pigs on either side of me"(p. 32), and he sketches one of them "posed in a pig-like position"(p. 33). It is the beginning of a systematic use of metaphor to transform instinctive feelings of respect for representatives of social authority into feelings of hostility and contempt.

After Cummings leaves the train and begins the long night journey by foot to the concentration camp, the pain and exhaustion of the journey bring him to a point of fierce hatred for the officialdom that has entrapped him. A hallucinated concept of the unreality of the "real" world disorders his mind. The transition from a superficial to a serious reversal of his relation to society is signaled by his nightmarish encounter with an image of something that might be a scarecrow, or himself, or a wayside image of the crucified Christ:

> every muscle thoroughly aching, head spinning, I half-straightened my no longer obedient body; and jumped: face to face with a little wooden man hanging all by itself in a grove of low trees. . . .
>
> There was in this complete silent doll a gruesome truth of instinct, a success of uncanny poignancy, an unearthly ferocity of rectangular emotion. . . .
>
> I had seen him before in the dream of some mediaeval saint with a thief sagging at either side (pp. 53–54).

From this point on, traditional religious rhetoric, symbols, and ceremonies take their truth from the narrator's individual, subjective perceptions and not from their conventional context. Cummings enters Ferté Macé as "a city of Pretend"; he finds himself in a chapel with an altar "on which stood inexorably the efficient implements for eating God" (p. 59); he discovers that he is in a chapel—that is used for storing mattresses. Dragging one of these he staggers into his prison: the liberating humanity of the enormous room.

Like Christian of Bunyan's *Pilgrim's Progress*, from which much of the imagery of *The Enormous Room* is drawn, Cummings seems to awaken to a reality that is a dream. Yet it is a dream dedicated to a devastating attack upon the cultural values of the world he had known. In America the experience of ambiguous arrest and brutal imprisonment could rarely have come to a man in Cummings's social position. As the muckrakers had repeatedly demonstrated, men could be and frequently were subjected to such arrest and imprisonment in America. On May 5, 1920, a few months before Cummings set about writing *The Enormous Room*, Sacco and Vanzetti were so treated by the Boston authorities. When the celebrated Unitarian minister Edward Cummings learned that his son had been taken under arrest to a detention camp, however, the monstrousness of the event seemed to him to call for action at the highest level. His letter to President Wilson (included in the Foreword to the Modern Library Edition) declares that, were he President, "I would do something to make American citizenship as sacred in the eyes of Frenchmen as Roman citizenship was in the eyes of the ancient world." In his cry of outraged patriotism can be heard at once the voice of American privilege and American innocence.

The experience of being held as a political prisoner, as Cummings re-created it, is anomalous in that Cummings's autobiographical-hero greeted his imprisonment with joy and recognized it at once as a way to salvation. Unlike the protagonists of Koestler, Malraux, Camus, and Silone, who struggle tormentedly to separate themselves from an ideology or to safeguard an identity, Cummings finds himself locked up with individuals who are rich in the very qualities he had come to admire. Like Bunyan's Christian when he is free of Giant Despair and in sight of the Delectable Mountains, Cummings breathes hope and joy and moves with a clear knowledge of the cultural traps he has managed to evade. His condition is similar to that of Henry Miller's auto-hero when he feels himself reborn, or to Hemingway's narrators discovering what they truly feel as distinct from what they are supposed to feel, or to that of James Baldwin, penniless in Paris, and free at last of the stereotypes of his native land.

The director of the camp is the archfiend Apollyon, "a Satan whose word is dreadful not because it is painstakingly unjust but because it is incomprehensibly omnipotent" (pp. 147–148). This man is a "perfect representative of the Almighty French Government" (p. 148). Like the God of the authoritarian culture, he rules through negative forces: fear of death and sexual repression. The Sunday Mass becomes a particular demonstration of his power, serving to intensify the fear and privation. On seeing the ferocious punishment to which one of the women was subjected, Cummings knew once and for all where he stood in relation to any society that could authorize such horror. "I realized fully and irrevocably and for perhaps the first time the meaning of civilization. And I realized that it was true—as I had previously only suspected it to be true—that in finding us unworthy to carry forward the banner of progress, alias the tricolour, the inimitable and excellent French Government was conferring upon B. and myself—albeit with other intent—the ultimate compliment" (p. 167). The special brutality that the women prisoners seemed to arouse in the guards and in the director revealed "those unspeakable foundations upon which are builded with infinite care such at once ornate and comfortable structures as *La Gloire* and *Le Patriotisme*" (p. 169).

While Cummings refers to the French Government, the tricolour, and *La Gloire,* he makes it clear in several places that he is dealing not merely with the French nation but with Western civilization. The object of his satire is the force exercised by society against some of the most precious qualities in human nature with the object of preserving a hierarchy of privilege and power. Apollyon sums up the culture. His self-righteousness is fused with a compulsive sense of order. He cannot tolerate the individuality of the prisoners and interprets as malice and recalcitrance the ways in which each of them is true to himself and not to the state's idea of what he should be. Cummings's refusal to dissociate himself from the attitudes expressed in Brown's letters is interpreted by Apollyon as a deliberate act of treason. Each prisoner, by the very fact of his being a prisoner, is guilty of treason in the director's judgment, even though no prisoner feels any guilt and most are innocent even of a conception of the state. The guards treat their charges as criminals, even though no one has been found guilty by lawful trial and the camp is technically a detention center, not a prison. As Cummings demonstrates, the real treason of the inmates of the enormous room is their incorrigible individuality. Prisoners and guards define one another. The individuality of the inmates and their responsiveness to subrational impulses is intensified by the conformity of the guards and their responsiveness to an abstract idea of the state.

On the dark night of his arrival at the concentration camp, Cummings mistook the camp building for a rural gendarmerie, and his heart sank "at the thought of sleeping in the company of that species of humanity which I had come to detest beyond anything in hell or on earth" (pp. 55–56). The prison guards were "the lowest species of human organism" (p. 152). They are but a part of their uniforms, and the chief guard is known simply as "The Black Holster." They are resolved into the element of force and their central objective is to annihilate the souls of their prisoner-victims. The degrading conditions of the camp were intended to reduce Cummings to mindless compliance, but their effect was precisely the opposite. For the first time he felt himself sharply dissociated from a repressive, authoritarian culture that had shaped much of his own character. He rejoiced in his alienation and in the opportunity to force the culture to show its tooth and claw and in being able to bear direct witness to the mutilations that it inflicted upon his fellow prisoners.

Being an artist and a poet, Cummings's response to his experience was strongly aesthetic. While capable of exclusively ethical or political or social judgments, he continually and spontaneously reacted on aesthetic grounds, and he kept notebooks of sketches and the few key words that would suffice to recreate a scene or a dialogue. The enforced, prolonged intimacy with his fellow prisoners gave him insight into the ways in which complex, delicate emotions would find expression in a simple gesture or a mere tone of voice or an absurd item of clothing. The physical necessities of the body, of which the inmates were always forcibly aware in the overcrowded room, play an essential role as a constant reminder of man's common animal nature and the shared denominator of mortality. Above this level the great gulfs of difference from person to person begin to open and Cummings had the leisure to explore personalities radically different from his own.

In trying to capture something of the nature of these personalities for *The Enormous Room,* he had to create a new idiom for the subject. His prose medium, instead of conveying a reasoned, conventional statement of an experience, would try by means of metaphors and symbols that bear the narrator's subjective, felt response to undermine conventional responses and evoke new cultural attitudes toward the primitive forces in human nature. Cummings's use of words and images was similar in many ways to Eliot's practice in *The Waste Land* and Joyce's in *Ulysses,* both of which appeared in 1922, the year in which *The Enormous Room* was first published (in incomplete form). For Cummings beauty and truth are one, the aesthetic and the social conscience are the same, and his work of art, *The Enormous Room*, is a manifesto of aesthetic radicalism.

Cummings's Harvard Commencement speech and the articles that he had published in *The Dial* prior to writing *The Enormous Room* show that he was aware of the implications for social revolution in the psychological forces liberated by the new forms of art—as well as his awareness of the representative "elderly Boston woman" who was not sympathetic to the new art and who would be most at sea when she believed she understood it and explained it to others. Cummings found in T. S. Eliot's technique an "alert hatred of normality" and a preference above everything for "the unique dimension of intensity," which replaces in the reader "the comforting and comfortable furniture of reality."[9]

In giving an expressive form to his experience at Ferté Macé, Cummings imagined the concentration camp as an individual, as he was to do later with his experience in Russia for *Eimi.* In his Introduction for *The Enormous Room* Cummings wrote, "Eimi is the individual again; a more complex individual, a more enormous room" (p. *viii*).

This meant that the dramatis personae, interacting with one another in their enormous room and with their guards and administrators, represent the elaborate mélange of impulse and repression that goes to make up a state of being. The concept is suggested by one of Cummings's poems, which begins as follows:

> so many selves (so many fiends and gods
> each greedier than every) is a man
> (so easily one in another hides;
> yet man can, being all, escape from none)[10]

Enclosed by the reality principle of the prison (itself an aspect of the personality) are the ugly and beautiful selves of this particular being. Pots of excrement and urine, hunger, thirst, and a variety of painful ailments are unpleasant evidence of its physical nature. Selves driven by hate, or love, or greed, or generosity must come to terms with one another. All are to some degree the victims of sexual frustration as a result of cultural barriers, and all are united in hostility toward the authority that continually makes incomprehensible demands on them and relentlessly seeks to violate, in Keats's words, "the holiness of the Heart's affections, and the truth of the Imagination."

For Cummings, who believed that all art was "strictly and distinctly a question of individuality," the camp at Ferté Macé provided a rare opportunity. The circumstances at the camp insured his encounter with "unaccommodated man," and in addition there was the extraordinary variety of nationalities and of occupations. The variety of forms of expression alone was all but incredible. The persona through which Cummings narrates the experience manages to use languages as an index to identities and to the vastly differing worlds that produced them. At the same time the symbols of his imagination, chiefly drawn from *Pilgrim's Progress,* unify all the bizarre eccentrics in a consciousness that has an astonishing capacity for compassion and love.

While Cummings had perceived his civilization as his enemy, the process of rooting its harmful elements out of his identity required time and patience, "that vast and painful process of Unthinking which may result in a minute bit of purely personal Feeling. Which minute bit is Art" (p. 307). In a way the camp functioned for Cummings as a kind of purgatory, one that he entered willingly in order to recognize his vices, to submit to forms of correction, and to have always before his eyes images of particular perfections—those inmates whom he named Delectable Mountains. After his own experience of unlearning, Cummings believed he knew how other artists had achieved their individuality. Cézanne, for example, "became truly naif—not by superficially contemplating and admiring the art of primitive peoples, but by carefully misbelieving and violently disunderstanding a second-hand world."[11] Such an observation is not anti-intellectual; rather it demonstrates Cummings's perception of a process whereby a person transcends intellectual formulae, *a priori* attitudes, and cultural conditioning and strives by an act of the imagination to feel the identity of his own primal nature with the forces that find expression in the art of primitive peoples. It is a process of reestablishing the mind's rapport with its nonrational life, a process in which the intelligence dissolves its own categories, "the negation on our part by thinking, of thinking."[12]

Cummings's point was anticipated emphatically by Henry James, who insisted upon the need of the creative artist to cultivate his personal, felt perceptions and who imagined "fine cold thought" as the looming menace of "some particularly large iceberg in a cool blue northern sea." These images referred to Mrs. Newsome of *The Ambassadors,* whom Strether came to "see" by unthinking the values of Woollett even as an earlier character, Newman of *The American,* disentangled his personal conscience from the cold logic of both Wall Street and the Faubourg St. Germain. Cummings's point about the recovery of primitive response is what Hemingway had in mind when he declared that the central difficulty he faced in his effort to become a writer was in recognizing the truth of his own emotions.

The inmates whom Cummings described as Delectable Mountains never had to undergo the process of unlearning or struggle to discern their own felt perceptions in the welter of cultural formulations. Birth and circumstances had endowed them with an uncorrupted simplicity. They were ignorant of governments and wars except as mysterious forces that thrust them into prisons. They had a resilient joy in life, although the inscrutable workings of officials tested this to the utmost. Each lived in the civilization of his own individuality, a civilization remarkable for its simplicity, independence, magnanimity, and trust—the qualities that Thoreau, in *Walden,* attributes to the life of the ideal philosopher. Indeed, Cummings gives his Delectable Mountains somewhat the same mythical qualities that Thoreau found in those drunken musquash hunters, "aboriginal men," "gods of the river and woods with sparkling faces (like Apollo's)" of whom he wrote in his journal.

The first Delectable Mountain, The Wanderer, seemed to Cummings a type of primitive, patriarch king. In recording how this man was separated from his wife and children, Cummings observes, "it takes a good and great government perfectly to negate mercy" (p. 228). Zoo-Loo, the second Delectable Mountain, cannot be described because Cummings finds him so much a part of himself that Zoo-Loo is not a thing but "a Verb; an Is" (p. 231). His lesson is Being. Surplice, the third Delectable Mountain, seems chiefly to have instructed Cummings by his exquisite combination of humility and dignity.

Jean Le Negre, the last of the Delectable Mountains, taught the redeeming capacity of living life as play. For The Wanderer and for Jean Le Negre life takes very different forms; but both live in the present moment, and for both life is a spontaneous game that takes its energy from an unrepressed sexuality. Prison could only modify, not destroy, the play of these images of the way to be. The fortresses of American culture, however, could produce the kind of repression that Cummings described in a sonnet published the year after the appearance of *The Enormous Room*:

> the Cambridge ladies who live in furnished souls are unbeautiful
> and have comfortable minds (also, with the church's protestant
> blessings daughters, unscented shapeless spirited) they believe in
> Christ and Longfellow, both dead.[13]

To such Americans Cummings held up as an ideal an unordered, unrepressed, unproductive mode of living, one that reveled in its sensuality and irrational response. He went on to affirm the ideal repeatedly in his poetry, drama, and miscellaneous writings. He directed the attention of Americans to the circus, for example, where "living players play with living,"[14] and where such law, order, and discipline as exist are wholly interrelated with the play impulse. It is the same fusion of discipline and instinct as that which characterizes the performance of the artist. It was the conviction that lay at the center of Hemingway's mode of living and writing.

Cummings invited Americans to look for images of themselves at the zoo: "What moves us is the revelation—couched in terms of things visible or outside us—of our true or invisible selves."[15] The true, the invisible self will try to refute the recognition of its relationship to the creature in the cage and protest, "I must be dreaming!—which conviction is well founded, for in a sense we are dreaming."[16] Even the fantasy world of the comic strip, Cummings pointed out to Americans caught up in the "Roaring Twenties," uttered its real cry of alarm to the true, invisible self. "The meteoric burlesk melodrama of democracy is a struggle between society (Offissa Pupp) and the individual (Ignatz Mouse) over an ideal (our heroine [Krazy Kat])—a struggle from which, again and again and again, emerges one stupendous fact; namely, that the ideal of democracy fulfils herself only if, and whenever, society fails to suppress the individual."[17] In the closing image of *The Enormous Room* New York looms above the waters much as the Celestial City appeared to Bunyan's Christian. But there are no Shining Ones and trumpet calls. America dawns on the reader as yet another enormous room, enclosed by walls and guards and the spirit of Apollyon, repressing its Delectable Mountains, who cannot comprehend the dread of death and love.

8
Hemingway and Life as Play

I

Hemingway's fiction demonstrates the evolution of his relationship to society from that of alienated critic to that of a man who is at the same time creator and actor in the drama of his social being. His early vignettes *(in our time)* and short stories express his maturing sense of American culture as having accepted a violent destructiveness toward human nature into its civilized formulae. An acute sense of the limitations of his culture had come early to Hemingway as a result of the rigid cultural attitudes of his grandparents and parents, attitudes that were thrown into vivid relief by the cultural attitudes of the Ojibway Indians, whom he began to know as a child during summers "up in Michigan," and by the cultural attitudes of the peasants and workingmen whom he was to encounter as a journalist and as a sportsman in such countries as Greece, Italy, France, Cuba, and Spain. A close involvement with nature, an involvement that intensified and deepened in meaning as his life progressed, gave him a clearly defined sense of his own individuality, his particular relation to the universe. His writing shows that he placed his ultimate trust in his personal, felt sense of experience and that, as with Whitman and Henry Miller, this trust was premised upon a sense of life and death as stages in a passage.

Given this fundamental condition Hemingway could accept the social process as shaping his consciousness while he also saw himself objectively in relationship to the process of history, and knew himself to be engaged actively in resolving the basic existentialist problem of alienation—of working through cultural barriers to a sense of one's share in humanness and in being. Henry James's character Strether, at the start of *The Ambassadors,* is anticipating experience with *a priori* assumptions; his relation to life is that of an observer viewing a landscape through a shop window, or of an uneasy spectator at a play. By the end of the novel he is part of the landscape, an actor in the human drama; he has changed his consciousness even though he once professed the belief that the affair of life is "a tin mould" into which "a helpless jelly, one's consciousness is poured." Very early in his life Hemingway "saw" Oak Park as Strether came to see Woollett. He deliberately cut the parental values out of his mind and chose ways of engaging meaningfully and imaginatively with life. He determined the values and the code as long as he could exert control, and *The Sun Also Rises* and *A Farewell to Arms* disclose stages in the process of moving from conditioned object to creative player in the game of life.

The bullfighter who chooses again and again to encounter the possibility of death in order to demonstrate his mastery of a contrived, deadly situation, a mastery that is an affirmation of youth and sexuality, of courage and grace—even, for aficionados, an affirmation of the human spirit—became for Hemingway symbolic of man's capacity to shape his own existence. The action of Robert Jordan in *For Whom the Bell Tolls* creates him as a social being, gives meaning to his personal life, is a working in and for nature and natural men, and his personal commitment is only extrinsically related to political parties and social goals. Even more, if possible, than Hemingway's critics, Colonel Cantwell plays with the role of "Hemingway hero"; unlike the critics, he suffuses with humor and grace and his sense of play the ceremonious farewell to life that is the subject of *Across the River and Into the Trees.* Stories centered about sports became an inevitable metaphor for Hemingway's sense of life. They demonstrated his belief that one only has his life when he plays for the sake of the game, according to the rules, and with the fullness of his being; that the game and the player are both destroyed when they become absorbed into such conventional goals as material profit and "success." The act of "liberating" Paris was a game for Hemingway, as well as hunting Nazi U-boats from his fishing-boat, or competing for trophies in Africa, or fishing for marlin in the Gulf Stream. He was an aficionado of living, and for him a game well played was a religious gesture. His last books conveyed the sense of men's lives as islands in a stream, moments in the process of being.

II

The many biographical studies of Hemingway that appeared shortly after his death and dealt, in whole or in part, with his early life describe Hemingway's family as ideally representative of the American middle class.[1] The Hemingway parents and grandparents were thoroughly devout men and women and patriotic citizens. This meant that they were in established businesses or professions, active in civic affairs, and involved in the activities of the church and in the work of such church-related organizations as the Y.M.C.A. They observed all the local social rituals and tried to bring up their children in what was unquestionably the correct Christian and American pattern. God and country were inseparable in their ideology, and both were conceived as being prime movers of the security, prosperity, and righteousness of the Christian, American middle class.

As this class defined a Christian American community, it excluded not merely the Indian, the Negro, and immigrant breeds, but also the poor, the mentally ill, and whosoever fell afoul of the law. In a society of intense economic rivalries, bitter jockeying for social position, and enormous intolerance for genuine individualism, Hemingway's parents and grandparents were indifferent to self-contradiction: they were prepared to affirm their belief that all men were essentially good. Hemingway's brother Leicester writes, "Ernest came straight out of the Midwestern Victorian era of the nineties. Our parents were an unusual pair for that middle-class society. But our grandparents were far more typical in their decorum—and in their unquestioning harking to that vast ground swell known even then as Public Opinion."[2] Hemingway's paternal grandfather, Anson Tyler Hemingway, amounts to a caricature of the type. As his funeral biography notes, he was an important fund-raiser for the Chicago Y.M.C.A., "an active and enthusiastic member of the First Congregational Church, serving as Sunday School superintendent, deacon, and finally becoming deacon emeritus."[3] He served "the cause of temperance," and all six of his children graduated from Oak Park schools and went to Oberlin College. Hemingway's mother, before her marriage, had initiated a career as an opera singer, but her sensitive eyes forced her to forego the career at its start. When it was clear that a career as a singer was impossible, she married. Music, however, remained her first love, and the chief room in her Oak Park home was the music room. The general care of the household and of the children fell to the respectful hands of Dr. Hemingway. In every possible way, the couple aspired to represent Culture and Conformity in the local community.

With his earliest published writing, Hemingway began his effort to detach his personal identity from that of the parental ideal. Writing for the high school's *Trapeze*, he sought to catch the ironic tone of Ring Lardner and to use a diction and to project a character purged of gentility. A mocking humor was to characterize his writing until his efforts to carve the vignettes of violence that became *in our time* broke through his protective pose and evoked a deeply personal commitment. Ironic humor was to be a pervasive element in Hemingway's mature work, but his sketches for the *Toronto Star Weekly* break repeatedly into burlesque, mimicry, and satire as well as irony.[4] Hemingway was mocking, with very slight disguise, the values that were most dear to the self-consciously American hearts of his parents. Well before he cited as an epigraph to *The Torrents of Spring* Henry Fielding's famous theory of the ridiculous in character and convention, Hemingway had discovered for himself the source of the ridiculous in affectation.

From his first to his twenty-first year, except for the momentous 1918, he had spent every summer at the Hemingway cottage on Walloon Lake "up in Michigan." These summers were of the greatest importance in providing him with the sense of a "counter-culture" to Oak Park. There he constantly associated with Ojibway Indians—including Prudence Boulton, sister of Billy Boulton, who gave him this lesson in sexual candor:

"You want Trudy again?"
"You want to?"
"Un Huh."
"Come on."
"No, here."
"But Billy—"
"I no mind Billy. He my brother." ("Fathers and Sons")[5]

The surface humor of this exchange deepens unexpectedly to cut into Oak Park mores where brothers and sisters scarcely dared to acknowledge one another's sexuality. Hemingway hunted and fished with the Indians for summer after summer and in sharing their way of life established a basis from which his parents' culture fell into a startlingly narrow perspective. The perspective on Indian life opened wide to include all of nature.

Upon graduating from high school, Hemingway seized the first opportunity for getting away from home and avoiding college. His job with the Kansas City *Star* was precisely what he wanted—an encounter with jails, courthouses, brothels, and slums. It was an exploration of the sexual and aggressive elements of human personality that his parents were concerned to deny even while they paid well to keep evidence of such elements at a distance. Only one irresistible opportunity drew Hemingway from his work as a cub reporter: the chance to go to Europe and participate in what promised to be the marvelous adventure of war.

Possibly the mass slaughter of World War I was robbing death of its tragedy for many Americans. If so, it was not true for Hemingway. Oak Park had anticipated the war in this respect by producing a culture in which there seemed to be no real sense of death. Like sex, it was heavily disguised by sentimental fantasies. Hemingway might work off his sense of violent death in stories for the school literary magazine (in which his protagonists were eaten by wolves, clubbed senseless, or run over by a train), but such violence came to him through the stories of Jack London and stories told by the Indians. They pulsed with the blood of a world far different from his own. Kansas City brought him close to human violence, and at Fossalta, Italy, he found himself an actor in the actual play.

III

Hemingway as a man embittered and disillusioned by his experience of warfare during World War I has been so much a part of critical legend that the gaiety and brevity of his actual involvement in that war are worth the reminder. He arrived in Milan, Italy, early in June, 1918, and was assigned to Schio, a post so comfortable that it was referred to as the Schio Country Club. After about a month of frustration, he volunteered to move to Fossalta where, as before, nothing happened. Then, while visiting a forward listening post on the night of July 8, as though by appointment he received his wound. Within six weeks of his departure from Milan he was back there, a victim of almost the only enemy action he had actually witnessed. Until the Austrian shell landed near him, he was a schoolboy anxious to see the big game. His convalescence at the beautiful, well-equipped hospital in Milan, where the eighteen Red Cross nurses had only four patients, was hardly typical of war experience, and falling deeply in love with one of the nurses, Agnes Hannah von Kurowsky, seemed more than to justify the wound.[6]

Nothing in Hemingway's first exposure to war embittered or disillusioned him. The terrible visions that came in the night during the first stage of recovery were, by the evidence of his short stories, sympathetic psychic trauma—visions of his mother's neurasthenic autocracy, her symbolic castration of her husband, and her efforts to extend her dominion to the rebellious Ernest.[7] For the time being, however, these visions remained secret, and Hemingway's letters home and to his friends were cheerful, even exhilarated. The wound proved a passport to fresh terrains of the imagination as he received two Italian medals, was reported in the Illinois newspapers as a war hero, and was received back in America with a hero's welcome; with his Italian officer's cape, his uniform, and a much-evident cane, Hemingway obligingly played the part. But when, toward the end of his first year back in the United States, the glamour had gone, Grace Hemingway once again sought to manifest her control. It appeared that he must play the role that his parents and middle-class America had chosen for him, and the elements of a serious identity crisis began to appear.

Leaving America to join the Red Cross unit in Italy had greatly weakened his already shaky sense of belonging to the cultural pattern affirmed in his home. The outspoken cynicism he had heard in Italy in reference to the war, the direct observation of the tolerance of conduct strongly disapproved at home—official brothels for soldiers and officers, the exuberant consumption of alcoholic drinks, the outspoken contempt of many Italian soldiers for their church, their government, their officers, and, in fact for all officialdom—made it difficult for him to treat with respect the long-resented lares and penates of Oak Park.

By the summer of 1920 Hemingway's opposition to his parents and to the kind of future they wanted for him had resulted in open antagonism. Greatly disturbed because her son refused to find a job, showed no interest in getting married and settling down, preferred to idle away his time with friends at the Walloon Lake summer cottage "sponging" on her hospitality, and rebelled at tending to the household duties usually performed by a docile Dr. Hemingway (who was away from the camp), Mrs. Hemingway ordered her son to keep away from the cottage until invited to return. She saw to it that Ernest promptly received a letter from his father reiterating her complaints and commands. The psychic rupture was complete.[8]

Hemingway's open break with his parents, a break that signified his conscious decision to pursue his own way of life, came in July, 1920, the month he came legally of age and the second anniversary of the wound that had been his initiation into a new way of being. As his short stories would soon demonstrate, far from operating as a catalyst of the horrors of war, the wound was linked to traumatic childhood moments out of which grew his hostile, contemptuous feelings for his parents and the kind of social life they embodied. In "Soldier's Home" Hemingway described in thinly veiled autobiography his own return home. Harry Krebs's way of escaping from the parental harassment was to turn back to the war: he wanted to learn all about the war; he had liked France and Germany; and he had not wanted to come home. In August, 1920, Hemingway made the fishing trip along the Fox River that he was to describe in "Big Two-Hearted River."[9] Unquestionably the young man of the story has been deeply alienated and is making a painstaking effort to recover his psychological balance. The story was viewed as field-and-stream writing until Malcolm Cowley, in 1944, presented it as a reaction to war, "an escape from a nightmare or from realities that have become nightmare."[10] Nothing in the story definitely links the young man's state of mind with the war, however, and while the story can be suggestively interpreted in this way, the biographical evidence strongly suggests that so far as the story is to be related to a personal crisis of the author, a different interpretation is called for. Given the nature of Hemingway's brief encounter with war, love, and heroism, his break with his parents, and his desire to return to Europe, it would seem that the "nightmare" or "realities that have become nightmare" issue from the young man's sense of the blighted nature of the American culture that he is expected to make his own, his bitter decision to turn finally away from his family, and his resolve to make his own way alone.

When Hemingway returned from Italy to a hero's welcome at home, like Stephen Crane's hero he had been wearing a false red badge of courage. Before the assembled high school students and various civic groups he displayed his shrapnel-shredded uniform and his scars. But, as with Krebs of "Soldier's Home," the pose wore thin, and, anyway, Americans were already bored with war heroes. The crisis that Hemingway faced in August, 1920, had to do with the lost generation only in the sense in which any generation becomes lost—when the sensitive young man finds that the values of his culture do not correspond to the truths of his experience; when he views nation, religion, and family as so many nets to ensnare his soul and desperately begins out of his response to his personal, felt sense of life to search for a direction in which he can commit himself.

Stephen Crane's Henry Fleming encountered a death figure in the forest "'chapel,'' a figure that, reinforced by further images of the dead, revived in him his spiritual sense of communion with his comrades and brought about his instinctive return to the battle line. Death, in Crane's story, is never a negative condition; it speaks miraculously to the living and guides the choices of the spirit. Hemingway's forest chapel might well have been the lonely reaches of the Fox River. In 1920 he wrote about his fishing trip on the Fox River in articles for *The Toronto Star Weekly*, but he did not write about the trip in its deeper dimension until sometime between January and August, 1924, when he was back in Paris. In "Big Two-Hearted River" neither his parents nor the war nor the war wound are mentioned; they were particulars that could be left out. What comes through the story is a sense of death, which gives life an entirely new meaning. Hemingway wished to keep vivid his sense of the reality of death and out of that awareness to forge a way of life that would be instinct with meaning. As Freud had observed, meditating on war a few years earlier, "Life becomes impoverished and loses its interest when Life itself, the highest stake in the game of living, must not be risked."[11] Hemingway's parents could never have conceived of life as a game. Hemingway could. In returning to Europe he turned his back on the whole complex forfeit summed up in "settling down," and in a spirit of play committed himself wholly to being a creative artist and to a mode of living that often put his life at stake.

IV

Hemingway's first truly original writing sought to show his countrymen truth in a handful of dust. The images that he painstakingly composed for *in our time* each held in suspension a moment of violence. The subject of each, however, is not the violence but the grotesquely civilized consciousness in which the moment hangs suspended. In each image there is the telltale thumbprint—a civilized voice exulting in slaughter, official executions, the ruthless transfer of a populace—that reveals the human mind as so numb to its arranged horrors, so civilized out of any compassion for its human and animal victims, that the images amount to an indictment of a culture for its fragmentation of the human community and its acceptance of all those artifices of the intellect that protect material interests and destroy the value of man. While Mrs. Grace Hemingway might be leading the Congregational Church choir of Oak Park in a confident hymn, "Give peace in our time, O God," her son held up images of a Kansas City policeman murdering "wops," of prison officials solemnly hanging Sam Cardinella, of professional soldiers gloating over the chance to kill enemy troops like targets in a shooting gallery, of merciless execution squads, and of a king turning phrases in his rose garden while his people endured the agony of their withdrawal from Thrace. In these moments of truth Hemingway was concerned not with the violence primarily, but with the mind produced by a civilization in which the individual human being has lost his sacredness, and the intuition of human community that had shaped the laws and institutions of the culture has been lost. Hemingway's social criticism is far more radical than that of the social realists of the thirties and forties who took him to task for being insufficiently concerned with the economic depression and the rise of fascism.[12]

When *in our time* became *In Our Time,* the short stories brought a perspective of space to the time dimension of the original images. The collection might well be called "The Education of Nick Adams," for, like Henry Adams's autobiography, it reflects a man's effort to understand the time and place in which he matured and his assessment of a culture. The screams of the squaw in labor ("Indian Camp"), a terrifying phenomenon to Nick, vibrate in unison with the pain of the Greek refugee giving birth to her child in a crowded cart herded in the endless procession through the mud and rain. Nick's civilized American father observes, " 'But her screams are not important. I don't hear them because they are not important.' " The uncivilized Indian husband could not bear the screams and cut his throat. In "The End of Something" Nick breaks off his love affair with Marjorie. It was leading to marriage, which meant, inevitably, joining the social treadmill. But in avoiding one trap, he entered another. The "something" that ended was a capacity for spontaneous, innocent love. The youth was conditioned for participation in the brutally calculated adult relationships in which material interests come first.

In "The Doctor and the Doctor's Wife" Nick watches his father submit to the insults of the Indian, Dick Boulton, and his father's failure in manhood is linked with his neurasthenic mother's refusal to recognize any realities other than those accommodated by her religious platitudes. She is as removed from the vital springs of life as the title couple of "Mr. and Mrs. Elliot," who try so very hard to have a baby. These overly refined sensibilities are placed in vivid contrast with the bullfighters who face death again and again, even though their bodies are broken and bleeding, driven by a commitment to the rules of their sport as binding as the instinctive reactions of the animal they seek to kill.

In subsequent short stories Hemingway moved on toward his personal revelations, yet he frequently touched deftly and corrosively upon the nature of the civilization he had left behind. After reading *In Our Time,* Hemingway's father wrote to him, "Trust you will see and describe more of humanity of a different character in future volumes. . . . The brutal you have surely shown the world. Look for the joyous, uplifting, and optimistic and spiritual in character. It is present if found. Remember God holds us each responsible to do our best. My thoughts and prayers are for you dear boy every day."[13] The son responded with stories ("Now I Lay Me," "In Another Country") describing how, lying awake in the dark after he had been wounded, he reached back for his earliest memory to the attic of his grandfather's house, where his father's collection of snake specimens was stored. He remembered how his mother burned the snakes and burned also his father's collection of arrowheads. The symbolic castration of the father-hunter did not extend to the son, who took up the gun and the two game bags and bore them to the house. Hemingway described the contemptuous treatment of the Indian subculture; his own love affair with Prudence Boulton ("Ten Indians") was destroyed by his father, who saw it as his duty to report to his son that he had seen the girl "threshing around" in the woods with a boy friend. Hemingway described in "The Battler" a Negro-White relationship that in its violent, inverted master-servant bond is another version of the sinister racial motif of Melville's *Benito Cereno* and of Poe's *The Narrative of A. Gordon Pym.* And in "The Light of the World" (Matthew 5:14: "Ye are the light of the world. A city that is set on a hill cannot be hid.") he presented to Oak Park the tale of a light-hearted, casual encounter with the adultery, fornication, homosexuality, and prostitution that were a tabooed aspect of its culture.

Europe provided Hemingway with a basis for comparative as well as objective analysis of American life. It offered, too, what it had offered American artists from early in the nineteenth century: inexpensive living, relief from family and social pressures, the opportunity for privacy and, when desired, for social involvement—particularly in Paris of the twenties. His was the American artist's typical discovery of individual freedom in Europe—a sense of escape from the relentless pressure for conformity that was possibly the most oppressive feature of American life, a feature singled out for especial comment by all the important European observers of American life since de Tocqueville. Among Europeans, Hemingway's preference was for the folk least conditioned by the sophistications of modern life and truest to folk ways, to natural instinct, and to the ceremonies and rituals through which their basic social needs had found expression for centuries.

While he associated in Paris with a group of men and women who were creating the art movements of the age, and while he adapted whatever he found useful in their theories to his own art, Hemingway ruthlessly held himself free of the influence of any individual, movement, or theory. The harshness with which he eventually turned on such teachers as Sherwood Anderson and Gertrude Stein is an indication of his sense that imitation is death, and of his instinctive knowledge that his personal sense of his experience was the basis of his worth as a writer. The choice of the Pamplona St. Fermin Fiesta as the central metaphor of his first major work of fiction was wholly the result of an instinctive, spontaneous, felt response to the festival. The moment of truth in the arena was the central meaning from which all other meanings fell away in a widening gyre.

V

In writing *The Sun Also Rises* Hemingway tried to express his personal revelation of an old ritual in which the virile identity of the male is affirmed and a sacrifice offered in celebration of the event. The narrator's consciousness through which the experience is given is crippled by the impotence of the culture that has made it, but his inward self moves toward a vital affirmation. Far from being an anti-war tract or a breast-beating for the disenchanted, the novel is an exaltation of the masculine principle—hunter, warrior, and blood-sacrificing priest—and of a people's spiritual community. Jake, the alien aficionado, has been crippled by the war and so has Brett; but their sexual disorder and social alienation are symptoms of a cultural sickness of which the war itself is a symptom. Jake and Brett are not poised in tension against one another as in a conventional love story. They are more the male and female elements of one psychically wounded protagonist. The action of the novel involves their desperate, futile efforts to rid themselves of their corrupt cultural identities. They are what time has made them, and Brett, although seeing in the matador Romero a masculine ideal, is resigned to the knowledge that for her there can be no union with such an ideal. She can never resolve herself into the natural feminine principle that such an ideal requires. For Jake, Romero's summation of courage and grace, his willing wager of a life for a life, is a demonstration of an heroic way to be—a way he can never be since his culture has maimed him with its manifold practical material considerations.

While *A Farewell to Arms* was written after *The Sun Also Rises,* in the emotional as well as the historical chronology of Hemingway's protagonist it precedes the latter. Jake Barnes is the destiny in store for Frederic Henry. In fact, when Hemingway completed *The Sun Also Rises,* he went back to ideas expressed in some of his short stories, particularly in "A Very Short Story," for the central theme of *A Farewell to Arms.* In this novel war and love are parallel metaphors to express the defeat awaiting the man whose culture has corrupted the possibility of an instinctual acceptance of his existence and of his spiritual bonds to his fellow man—an acceptance unconditioned by institutional, or intellectual, or material ends. Lieutenant Henry tries to believe in the war, but the superficial motives that led to his associating himself with the Italian army dissolve under the first challenge of events. In the famous scenes describing the retreat from Caporetto (which drew upon Hemingway's experience while reporting on the Greek evacuation of Turkey and scarcely at all upon his experience at Fossalta) Lieutenant Henry knows himself to be the complete alien. Friendship, loyalty, love, all dissolved in the symbolic rain.

The love affair with Catherine is a parallel instance of his incapacity for belief. Everything about the relationship is cast in terms of withdrawal and escape; it is a prolongation of Nick Adams's experience in "The End of Something." Hemingway had already made clear in the short stories "In Another Country" and "Now I Lay Me" his belief that if a man commits his self to a cause, as in warfare, or to love of another, as in marriage, he gives up control of his emotional being to the indifferent chances of life. The war may ravel into a meaningless disaster and marriage may be broken. It is Hemingway's view that a man must live out of his own sense of values and out of loyalty to his own ideals. If he engages in war or love, it must be for the nature of the life it brings him with each moment, and in full awareness that nothing is ever finally won or lost, that the only achievement is in playing as truly as one can, and that to play at all one must bear in mind that the game will end. He does not win—despite whatever victories may come to him in war or love; and he does not lose—even though, like Robert Jordan, the side on which he is fighting loses and he loses his loved one and his life. After all, he has had his own life and on his own terms.

Lieutenant Henry and Jake Barnes, as witnesses to their own experiences, convey a kind of wisdom through the tone of their narration that transcends the usual concepts of satisfaction in good fortune or bitterness in loss. Lieutenant Henry tells of his having been in a game devised by others, one in which he was more a victim than a player, "You did not know what it was about. You never had time to learn. They threw you in and told you the rules and the first time they caught you off base they killed you."[14] In the narration, however, both he and Jake Barnes seem to view the game of life in terms of the epigraph that Hemingway devised himself, with deliberate overtones of the age of chivalric games, for his volume of short stories, *Winner Take Nothing* (1932): "Unlike all other forms of lutte or combat the conditions are that the winner shall take nothing; neither his ease, nor his pleasure, nor any notions of glory; nor, if he win far enough, shall there be any reward within himself."[15]

VI

Hemingway's concept of life as play was first suggested to him in the 1918 Milan days by Captain Dorman-Smith by means of the same fragment of philosophy which, in "The Short Happy Life of Francis

Macomber" (1936), another professional hunter (this time of animals) employs in connection with Macomber's initiation to his short, happy life: " 'Shakespeare. Damned good. . . . "By my troth, I care not; a man can die but once; we owe God a death and let it go which way it will he that dies this year is quit for the next." ' "[16] These words formed a talisman for Hemingway to the world of professional soldiers, matadors, and others involved in a repeated confrontation with death. What followed from this was the transforming discovery that life was to be played as a game.[17] At the Nick Adams stage, games had been esteemed largely as a diversion from the serious business of life even when, as with hunting and fishing, they provided him with his most meaningful sense of himself in relation to nature. Like Lieutenant Henry he had tried war and love and been hurt by both. With Jake Barnes he created a transitional figure. Jake has discovered a ceremony to which he can respond with primitive energies, but the great degree to which society has alienated him from his natural self incapacitates him for full participation. Robert Cohn, Jake's thoroughly civilized counterpart, is someone who will never know about life as play despite his shining competence as a sportsman. At this stage in Hemingway's career a "transvaluation of values" was complete, and he could enter fully into his role as a player in the game of life, a role that takes as its premise that reality is the supreme fiction.

Implicit in Hemingway's fiction is the judgment that American culture is characterized by excessive seriousness, excessive practicality, and insensitivity to natural patterns of living. The individual under such conditions does not mature as a social being; he is adapted to form a part of a social machine. Life as play, while it might be a concept that characterizes the philosophical attitude of the American transcendentalists and of the adventuresome American spirit associated with the founding, the exploration, and the settling of America, is a concept inimical to what had become the predominant American cultural attitude. With *Death in the Afternoon* Hemingway set out to provide a handbook on tauromachy only in the sense that *Moby Dick* is a handbook on whaling. He wished to demonstrate that bullfighting, considered by most Americans to be a decadent, cruel amusement, was in fact a religious ritual. He wished also to assert his arrival at an outlook on life wholly different from the one prevalent in his homeland. As he stated in *Death in the Afternoon,* he was in rebellion against death. Like the metaphysical poets, he would destroy death in his metaphors by proving death to be but a stage to a new order of being. Killing the bull was a ritual victory over death; it was also, in its permitted unleashing of destructive powers, a victory that could be tolerated only under elaborate disguise in America, where a moralizing sentimentalism, well illustrated by the behavior and letters of Hemingway's parents, sought to deny the destructive forces in the human personality and inadvertently brought about a corresponding denial of Eros.

Hemingway's celebration of bullfighting can be taken as part of his anti-intellectual stance. He was, however, an intelligent man given to the pursuit of many intellectual activities. His concern with bullfighting and, in general, with the need to confront death, to accept danger and violence as part of life, is related to the idea expressed by Freud in both *The Future of an Illusion* and *Civilization and Its Discontents* that neuroses are frequently the result of a civilization imposing upon the individual cultural ideals that frustrate primitive impulses of aggression and self-destruction. Hemingway's view is even more akin to that of those modern social psychologists who feel that excessive repression has made the culture itself neurotic.

In addition, the insistence upon the need to accept death was a way of insisting upon man's individuality. Through its many devices for obscuring the reality of death, American culture promotes the loss of individual identity; a sense of the cycle of the individual life is lost in the onward movement of the democratic mass. Values of love, justice, man, all are given over to general opinion instead of being weighed anew in the light of individual experience. Hemingway's later fiction repeatedly offers the consciousness of an individual awaiting death and struggling for one final time to clarify the values by which he lives. The nearness of death is a reason the more for the Hemingway protagonist to cultivate his personal vision of how he has played, or misplayed, the game of life. Freud, in *Civilization and Its Discontents,* suggested that American democracy by its nature prevented the emergence of great individuals: because of its democratic nature members of the culture sought to identify with one another rather than cultivate their individual sense of life.

In his *Address* to the men destined to be the most serious, dedicated enforcers of America's cultural ideals, the graduating class of Harvard Divinity School, Emerson said, "The child amidst his baubles is learning the action of light, motion, gravity, muscular force; and in the game of human life, love, fear, justice, appetite, man, and God, interact." Emerson's use of the word *game* was not a metaphor, and his repeated description of life as "play" was calculated to shock his listeners into a radical reassessment of their concepts;[18] and so, too, was Hemingway's glorification of the *corrida.* Both men believed in what they were saying, and they said it in such a way as to startle others into an appreciation of their views.

When the novel first appeared, it is unlikely that many Americans saw in the bullfight scenes of *The Sun Also Rises* the expression of a spiritual idea that would shock them into any reassessment of their own spiritual ideas. Jake's empathic victory with Romero over the bull was not seen as intrinsically related to the quickened sense of life that comes to him when he is fishing the mountain streams or plunging into the sea, and his sense that all is vanity except those actions which bring a sense of oneness with natural things. But Hemingway's appreciation that the bullring expressed more of the Spaniard's feeling of life and of death than did the rites and ceremonies of the Catholic Church is paralleled by perceptions of André Malraux, Ignazio Silone, and Carlo Levy, who found genuine religious impulse in the folk festivals of Spain and Italy and a waste land in the official church.[19] Jake Barnes led the way to the nature rituals of Robert Jordan, to Hemingway's ritual of blood-brotherhood with Masai tribesmen in *Green Hills of Africa,* and finally to Santiago of *The Old Man and the Sea,* whom Americans could accept as expressing a religious idea although, perhaps, not quite in the way in which the old man is a trenchant indictment of their materialistic, self-alienated culture.

VII

Mining his creative perceptions out of his innermost experience, Hemingway was arriving at a concept of religion that was radically at odds with the popular concepts of religion prevalent in America. He fastened the idea of religion not to theology, institutions, and conventional mythology, but to the process by which life itself—lived in reverence for being, in responsiveness to nature, and in accord with a felt sense of ideal conduct—assumes the form of play and is a continuous worship. He had devised his personal strategies for what Emerson termed "the game of life." To regard play as prayerful was not to view life indulgently, or selfishly, or frivolously. It might involve the rigid self-discipline of Romero, the bullfighter, whose dedication requires the utmost control. It might demand the political involvement of Robert Jordan, whose personal mission becomes part of a greater cause. Or it might, as with Santiago, convey a state of grace, his perfectly unself-conscious quality of belonging to a divine creation as he hooks the great marlin and heads to port.

Man, in this view, accepts the mysteries of birth and being and death. But, while he must play out his life within the civilization of his time and place, he struggles to an awareness of his personal sense of life and to create his own goals. For this reason the concept of "game" is appropriate, and for the deeper reason that he recognizes the illusory nature of all that time and place can offer him, and, indeed, of anything to be gained other than that which comes from living in accordance with his deepest sense of the rules of the game.[20] In Hemingway's later work the greatest sense of loss comes from a protagonist such as Harry of "The Snows of Kilimanjaro," who gradually discloses his sense of self-betrayal at having sold out to the things of this world. He began as a joyous player and ended as a culturally manipulated plaything. Robert Jordan, Harry Morgan, Colonel Cantwell, Santiago, and the narrator of *Islands In the Stream* have all played well, and the slow or sudden arrival of death does not alter their style of being. From most social points of view the lives of such men might well be considered worthless or even corrupt; but from Hemingway's point of view they were lives lived in response to a deeply felt inner direction that made them part and parcel of nature, and as such they were holy. One of the oldest philosophic formulations of what Hemingway had in mind is given by Plato in *Laws* (VII, 803), where he concludes that life must be lived as play. This passage led Johan Huizinger, in *Homo Ludens,* to conclude "Play consecrated to the Deity, the highest goal of man's endeavor—such was Plato's conception of religion."[21]

The irony in Hemingway's work is directed continually against whatever tries to bring stasis to what is process, or tries to give permanent social form to something that must arise spontaneously from the heart of man. In this critical spirit he directs attention to the monument that is a parody of what it seeks to memorialize; to such words as *patriotism, glory,* and *in vain,* which pretend to give an abstract value to sentiments of partisan politics; to the architecture, meant to immortalize an idea, that succeeds only in petrifying a social pose; to flags, uniforms, and medals that too often mock an outmoded ambition. The same is true in his writing of official ceremonies, or political programs, or cultural status based upon wealth, or professional status (doctor, hunter, soldier) when the social role is opposed to the individual man. A repeated, symbolic failure is the athlete (jockey, boxer, bullfighter, big-game hunter) who has allowed money to corrupt his relation to his sport.

In an article for *The Toronto Star Weekly* (February 18, 1922) written when he was a beginning journalist, Hemingway ranted, ". . . if you land a big tuna after a six-hour fight, fight him man against fish when your muscles are nauseated with the unceasing strain, and finally bring him up alongside the boat, green-blue and silver in the lazy ocean, you will be purified and be able to enter unabashed into the presence of the very elder gods and they will make you welcome."[22] By 1935, when *Green Hills of Africa* was published, this rhetoric had deepened into an abiding faith in a way of being. Hemingway at one point in that work comments on the behavior of camel flies tormenting a horse; this leads him to recall a time when he himself was badly wounded and how, in his suffering, he thought of what a wounded animal must feel. This in turn leads to the reflection, "I had been shot and I had been crippled and gotten away. I expected, always, to be killed by one thing or another and I, truly, did not mind that any more." Then, quite unexpectedly, he expresses his deepest belief about how to live in a passage that links his past, his writing, his love of sports, and his sense of unity with natural things:

> If you serve time for society, democracy, and the other things quite young, and declining any further enlistment make yourself responsible only to yourself, you exchange the pleasant, comforting stench of comrades for something you can never feel in any other way than by yourself. That something I cannot yet define completely but the feeling comes when you write well and truly of something and know impersonally you have written in that way and those who are paid to read it and report on it do not like the subject so they say it is all a fake, yet you know its value absolutely; or when you do something which people do not consider a serious occupation and yet you know, truly, that it is as important and has always been as important as all the things that are in fashion, and when, on the sea, you are alone with it and know that this Gulf Stream you are living with, knowing, learning about, and loving, has moved, as it moves, since before man . . . and the palm fronds of our victories, the worn light bulbs of our discoveries and the empty condoms of our great loves float with no significance against one single, lasting thing—the stream."[23]

By the time Hemingway came to write *The Old Man and the Sea,* these words had an even deeper truth, for he knew his existence to be an island in the stream. The "monkey-rope" that bound Melville's Ishmael to Queequeg is emblematic of man's evolutionary ties. Santiago feels himself bound by a similar line not merely to the great marlin, which he calls brother, but to the dark, flowing water that sustains them both. All man-made, mind-made distinctions are lost to the old man's dreams of Joe DiMaggio or of lions playing on a seashore, and to his transcendent conception of existence as a vast Gulf Stream of being.

9
Henry Miller's Democratic Vistas

I

When Henry Miller settled down in Paris in 1930, it was with no mere sense of being an expatriate. He believed that he had died and been reborn. From this time he dated his birth as a creative artist and the beginning of the "auto-hero," "Henry Miller," whose past and present being he was to examine throughout the whole decade of the thirties, which he spent mainly in Paris. From this time he became a citizen of the universe, occupant of that "enormous womb" that reached to and included the most distant stars. And from this time he began once more to be an American. He felt that he was American in a sense of the term that would have been meaningful to the great transcendentalist writers of America's literary renaissance. In *Democratic Vistas* Walt Whitman had tried to formulate anew what he felt to be the motivating ideals of America, and Miller's work gave expression to similar vistas: a recovered awareness of the roots of democracy in spiritual community; a reorientation in human as distinct from commercial and technological values; the effort to liberate individual identity from conformist pressures and from the "City"; the acceptance of change and of suffering; faith in individual creative power as a force for transforming society; and—here, perhaps, most of all like Whitman—a profound acceptance of love and of death.

In the neighborly life of Parisian middle- and lower-class quarters, Miller recognized a sense of the life he had known as a child in the 1890s in Brooklyn's 14th Ward. In the working-class, largely German-speaking neighborhood (Miller's grandparents had emigrated from Germany), there had been the same openness and intimacy and humanness of life, or so Miller remembered, as he found in Paris. The animal and the god in man were one in the 14th Ward; but the family moved to the more prosperous Bushwick section of Brooklyn when Miller was ten, and a process of denying the animal and abstracting the god set in, splitting his being apart, Miller felt, until he was made whole again in Paris, where he could admire Montmartre's *Sacre Coeur* while emptying the garbage, or, from the public urinals, adore the cathedrals of Paris, or the Palace of the Popes in Avignon, or the Citadel in Carcassonne. "Nearly always the French have chosen the right spot for their urinal."[1]

Miller's family had moved from the 14th Ward, in part, to get away from the Jewish families who were spilling over the newly opened Delancey Street Bridge from the lower East Side. When Miller chose to go to the high school in his old neighborhood, he was amazed to discover that the student body was eighty percent Jewish. Miller's reaction to his discovery of the expanding Jewish ghetto[2] is strikingly similar to that recorded by Henry James in *The American Scene,* based upon observations made during the same period. Both writers were impressed by a sense of the Jews as aliens, as an enormously multiplying people with an intense quality of "race," and as a people confronting the terrible fate of having to come to terms with the impersonal, mechanical, economic world represented by the clifflike skyscrapers that were already towering above them. Both saw the Jewish ghetto as vividly European; but whereas the presence of such a thriving element led James to wonder what was to happen to America's unity of character (led him eventually to wonder if there really had ever been such a thing as an American character) and to foresee dread possibilities for the language, Miller, on the other hand, was deeply attracted to the Jewish people because of their "foreignness." "In fact," he wrote, "the difference between me and the other Gentiles was more threatening than the difference between me and the Jews, so it seemed at the time. And so, out of pure strategy, I suppose, I began, in short, to *cultivate* them. It is to them I owe my initiation into the arts."[3]

Neither James nor Miller questioned for a moment the right of any foreign element to present itself in an American city. To James the phenomenon was but another aspect of the formlessness, and hence in part the meaninglessness, of American life. Miller caught the same idea in complaining of how the successive generations in American cities were more hostile in spirit to the founders of the American nation than they were to the rulers from whom they had fled. Each generation built on layers of fossil, each separate and distinct, "and at the bottom, instead of the solid core of earth, is quicksand and quagmire in which the historical and the biological alike will perish without trace."[4]

When Miller was old enough to handle the ledger of his father's fashionable lower-Manhattan tailor shop, he came in close contact with a nineteenth-century style of New York life which, in the new century, was swiftly disappearing. Calling on clients whose names were in the ledger introduced Miller to men whom he remembered as being "weak and lovable," generous, emotional, and devoted far more to a hearty style of living than to business achievement. Miller's use of the ledger in *Black Spring* suggests Faulkner's use of a ledger in *The Bear,* in that both writers sought to recreate the personalities and values of a past era in American life. But where Faulkner demonstrates how the forces at work in the ledger persisted vengefully into succeeding generations, Miller regarded the life in the ledger as fossilized, buried beneath the ghetto and the skyscrapers. He describes the ghetto as "a huge festering sore that runs from river to river along Fourteenth Street. This line of pus, which runs invisibly from ocean to ocean, and age to age, neatly divides the Gentile world that I knew from the ledger from the Jewish world that I am about to know from life."[5] Henry James had but a brief, superficial visit to the ghetto, but he was struck by the degree to which life there seemed more prosperous than in the squalid, sordid ghettos he had seen in London, Paris, and Rome. The improved quality of life, however, he foresaw as something that was doomed to "shrink and dwindle under the icy breath of Trusts and the weight of the new remorseless monopolies that operate as no madnesses of ancient personal power thrilling us on the historic page ever operated. . . . There is such a thing, in the United States, it is hence to be inferred, as freedom to grow up to be blighted, and it may be the only freedom in store for the smaller fry of future generations."[6]

In order to understand Miller's response to Paris and to European life in general, and his bitter rejection of American life, it is necessary to see how his life had its beginning in a German immigrant culture, and how it was nourished and matured in a Jewish immigrant culture subject to the remorseless pressures James had described. Until he was in his twenties, Miller knew almost nothing of American literature. No American novelist excited him, but the work of Dostoievski and of Knut Hamsun affected him intensely; while he accepted the wisdom of Emerson's and Thoreau's writings, those of Nietzsche and Spengler made a profound impression on his imagination; and while he hailed Whitman as a fellow spirit, he felt that Rimbaud's voice cried out from the depths of his own nature. Even the great figures of English literature meant little to Miller (he gave lip service to Blake as an exception), while Goethe so impressed him that at one period in his youth he sought to memorize all of *Faust.* Shortly after settling in Paris he was at work upon a long study of D. H. Lawrence (largely due to the influence of Anaïs Nin's work on Lawrence), and while at work on *Tropic of Cancer* he carefully analyzed the work of Proust, Joyce, and Céline. But even the famous departing American "exiles" held little interest for Miller.

Through his constant wandering about New York and his work as a personnel manager in charge of hiring and firing messengers for the Western Union Telegraph Co., Miller knew the city intimately. He also had some knowledge of America as a result of hitchhiking across the country and back and working at odd jobs on the way. As a result he knew precisely what James meant in his prophecy about the freedom to grow up blighted, and well before he left the country he was determined to grow up whole. There was no need for him to become disillusioned; he had grown up with the awareness of what he had to fear from America. *Black Spring* describes his sense of self and his close personal associations as a river flowing inside him, and "out of this black, endless, ever-expanding girdle of night springs the continuous morning which is wasted in creation."[7]

Threatening this existence, the "cunning, abstract world rises like a cliff in the midst of which are buried the fires of the revolution";[8] and the threat of personal annihilation was ever greater: "Steel and concrete hedging me in. The pavement getting harder and harder. The new world eating into me, expropriating me. Soon I won't even need a name"; he would be "swimming in the crowd, a digit with the rest."[9] Repeatedly Miller makes the point in his work that America is destructive of life: "Here nobody can have a clear conscience: we are all part of a vast interlocking murdering machine."[10] He emphasizes that in going to Europe he is leaving a recent offshoot and rejoining the main trunk of Western culture, the "heavy tree of the past." He arrived in Paris in 1930 with ten borrowed dollars and joyously embarked upon his "Song of Myself," the creative examination of his personal and cultural history. "Here I sit in the open street composing my song. It's the song I heard as a child, the song which I lost in the new world and which I would never have recovered had I not fallen like a twig into the ocean of time."[11]

Miller had no sense whatsoever of expatriating himself from a political structure, "The United States of America," since he had never felt its existence. His political attitude in this respect recalls pre-Civil War attitudes when the idea of *nation* was still a loose abstraction for many Americans, and patriotism was associated with a familiar plot of land. Miller began *Black Spring* by describing himself as a patriot of the 14th Ward, Brooklyn: "The rest of the United States doesn't exist for me, except as idea, or history, or literature." Home, school and church, the traditional molders of America's youth, seem to have made little impression upon the willful young Miller. His extensive firsthand acquaintance with American immigrant life, however, had introduced him to spiritual community; and his sense of the immigrants' faith in democracy was supplemented by social and political analysis as provided by men connected with the I.W.W. and the Socialist movement. Emma Goldman helped to form his literary as well as his political views. One speech by W. E. B. Du Bois profoundly affected him with its message, "Assume the spirit of liberty and you will be free!"[12] Radical political philosophy was in the streets, especially in the streets and cafés of the ghetto. "Certainly the Jews I met and loved on the East Side, Manhattan, were 'intellectuals' and 'radicals,' as well as chess players. The Café Royal on Second Avenue, N.Y., was a great meeting place—even Huneker used to write his column there. It was like old Europe—Vienna or Budapest."[13] The "radicals" and "intellectuals" were seeking "a new birth of freedom," and it was with this revolutionary vista that Miller began his life in Paris.

II

Miller was fond of quoting a maxim by Jacob Boehme, "Who dies not before he dies is ruined when he dies." Walking out on his job with the Western Union was death to a Miller existence. Rebirth occurred with the discovery of living now, of living in utter simplicity, of accepting his own nature, and of trusting to life. "All growth is a leap in the dark, a spontaneous, unpremeditated act without benefit of experience."[14] As part of his new truth, Miller had to acknowledge the extent to which he was "American." In 1936 he wrote, "The Americans themselves are naturally unable to see clearly—they are floundering. Being an American myself, not just a hundred percent, but a hundred *and one,* I think I can offer a corrective to your otherwise splendid vision. Having lived through, *lived out,* probably, my American life, I *know* whereof I speak. I know it in my guts, as it were—not intellectually, not philosophically."[15] As he was to remark in connection with Rimbaud, the "chimeras" (of church, state, custom) that a man gradually drives out of his mind are never slain, but return continually in new forms.[16] As did others before him, and especially the transcendentalists, Miller found that the most insidious form of the demonic in American life was conformity. Behind all the hatred and vengeance that went into *Tropic of Cancer* was his effort to separate his own self from the culture in which it had matured. He felt that he had to break completely with his past.[17] When he left America, he left wife, former wife and child, parents, friends and, what he most desired to leave behind, any possibility of becoming a responsible member of society.

As Thoreau moved to Walden Pond, Miller moved to Paris to live deliberately and not to discover too late that he had not lived. He wished to possess himself and to be aware. And like Thoreau's *Walden*, Miller's *Tropic of Cancer* is a mythic birth of personality, a self sculptured into full separateness from the cultural clay that would have leached away the individual nature. Miller saw the threat to individuality as more terrible than mere dissolution in its action: "By simple external pressure, by force of surroundings and example, by the very climate which activity engenders, one can become part of a monstrous death machine, such as America, for example."[18] Paris was a home; New York was a prison constructed over nothingness. Absolutely meaningless.[19] Everywhere the same smile, "America smiling at poverty,"[20] Americans dreaming American dreams, insisting absolutely on sameness; "between the cop on the beat and the director of a big corporation there is no difference except the uniform."[21]

In making his move to Paris, Miller believed at the time that his chief objectives were to be an artist and to live like an artist; subsequently he realized that his deepest motivation had been spiritual, the need to satisfy a craving that life in America had intensified but was unable to satisfy. It seemed to him that in Europe there was still a sense of the sacredness of the individual as well as a felt spiritual bond in the social community; these qualities had survived a thousand years of war and revolution in Europe, but America had lost them in a hundred years of "peace and progress."[22] While Miller frequently raged at America's highly technological society, he believed that the root of its troubles lay in a pseudo-democratic political and social structure, one in which the common man's worst qualities flourished, power and riches were garnered by a few, and there was no foundation of respect "for the sacred human individual who in aggregate makes a democracy and in the ultimate will make divinity."[23]

While America had a spiritual history, a record of harrowing struggles with the wilderness, Civil War, World War, and grim battles associated with industrialization, Miller came to the conclusion that Americans were cut off by their very prosperity from any sense of being the sons and daughters of martyrs. They had a synthetic security.[24] The young Americans who were slaughtered in World War I vanished from the American consciousness like the Aztecs, the Incas, and the buffaloes. There was patriotic pretense, but no American lost his appetite or rang the fire alarm. Miller recalled, "The day I first realized that there had been a war was about six months or so after the armistice."[25] In Europe history was an agony felt in the bones, an agony which, despite recurrent battle, made for spiritual awareness and communion. It seemed to Miller that the European shared in "a group soul"; beneath the outward differences was an instinct for community. But "the American, while moving with the herd is instinctively a traitor—to group, country, race, tradition."[26] Miller found Americans to be "the most collectivized people in the world," and yet, "a lonely people, a morbid, crazed herd . . . not really united, not really devoted to one another, not really listening."[27]

While the twenties were "roaring," and America's famous literary exiles were enjoying the luxuries afforded by the unbalanced exchange rate, Miller was in America living under conditions of complete economic insecurity and associated constantly with society's "misfits." In his work for Western Union, he dealt continually with the sordid world of men who for various reasons are unemployable. He had to cope with men who drifted from job to job, with men who were unemployed for discriminatory reasons, and with immigrants. He knew their hardships at firsthand. After quitting his job he lived by various expedients, including begging. He refused to accept the values that made up the reality of American life; he insisted on his indifference to job, financial security, social acceptance, family loyalty, and service of any kind. Although he earned the reputation among his friends of being a buffoon and enjoyed playing the role, in his judgment society was the grotesque. To Miller it appeared that he was consciously alive, while the serious, well-adjusted citizens were busily embalming themselves.[28]

When the stock market crash devalued the dollar and the Great Depression settled upon America, Miller confidently chose that hour, without money, job, friends, or knowledge of the language, to commence the life of the creative artist in Paris. In addition to self-confidence, he had confidence in the Parisian community as one that would have respect for a genuine artist and provide him with essential spiritual support. Economic support would be harder to find in Europe, but the spiritual support was absolutely lacking in America, and of the two, the spiritual was by far the more important. "In Europe," he wrote, "the artist usually had a much harder time of it, but he was never terrified. He was part of the grand old oak tree which had weathered every storm; he would go down when the tree fell, not before."[29] Miller did not greatly care that in America to be poor was to be regarded as lazy or ignorant or in some way deficient; there were kinds of poverty, and the kind that bothered him was "a more sinister kind of poverty, a veritable deprivation, which life in America entails. I was made aware of it the moment I set foot on French soil. I mean —the lack of communion with one's own kind."[30]

When he had wandered from New York to California and back in 1913, Miller had been disheartened by the sameness and triviality of the culture and by the supicion and hostility he evoked as a migrant job-seeker. Moving about Europe, by contrast, brought him a "resurrection of love," and he was overjoyed at encountering on every hand works great and small that had been shaped by man's religious and aesthetic impulses. It was always possible to accommodate the impulse to bow down before something and to give expression to the need to adore. In America there had been Nature, but now even that was being defaced at every turn. Miller described himself as "alone in a land where everyone was hopping about like mad. What I craved was to worship and adore. What I needed was companions who felt the same way. But there was nothing to worship or adore, there were no companions of like spirit. There was only a wilderness of steel and iron, of stocks and bonds, of crops and produce, of factories, mills and lumber-yards, a wilderness of boredom, of useless utilities, of loveless love."[31]

III

In the process of creating the material out of which he assembled *Tropic of Cancer,* Miller sought with hatred and contempt to cut away from himself those portions of his identity which he conceived as being the cancerous "City," and to bring into recognizable being his separate and unique personality. The narration is autobiographical, but only if one allows for the possibility that dreams, wishes, and lies are essential parts of the central consciousness. Although the narrator is in Paris, he is cutting himself free of the disease of civilization that he had absorbed in America; he has reached Cancer, "the extreme point of realization along the wrong path . . . the apogee of death in life," and must reverse his course.[32] The novel begins abruptly, and unlike the stream-of-consciousness novels, which seek to reproduce an *apparent* discontinuity of thought and an *apparent* dissociation from reality, *Cancer,* in form and subject, responds to the narrator's effort to be true only to his nature as animal and as god and thereby to betray his cultural conditioning.

Order, system, pattern, these are aspects of the disease that must be destroyed. All taboos must be challenged because they are taboos; the only authoritative totem is the self. Miller was to describe America as "the schizophrenic Paradise" and as "a far-flung empire of neurosis";[33] in *Cancer* what is given is the process of analysis through which the author heals himself. Other American characters in the novel, like Biblical scapegoats, are heaped with the narrator's afflictions and abandoned to the devils of the American wilderness. A young Hindu, infected with the virus of America, demonstrates that "America is the very incarnation of doom. She will drag the whole world down to the bottomless pit."[34] The auto-hero's temporary job as proofreader of the stock market section of the Paris edition of the *Chicago Tribune* (a job Miller actually held) provides a metaphor of his indifference to the statistical heart of American life.

While Miller hires himself out when it becomes absolutely necessary to earn money, he contrives to make each job serve his purpose of self-creation. The making (of the self, of the book) is always going on. Like Hemingway, he, too, has arrived at a sense of life as play: "Cease laboring altogether and create! For creation is play, and play is divine."[35] Play has its own law, spontaneous and compulsive, operative always at the borderline between exterior and interior life.[36] Early in *Cancer* Miller states his Dadaist determination not to let will, ethical or aesthetic, affect his creation, and his determination to make no resistance to his fate—to pass, as it were, out of the menagerie into the jungle.

He had found himself becoming, in New York, "a city, a world of dead stone, of waste light, of unintelligible motion, of imponderables and incalculables, of the secret perfection of minus,"[37] whereas he wished to become "a wild and natural park," where people go to rest and dream.[38] Once, while he was struggling to be a writer in America, he had walked from the daylight world into a theater just as the curtain was rising. The action suddenly struck him as symbolic of what happened each time he fell asleep—a curtain rising *in man*,[39] with the players who act out his true drama on the stage that in the waking world is mounted by the abstraction "Man." Only in Paris, however, did the implications of this discovery become the Lear-like imperative, "Crack Nature's molds." In his efforts to become a writer, Miller had copied pages of the work of Hamsun, Dostoievski, and Céline, fascinated by the way in which these authors could create a protagonist who threaded his holistic way through frenzy like the still eye of a hurricane. While Miller shared the destructive need of these authors, he did not as yet possess the deep, upwelling strength—a different kind of strength in each case—that enabled them to hurl their anathemas. With *Cancer* Miller for the first time got off "the gold standard of literature," and instead of creating from what he had drawn from the "City" and "Man," sought to be incorruptibly true to his inner generation, "in short, to erect a world on the basis of the omphalos, not on an abstract idea nailed to a cross."[40] Even twentieth-century Manhattan, given this vision, could become a cradle endlessly rocking.

In creating the chthonic disorder of *Cancer*, he created the rebellion of his actual life. He opened the black spring, the "dark, mysterious realm *in the absence of which nothing could happen*,"[41] and made himself into the sublime, absurd rebel who, he believed, was closer to Divinity than was the saint with his revelations, in that the rebel was responsive to the sources of human nature. A passage to union with the divine nature of things, "this is the true significance of the plunge into life's stream, of becoming fully alive, awakening, recovering one's complete identity."[42]

IV

Paradoxical as it might seem, Miller pointed out that European life fostered change *because* of the feeling of continuity everywhere. Out of a rich tradition came the inspiration that nourished the varieties of thought and feeling that resulted in change.[43] Unconsciously echoing Henry James's famous exchange with Howells, Miller argued that the only experience that has significance is that which becomes art. To the extent that tradition was absent from American life, the possibility for creating something new was the less; and the result of this, for America, was a fear of change, of creation, and an incessant effort to make permanent the *status quo*: "Are we not always trying to circumscribe, erect barriers, set up taboos? . . . *Civilized,* we say. What a horrible word!"[44] Real change, that is to say, creation, alters form. Taken literally, Miller's view sees form as an artificial stasis, an intermittent measure of what is in continual flow. For this reason, "the worst sin that can be committed against the artist is to take him at his word, to see in his work a fulfillment instead of a horizon."[45]

Miller's concern with change and his contempt for the institutions of Western civilization are not necessarily related. He felt that contemporary institutions were particularly destructive of the human spirit, but his concern was almost exclusively with changing the individual—almost exclusively with the creation of that individual, Henry Miller. As an American in Paris he found it possible to stay free of institutions, and to live as though governments, religions, laws, political organizations, social movements, and the rest did not exist. The incredibly complex social infrastructure of American life has come about through men freely organizing to promote their interests, and Americans take for granted the essential role that organizations play in their lives. The assumption is that the individual interest will find its expression and development in an organization. Miller contended, however, that organizations were inimical to the individual, and that the state had replaced the old tyranny of the church, seeking "to make of its citizens obedient instruments for its glorification."[46] The French, on the other hand, while living amid ancient institutions, went their individual way relying on their spirit: "On the naked stage of the world they improvise their lines according to an inner dictation . . . obsessed with one idea—to act out the drama which is in them."[47] During his visit to Greece Miller encountered isolated men in the countryside who astonished him with their qualities of peace and joy, their sense of being linked to nature and the divine. But such a provincial town as Nauplia, ridden with institutions, caused him to burst out, "Warrior, jailer, priest—the eternal trinity which symbolizes our fear of life."[48]

Miller was not singing the romantic praise of Arcadia. He preferred to live in cities because he could lose himself in their labyrinths. He was not for revolutions, because "they always involve a return to *status quo.* I am against *status quo* both *before* and *after* revolutions. . . . The fact is, to put it simply, I am positively against all this crap which is carried on first in the name of this thing, then in the name of that. I believe only in what is active, immediate and personal." [49] In 1940 when he wrote "An Open Letter to Surrealists Everywhere" Miller wished to make it plain that he was not to be considered as pro-Fascist or pro-Communist in the matter of the Spanish Civil War. Where he stood had been made clear in *Cancer*: he emphatically dissociated himself from humanitarian causes, indeed from the "creaking machinery" of humanity itself, and affirmed, "I belong to the earth!"[50] Unlike the great satirists whose shafts pierced through cultural behavior to attack the nature of humanity itself, Miller finds his salvation in his nature. And despite the shortcomings of the culture, he does not hold it to blame for his misfortunes. The self-analysis he engaged in after his arrival in France startled him with the discovery that he alone—not his parents, or society, or the country—was responsible for his condition. In accepting the responsibility for his suffering, he found that the suffering turned into joy.[51]

Being concerned with self-fulfillment, Miller felt that the men devoted to social reform were caught in an imaginary wheel rolling clockwise into the future.[52] In their concern with the problems of arranging life to come, they failed to solve the problem of living. Their action was evidence of individual failure.[53] Miller believed in "spreading" nothing—neither gospel, nor education, nor the wealth, nor brotherhood. To try to do so was to interfere with the sacred privacy of others. He saw "the brotherhood of man" as a permanent delusion common to idealists everywhere in all epochs; it always fails because it reduces men as individuals "to the least common denominator of intelligibility."[54] Individuals and peoples, he believed, can only be helped—and should only be helped—after suffering has played its necessary part in the resurrection of the spirit. "The *human* instinct to spare the other person his agony (which is his means of salvation, in any sense of the word) is a fallacious instinct. Here the subtle temptations, the vicious and insidious ones, because so confused and entangled, enter in. On this so-called 'human' plane it is the ego which commands—often in the most amazing disguises. The temptation to be good, to do good, gets us all some time or other. It's the last ruse, I feel, of the ego."[55] Like Thoreau ("Set about being good") and Emerson ("Are they *my* poor?") and post-Brook Farm Hawthorne, Miller viewed reformers as projecting their own maladies upon mankind, and while society at large might be thoroughly diseased, a man should accept it as such and proceed to heal himself. "When you accept the world as it is you alter it profoundly," he wrote, "because you have first altered yourself."[56]

Miller's indifference to political and social movements won him the hostility of those literary critics in the thirties who were indignant with any artistic effort that was not harnessed to humanitarian goals —and Miller has continued to enjoy the virulence of such critics, coupled with that of formalist critics who do not respond to his original concept of form. Behind the clowning with which he sought to exacerbate his critics, Miller understood very well that "war, like peace, involves us all."[57] In the hurly-burly of actuality, however, he believed it was more important than ever to "remember to remember," and those who remember are those who are "pure." They are aware of an order and law underlying events and serve a principle of life that runs deeper than actuality. They are immortal because they have life—they have renounced personal survival, and in remembering the road back to their birth, back to the birth of mankind, they place themselves outside the tragedies and deaths of the world. They see how the complex web of experience has been spun out of their own consciousness. Being free of the world, they are able to live.[58]

The struggle of the creative artist is not with politics and social reorganization; it is a personal and religious effort to make life a poem.[59] Such an effort, because it is creation, is play, "which just because it has no raison d'être other than itself is the supreme motivating power in life."[60] Instead of trying to impose his ideas of order upon the world, the individual had to learn acceptance, to put himself in order with the world. How? "Through art then, one finally establishes contact with reality: that is the great discovery."[61]

V

Spengler observed, "It is not products that 'influence,' but creators that absorb." This perception describes aptly Miller's use of books. Although the autobiographical material of the *Tropics* might suggest otherwise, even in the Paris years he was an avid reader and absorbed much of what he read into his creative process. The growth of his theme of the disease of American life found rich nutriment in the prophecies for Western culture made by Nietzsche and Spengler. Civic decay, he discovered, had been richly imaged by the French symbolist poets. Joyce, Proust, Lawrence, Céline, all were converted to use in Miller's varied denunciations. A civilization was dying and Miller said bad cess to it in hundreds of pages purportedly dealing with Shakespeare's *Hamlet*. The prospect of the decline and fall of America was to Miller something to be regarded with great joy, for only through its suffering and death could America be reborn. The nation, too, must have its rosy crucifixion. To elaborate this fundamental theme, Miller absorbed Walt Whitman (albeit first through parallels drawn from Balzac novels) into his process of creative realization.[62]

Miller was struck by the similarity between the view of France given in the 1830s by Balzac in *Louis Lambert* and *Seraphita* and the view of America expressed in 1870 by Whitman in *Democratic Vistas*. Even more striking to Miller was the coincidence of Balzac and Whitman's views with his own view of America in the 1930s. In exploring these related views, especially Whitman's concept of death, Miller arrived at his deepest understanding of the relation of America to his "being." Unlike the successive generations of Americans who have gradually come to a recognition of the virtues of many elements in Whitman's poetry but still cannot truly accept his views of love and death, Miller at once absorbed these views into his own. What America needed, both agreed, was great poems of death.

To Whitman and to Miller it was essential to sing of death in its relation to divinity and to democracy. The civilization dominant in the United States, in the estimation of both men, had lost the sense of death wherein each man, individually, knew his death as passage —a stage in the process of being—a part of divinity being restored to the whole. Out of their separate experiences, both men had arrived at the concept of America as *idea.* America was an idea synonymous with the idea of "Religious Democracy." Like Emerson they believed each individual to be "part or parcel of God," and in this divinity and in this being part of a whole lay the essence of democracy.

The result of living in Europe, where he was constantly aware of living in the midst of the great conventions which for centuries had shaped civilization and the individual consciousness, was for Miller a continual necessity to create his separate nature. He recognized in his readiness to be separate a distinctively American heritage. But if tradition lay far more lightly on the minds of Americans at home, the result was not a quickening of the inherent individual spirit but an abandonment to immediate conformist pressures, to deeds related solely to accepted material values, and to a dread and suppression of death. "The self-sufficient finitude," as Paul Tillich has described the capitalistic spirit, denied Americans their relationship to eternity. The result was that in the United States neither democracy nor America existed as Whitman and Miller understood them.

In *Democratic Vistas* Whitman remembered how when he was a boy he heard the old men always talking of American independence and that this independence meant a freedom from all laws and bonds except those a man discovered in his own being. Such was Miller's sense of the matter also, and was the substance behind his diagnosis of the nation as schizophrenic in that it had lost contact with nature, with divinity, and with the sources of its identity as a democracy. As his idea of what a democrat and an American should be, Miller presented Whitman, a citizen of the universe, accepting eternity, "living not in the times but in a condition of spiritual fullness."[63] Whitman's view that a race that grew up in a harmonious, active relation with nature would find it enough merely *to live* and "in the fact of *life* itself, discover and achieve happiness" was to Miller "absolutely American";[64] more than this—it meant that "Whitman is a hundred, a thousand, times more *America* than America itself."[65] The special sense in which, for Miller, Whitman was "America" was expressed in *Tropic of Cancer* as follows: "Whatever there is of value in America Whitman has expressed, and there is nothing more to be said. The future belongs to the machine, to the robots. He was the Poet of the Body and the Soul, Whitman."[66] When Miller ends *Tropic of Cancer* he is at rest where the Seine leaves Paris and flows on toward the sea. "I feel this river flowing through me—its past, its ancient soil, the changing climate. The hills gently girdle it about: its course is fixed." He is one of Whitman's "identified souls," at one with the flowing river of Man's past, part of nature and part of divinity. In leaving his homeland he was not the man who ran away from something, but "the man who ran *towards* something"[67]—toward those timeless democratic vistas that had the local and temporary name of "America."

Part Four
NATIVE SONS

Keep the habit of the observer, and, as fast as you can, break off your association with your personality and identify yourself with the Universe.

—Emerson, *Journal*, 2 October 1837

10
Richard Wright: The Expatriate as Native Son

I

Such American novelists as Henry James, Hemingway, and Henry Miller did not discover how to cope as an artist with their experience until their sense of American life had been placed in the focus of a European perspective. With Richard Wright the opposite was true. When he left for Paris in 1946, where he was to make his home until his death in 1960, his best fiction had been written and exile was only to dilute his capacity for dealing with American life in those works of fiction, principally *The Outsider* and *The Long Dream,* which he wrote abroad. Critics of Wright's work seem fully agreed that as a result of leaving America he lost touch with the source of his strength as a writer, namely, his being a Negro, a man immersed in the American Negro experience, and a spokesman for black causes.

There are two fundamental conditions, however, that should qualify this prevalent view of the relation of Wright to his American experience and the part that his activities as an expatriate played in affecting his thinking and writing. One condition is that Wright may be said to have gone into exile from that moment in early childhood when he began his long migration from the shack near Natchez, Mississippi, where he was born; so that all of his fiction written from, and at times about, the "alien" lands of Chicago and New York bore the mark of an outsider not responding to felt, personal experience, but consciously shaping an intellectual criticism of specific aspects of

American life. A second condition is that only after he had left the United States was Wright able to acknowledge—in Africa, in Indonesia, and in Spain—the manifold ways in which, beneath the shifting façade of formal institutions, a people sustained its folk identity, the kind of folk identity he had responded to only as a monstrous caricature in the U. S. A. It was in "savage" and "pagan" lands and in the privileged role of neutral observer that Richard Wright finally "came home." In African, Asian, and Spanish life he found a universal significance for the Negro, who had been America's Metaphor. It is necessary, then, first of all to clarify Wright's relation to his American experience and the effect of this relationship upon his fiction; and second, to examine Wright's nonfiction of the 1950s in order to observe his recognition of the roots of separate cultures, and the implications this had for his sense of himself as a black American.

When he drew his self-portrait in *Black Boy,* Wright went to some pains to make clear that his cultural alienation had begun in his black home and in a black community where, as a small child, he was scarcely aware of the existence of a white race. Writing in his early thirties, Wright insisted upon the fact that his family had tried to beat fear and submission into his nature years before interracial contacts made evident the rationale for a "nigger" identity. Creating the image of himself as a perceptive child, sensitive and imaginative and forever trying the conduct of his elders in the court of his innocent intellect, Wright seeks to demonstrate that from the start he was never able to accept the role being foisted upon him by the black community; that when the time came for participation in the Southern racist assumptions he could not make the instinctive adjustments that both black and white accepted as an inevitable way of life; and that his flight to the North was as much a flight from the black as from the interracial community. In fact he saw black and white as inseparably fused in their acceptance of a grotesque racial myth. What angered many black readers of Wright's autobiography even more than the disclosure of Negroes as leading shabby, empty, fear-ridden, tyrannized lives was his portrayal of them as yielding mindlessly to such degrading tyranny and positively insisting on preparing their young by what Ralph Ellison termed the "homeopathic method" for submission to such a mythos.

Possibly Wright believed in the truth of the picture of the culture presented in *Black Boy*; it is more probable that even as he tried to reconstruct his early years, at a time when he was making his traumatic break with the Communist Party, his creative memory chose those events which reflected his own rational integrity in a world of irrational elders. Neither land nor race had ever held possession of his mind, he believed, as they had possessed the minds of his family and friends; so that in looking back he recorded, not the felt life itself, but the reasons why he had been an alien in his own home. The reasons, brilliantly dramatized, are those to which a Northern, liberal mind would respond with an appropriate compassion and outrage. The portrait is of the artist as a black boy, but it is primarily the portrait of an artist.

If Wright was in individual exile in the South, flight to Chicago, while it greatly eased the conditions of his exile, did not change his analysis of, or his relation to, the racial condition. Black men in Chicago were still the children of Uncle Tom, as the name-play "Bigger Thomas" suggested. In *Uncle Tom's Children, Lawd Today,* and *Native Son* Wright made fewer cultural concessions to the blacks than to the whites. Victim and victimizer are locked together, the fear and violence of one inevitably producing the fear and violence of the other. Wright felt that his personal escape had not come from playing the racial game with greater skill, or from manipulating its centuries-old rules, but through the process of altering his own mind. With all but incredible tenacity he had held to an image of himself antecedent to the concept "American Negro," and largely by reading kept alive his ability to dream of possibilities in life wholly other than those which made up the reality in which he lived. He wrote in *Black Boy,* "I hungered for books, new ways of looking and seeing. It was not a matter of believing or disbelieving what I read, but of feeling something new, of being affected by something that made the look of the world different."[1] "Accidental" reading of fiction and criticism nourished his sense of possibilities, not simply in that they presented glimpses of other cultural worlds, but in that they persuaded him "that America could be shaped nearer to the hearts of those who lived in it."[2] Literature, which had been so instrumental in enabling him to become a person wholly different from the being predicated by his environment, served, through the literary magnet of the John Reed Club in Chicago, to bring Wright into the organization of those whose commitment to political goals allowed no tolerance for the creative imagination of the individual artist. Wright never ceased completely to trust himself or to keep for himself the essential control of his identity; but he allowed himself to become further estranged from a sense of being part of a people, of a landscape, of songs and rhythms and gestures that made up the Negro-American folk heritage.

In almost all of Wright's work, from *Uncle Tom's Children* to *The Long Dream* and *Five Episodes,* there are passages of dialogue, glimpses of river life, snatches of song, interior scenes, and perceptions of character that give a flickering sense of a folk heritage; but overwhelmingly his black characters are shaped to fit a literary strategy. The havoc worked on such promising stories as "Fire and Cloud" and "Bright and Morning Star" as well as on *Native Son* by the obtrusion of Party doctrine has been much lamented. But what is more lamentable is that Wright should have been so outraged by the black man's acceptance of the role defined for him by American culture that he responded to no impulse to discover what was fine in the black culture, what was noble in its heritage, what brighter side of generosity and love might exist on the coin that bore the image of poverty and despair, or what meaning there might be in the special responsiveness to things not of this world. Faulkner wrote, "They endured." The words summed up a long history which he had evoked aesthetically. Wright, however, was caught up in a hideous present moment, the Great Depression years and the Chicago black ghetto, when it was an achievement to survive, and when the Communist Party seemed to offer him an undreamed of freedom, an unqualified social acceptance, and—what indeed it did provide him—the only hope for his existence as a writer.

In sum, and paradoxically, Wright joined the Communist Party for what were, from the Party's point of view, all the wrong reasons. He wished to enlarge his mind through association and discussion with other artists, to cultivate his individuality, and to realize his powers as an artist. In the process of transforming himself he hoped to promote the transformation of society. Such ambitions tend to place

Wright in the American transcendentalist tradition, and as he was later to remark in his essay "I Tried To Be a Communist," he was "fantastically naive" to believe that he could fit into the Communist program.[3] But where Wright up through the thirties differed fundamentally from the transcendentalists was in his refusal to trust his intuitive sense of things. In fact, he ruthlessly insisted upon denying those intuitive promptings which might have led him to respond to the deep cultural roots to which he was perversely insensitive. Of the period preceding his joining the Communists he wrote, "So far I had managed to keep humanly alive through transfusions from books. In my concrete relations with others I had encountered nothing to encourage me to believe in my feelings. It had been by denying what I saw with my eyes, disputing what I felt with my body, that I had managed to keep my identity intact."[4]

Like his family and his associates in the South, the Communists grew to fear and distrust Wright because of his irrepressible individuality. Ostensibly he broke with the Party because he would not submit to the Party's manipulation of Negro causes to suit its international policies. But as Wright himself recognized, the true reasons were emotional. Despite his ideological commitments and his long involvement in political action programs for Negroes, he had an overwhelming sense of working in a void. Negroes were the central subject of a series of brilliant books by Wright, books in which he endeavored to force Americans to realize the humanity of the Negro; but his burning sense of the degraded image of the Negro in American life drove him in every book to reproduce an image of the Negro in his most brutalized condition. Finally, in the most effective literary passages of *Native Son,* he produced a scarcely human creature—not an imaginary monster, in Wright's opinion, but a faithful rendering of America's idea of "the American Negro," and thereby a mirror image of American civilization itself.

Early in *Native Son* Bigger Thomas kills a rat in the grim apartment he shares with his mother and sister, and he holds it up to their faces; by the end of the novel the white society is the "Bigger Thomas" holding up its victim in bitter acknowledgement of the sordid world in which it lives. The windy harangues and stilted confrontations of the last third of the novel have little dramatic force; but in the powerful first two-thirds Wright's artistry is driven by the hatred he feels for the total culture, black and white. The philanthropic Daltons, the liberal reformers, the Communists, *and* the degraded blacks are the loathsome generative stuff out of which emerge the murderous Biggers. Borrowing journalese to describe an ape-like Bigger from the Chicago newspapers' actual reports of a Negro's murder trial, and possibly hoping to suggest to the minds of his readers a parallel with Poe's account in "The Murders in the Rue Morgue" of a terrified orangutan stuffing its female victim up the fireplace, Wright piled horror upon horror in the most fully realized parts of the novel as though probing the limits of the public's capacity to accept the monstrosity of "the American Negro."

With Jake Jackson in *Lawd Today* Wright had proceeded with a controlled naturalism to present in unrelieved contempt a portrait of a black Chicago worker. The man is created in terms of every popular cliché of Negro homelife, tastes in food and clothing, attitudes toward work and play, his uses of being a Negro, his utter emptiness of value. Other writers have from time to time invoked the Biblical passage of God's creating man in His image for ironic effect; Wright uses Lincoln for this purpose, setting the entire novel on Lincoln's birthday, and he repeatedly intrudes the great promise of emancipation into Jake Jackson's day in a counterpoint of contempt. *Lawd Today* the title exclaims; so many decades later and the work of emancipation has not yet begun! If this attack upon the concept of "the American Negro" —a concept, Wright insisted, operative with both black and white men—was drawn in ironic contempt, the conception of the American Negro as a Bigger Thomas was drawn in wrath and despair. It is essential to bear in mind, however, that in both *Lawd Today* and *Native Son* Wright is not presenting a natural human being. With great creative power he is drawing "the American Negro" of popular mythology, breathing life into a vicious caricature in the desperate hope of rooting the myth out of the American mind where for three centuries it has, with variations according to time and place, played its pervasive, corruptive part.

Wright's personal escape from the cultural caul of "the American

Negro" had been primarily engineered through literature and through a persistent belief in scarcely dreamed possibilities that were violently contradicted by the facts of his everyday life. He had, at least to his own satisfaction, reached the point where his dream of humanity was sufficiently strong to permit him with radical irony to deny "the American Negro" construct in its own terms—the self-negating "reality" of Jake Jackson and Bigger Thomas. The fact that he could through his artistry create such figures was sufficient proof that America's conception of the American Negro did not exist. But to the American public Richard Wright remained invisible; his artificial "niggers" were visible to all.

In 1941, the year following the publication of *Native Son,* Wright produced a commentary for a group of photographs supposedly recording the folk history of the black American, although the book actually had to do not with folk history but with desperate poverty. In 1941 *12 Million Black Voices* went unheard, although Wright's text included this observation: "The word 'Negro,' the term by which orally or in print, we black folk in the United States are usually designated, is not really a name at all nor a description, but a psychological island whose objective form is the most unanimous fiat in all American history; a fiat buttressed by popular and national tradition, and written down in many state and city statutes; a fiat which artificially and arbitrarily defines, regulates, and limits in scope of meaning the vital contours of our lives, and the lives of our children and our children's children."[5]

Some criticism of Wright's Bigger Thomas has claimed that the almost subhuman nature of the character detracts from the realism of the work. But Wright's point is in the caricature, not only of Bigger, but of the whole black and white cultural context operative in the novel. The critics were thinking within the very plane of consciousness Wright wished to destroy. They believed in the monster Bigger, because the myth, as critical studies by Ellison and Baldwin have pointed out, was firmly lodged in their minds. The pathos of the situation, Wright suggested in his continuation of *Black Boy,* reprinted as "The Man Who Went to Chicago," was in the sordid cultural objectives of white America. The Negro "is doomed to live in isolation, while those who condemn him seek the basest goals of any people on the face of the earth. Perhaps it would be possible for the Negro to become reconciled to his plight if he could be made to believe that his sufferings were for some remote, high, sacrificial end; but sharing the culture that condemns him, and seeing that a lust for trash is what blinds the nation to his claims, is what sets storms to rolling in his soul."[6]

Like the great American novelists who tried to break through the vainglory of American self-deception and to bring Americans to a self-knowledge on the basis of which something genuinely constructive might grow, Wright pleaded, "We black folk, our history and our present being, are a mirror of all the manifold experiences of America. What we want, what we represent, what we endure is what America *is.* If we black folk perish, America will perish . . .

"The differences between black folk and white folk are not blood or color, and the ties that bind us are deeper than those that separate us . . .

"Look at us and know us and you will know yourselves, for *we* are *you,* looking back at you from the dark mirror of our lives!"[7]

12 Million Black Voices and *Black Boy* were efforts to bring to America's attention the condition and history of its black people, but while the two works represented successful sociological and artistic achievement, the writing of them must also have brought to Wright a private conviction of his personal separateness from the folk whose condition he had set forth. He had become a city man, an intellectual, and from the time of the John Reed Club was more at ease with mixed racial groups, or even with white friends, than with black groups. By 1945 Wright was sure of one thing: his loathing for the values of American culture and its mirror image, "The American Negro." And he had become "The Spokesman for His Race," an unofficial office that had as its function the task of reconciling the American black to the American way of life.

Wright's books added very little to black folk history, a folk history that had already been richly documented by both black and white writers. His eyes had been for so long a time trained to see the horror in the lives of black Americans that he could see little else. Wright's "color-blindness" had begun very early in life, not when he went to live in Europe.[8] When he came to deal with Negroes in extended works of fiction he was a mature man, well acquainted with the harsh side of Chicago's life, and an effective political organizer and propagandist; while he could depict the intimate lives of poor Negroes with convincing authority, he dealt with them as an outsider uninterested in their folk history and folk identity.

In a revealing passage in *Black Boy,* Wright offered this speculation: "Whenever I thought of the essential bleakness of black life in America, I knew that Negroes had never been allowed to catch the full spirit of Western civilization, that they lived somehow in it but not of it. And when I brooded upon the cultural barrenness of black life, I wondered if clean, positive tenderness, love, honor, loyalty, and the capacity to remember were native with man. I asked myself if these human qualities were not fostered, won, struggled and suffered for, preserved in ritual from one generation to another."[9] Wright's remarks, as Ralph Ellison has noted, recall Henry James's complaint of the absence of ritual and tradition in American life as compared with European life. What James wished to emphasize, of course, was that the novelist who would lay hold of the forms and rituals of American life had to exercise a positively "grasping imagination." The unfortunate fact is that far from using his imagination to grasp at such forms and traditions as *did* exist in American black culture, particularly that of Southern Negroes, and thereby growing aware of their possibilities for his life and his art, Wright had allowed his limited recollection of his childhood years to fill the need of his large, immediate concern with political and social justice.

Joining the Communist Party, as was noted above, paradoxically satisfied primarily a *human* need with Wright, and when he left the Party it was with a sense of being drained of human warmth. In his essay, "I Tried To Be a Communist," Wright spoke of how, after he had separated from the Party, he tried to rejoin his former comrades during their May Day parade and had been physically cast aside. It seemed to him that in all the mighty continent "the least known factor of living was the human heart, the least-sought goal of being was a way to live a human life." He wanted "to create a sense of the hunger for life that gnaws in us all, to keep alive in our hearts a sense of the inexpressibly human."[10] Yet despite this need to be accepted in terms of the essentially human, Wright strove continually to be accepted wholly in terms of the image that his intellect had created and apart from the historical reality that had its great share in his making.

Images of burial, of living underground, crept into his writing of the early 1940s. In "The Man Who Went to Chicago" he described how he and three other Negroes worked as obscure creatures, scarcely tolerated in the basement corridors of a great hospital: "we occupied an underground position remembering that we must restrict ourselves . . . so that we would not mingle with white nurses, doctors, or visitors."[11] Wright's efforts to understand something of the experiments being carried out on the caged animals they tended were brusquely cut short. In their empty, degraded isolation the black men turn violently on one another, upset the cages, and recage the animals haphazardly, thereby destroying the validity of the records. The episode is a miniature allegory. It seemed to Wright that if the State were to guard itself from the men who truly threaten it, it would not club workers and union men, but would "ferret out those who no longer respond to the system under which they live." It would "fear those who do not dream of the prizes that the nation holds forth, for it is in them, though they may not know it, that a revolution has taken place and is biding its time to translate itself into a new and strange way of life."[12] In his story, "The Man Who Lived Underground," first published in 1942 (*Accent*, 2, Spring), the fugitive Negro rejoices in his perspective of life from the public sewer. In the version of the story published two years later, the sewer-dweller is murdered while trying to communicate his gospel of joy and love to the white police. The policeman who killed the underground man explains, " 'You've got to shoot his kind. They'd wreck things.' "[13]

Although he attributes the noblest motives to his underground man, Wright was aware of other motives possible to the ignored and alienated. He drew attention to a remark by William James as to how fiendish a punishment it would be to live in society and yet remain absolutely unnoticed by all. If every person "acted as if we were non-existent things, a kind of rage and impotent despair would ere long well up in us."[14] This was more in tune with his personal reaction to being unseen and excluded as an individual person, apart from his race or politics, the reaction he expressed in metaphors of alienation that were to be extensively developed by later black writers.

II

In her biography *Richard Wright*, Constance Webb relates how the French Government plucked Wright up from his underground. In response to an unexpected invitation from the French Government (and after overcoming passport obstacles erected by the U. S. State Dept.), Wright found himself in May of 1946 in the very heart of expatriatedom, Gertrude Stein's apartment in Paris. He responded to his hostess's declaration of her debt to William James by quoting from memory James's words, "a man has as many social selves as there are individuals who recognize him and carry an image of him in their minds," and showing her his quotation from James about the hideousness of treating men as "non-existent things" in the copy of *Black Metropolis* that he presented to her. In Paris the literary vogue of existentialism was at its height, and, utterly miscomprehending Wright's intention in *Native Son,* French critics had seized upon Bigger Thomas as an existentialist hero and upon the author of *Black Boy* as an existentialist man. Thus Wright found a new visibility, and his friendships with Sartre, Simone de Beauvoir, and Camus must certainly have helped determine the direction of his next novel, *The Outsider.* He had not intended to settle permanently in Paris; but a return to New York and the depressing experience of being turned away from restaurants and hotels, of encountering hostility because of his marriage to a white woman, of having to conceal the fact that he, a Negro, owned his Greenwich Village home, of having to consider what his child would soon encounter when she entered school —all this must have seemed to him too grim an echo of the occasion in 1940 when he had revisited Natchez and had had to submit once more to the humiliating Jim Crow treatment. Having always fought against an "American Negro" identity in America, he found it easy to lay that particular burden down on what he described as the "free soil" of France. In an article, "I Choose Exile," which, according to Constance Webb, was written for *Ebony* magazine but rejected as too severe an attack against the United States, Wright pointed out that something was basically wrong with a nation that, in its denial of rights to the Negro, "could so cynically violate its own Constitution and democratic pretensions." Once more he insisted that the treatment of the Negro produced a dislocation of values that was essentially a destructive war waged by the nation against itself.[15]

Henry James and Mark Twain, writing out of their nineteenth-century expatriate experience, tried to persuade Americans of the errors of their ways—although the ending of *A Connecticut Yankee in King Arthur's Court* suggests that Twain despaired of ever effecting improvements in the damned human race. Hemingway and Henry Miller, instead of persuasion, tried to hold before the eyes of Western culture images of its violence and sterility and to communicate their personal transcendence of cultural problems. There is something of Miller's apocalyptic attitude in Wright's first novel written in Europe, *The Outsider.* Like Miller, Wright had a sense of rebirth in his new life; and, like Miller again, Wright seemed to have come to the transcendentalist conclusion that one must remake one's self before undertaking to remake the lives of others. But Wright could never go the whole mystical way; he could never quite abandon, even while he looked back in anger, some hope for a rational solution to America's problems.

Although *The Outsider* has been frequently regarded as an existentialist novel and interesting parallels can be drawn between elements in it and in existentialist novels by writers from Dostoievski to Camus, whose works were quite possibly in Wright's mind as he composed his novel, *The Outsider* bears at its deepest level the hallmark of Wright's compulsion to shape society in accordance with some ideal conception of social justice; there is no consideration of ontological solutions. Other "outsiders" would appear, a "tragic elite" as Wright was elsewhere describing them, to revolutionize the ways men thought, felt, and lived together. As with *Native Son*, *The Outsider* ends with wishful philosophizing and the author's persona shifts from the black Damon to the white D. A. Other shifts in the novel are interesting for the light they shed on widening divisions in Wright's mind. Early in the novel Cross Damon expresses his strong dislike for all men of religion because "they could take for granted an interpretation of the world that his sense of life made impossible."[16] Unlike the priest who is "a kind of dressed-up savage intimidated by totems and taboos," Cross Damon, as existentialist, had to make his own way alone and bear the brunt of the consequences without hope of grace or mercy. By the end of the novel, however, Cross has reached a position that has strongly Emersonian overtones:

> Religion was once an affair of the church; it is now in the streets in each man's heart. Once there were priests; now every man's a priest. Religion's a compulsion, and a compulsion seems to spring from something total in us, catching up in its mighty grip all the other forces of life—sex, intellect, will, physical strength, and carrying them forward toward—what goals? We wish we knew.[17]

Early in the novel civilization "is simply man's frantic effort to hide himself from himself."[18] Toward the end of the novel "civilization" has been limited to the creation of the industrial-capitalist leaders who "preach to their rats that their nation is the best of any of the nations, and that as rats they are the best of all possible rats."[19] But the day will come when "outsiders," "who seek to change the consciousness of the rats who are being controlled," will prove to be the real enemy of the system by altering the public consciousness.[20] Dialectically, Wright was the same outsider he had always been, only now he was much farther removed from the humanity he proposed to save and his aesthetic imagination had lost its grasp upon American life. Depending on newspaper clippings, Freudian, Marxist, and existentialist "theories," and old memories, Wright's fictional treatment of the American scene spluttered out in *Savage Holiday* and *The Long Dream.* He had turned in fascination to Europe, Africa, and Asia, and it was in recording the illuminations that his visits to these foreign lands brought him that his imagination finally fastened upon America.

III

In June, 1953, Wright began his visit to the Gold Coast, a visit that was to take him to its ports, villages, and high rain forests, and was to result in hundreds of interviews with natives of all degree. Typically, he had fortified himself with political theory about the emergent nations, with anti-colonial statistics, and with "black power" concepts to explain the "tragic elite" who were to lead the new nations on a new course. Typically, he deliberately examined his reactions for evidence of any personal sense of racial identity with the African natives and, like a good Marxist, found none. As his visit progressed, Wright kept a record, which became *Black Power, A Record of Reactions in a Land of Pathos.* In this work, more than ever before, Wright displayed a split that had been present in his work from the beginning—the divergence between the intellectual theories he felt compelled to state and the truth of his acute perception of human experience. *Black Power* from time to time records Wright's political theories and concludes with a fiery letter to Kwame Nkrumah, Wright's Gold Coast host, exhorting him to sweep away tribal cobwebs, to assume dictatorial powers, and through stern social discipline forge the new industrial state. "African life must be militarized," not for war, but against its own tribal heritage and the possible return of colonial powers (p. 347).[21] Contradicting this fierce call to arms at the opening and at the closing of the book are the mystical utterances of Walt Whitman breathing peace and acceptance: "Not till the sun excludes you do I exclude you," and "Turn back unto this day, and make yourself afresh." It is the spirit of Whitman that informs the essential theme of the book, for *Black Power* records Wright's gradual discovery and absorption in the role the spirit plays in African life and—since Africa comes to operate for Wright as a metaphor—in all life.

The subtitle of the book, "*A Record of Reactions,*" describes accurately how the book was composed. When he submitted the manuscript to prospective publishers, Wright encountered various objections from them in regard to the content of the book—to the effect that he was too harsh on the British and on the Dutch, that he was not making sufficiently clear his separation from Communism, that the book was too long. In his letter to his agent explaining why he could not cut portions out of the book, Wright made this significant disclosure: "The trouble with writing a book like this is that the reality of a given phase of the life does not come upon one all at once; for instance, the religion of the people came to me in bits, each bit extending my comprehension of the reality a little more . . . by going from spot to spot, talking to this person and that one, I had to gather this reality as it seeped into me through the personalities of others."[22] Even as on one level of his consciousness Wright was comprehending the spiritual reality of African life, on another level he was still thinking in terms of his political rhetoric. His early impressions led him to believe that Nkrumah had "fused tribalism with modern politics," since the natives swore an oath to Nkrumah (p. 59). The British, he decided early, had slowly destroyed the African's faith in his own religion and customs (like American slaveholders?), "thereby creating millions of psychologically detribalized Africans living uneasily and frustratedly in two worlds and really believing in neither of them" (p. 65). Religious meetings were "a mixture of tribal ancestor worship, Protestantism, Catholicism—all blended together and directed toward modern political aims" (p. 89). Since Wright had decided on new political goals for the Africans, he "saw" that their old patterns of life were being transmuted to the new. "Mass nationalist movements were, indeed, a new kind of religion. They were politics *plus*!" (p. 56).

As his visit progressed, however, he sensed that the changes were only apparent. The Westerners (i.e., European and American whites) and the Africans, he began to see, lived in worlds based on assumptions that seem fantastic to one another. Each comes to accept, from necessity, the "false" assumptions of the other and thereby creates a new reality: "Men create the world in which they live by the methods they use to interpret it" (p. 118). As for the African, "the African's whole life was a kind of religious dream" (p. 124). Wright described the African's life as rational, but only in terms of his assumptions—such assumptions as the control of the living by the dead. Compared to a pagan funeral, it seemed to Wright that a Christian funeral was a mockery of religious conviction. Like Twain observing the work of the missionaries in the Sandwich Islands and later in the Holy Land, Wright reported himself as "stunned" at their perverse folly. "They had, prodded by their own neurotic drives, waded in and wrecked an entire philosophy of existence of a people" (p. 152). Unquestionably Wright had in mind what had happened to the Africans who had been torn out of this culture centuries earlier and shipped to America—a thought that becomes explicit when he visits Cape Coast Castle, where slaves had been held prior to shipment to the West. Bit by bit, as he said in his letter to his agent, he grew aware of the spiritual dimension of African life; bit by bit, and against all his intellectual conditioning, he saw that he could respect this African consciousness and feel honored to claim it as his heritage.

But this link between African culture and that of the American Negroes comes in the final chapter of the book, when Wright's record of reactions had finally overcome his *a priori* assumptions—and even then the record was not strong enough to prevent his resurgence as tactician in the letter to Nkrumah saved for a conclusion, with its manifesto: "Our people must be made to walk, forced draft, into the twentieth century!" (p. 345). On the level of his felt perceptions, the more Wright talked with Africans the more he came to admit that the Africans would indeed have lost if they sacrificed their tribal gods and their magic world to achieve a Chicago or a Detroit. Capturing superbly the essence of the matter, Wright asked, "Would an African, a hundred years from now, after he has been trapped in the labyrinths of industrialization, be able to say when he is dying, when he is on the verge of going to meet his long dead ancestors, those traditional, mysterious words:

I'm dying
I'm dying
Something big is happening to me . . . ?" (p. 227).

It is Wright, the fervid exponent of industrialization, who declares that the gold can be replaced, the timber grown again, but that the mental habits and the vision cannot be restored to a people: "Nothing can give back to them that pride in themselves, that capacity to make decisions, that organic view of existence that made them want to live on this earth and derive from that living a sweet even if sad meaning" (p. 153). Like the writers in America's transcendentalist tradition, Wright saw, as a result of his African reactions, that religion was not an affair of institutions but of life lived: "Africa must and will become a religion, not a religion contained within the four walls of a church, but a religion lived and fought out beneath the glare of a pitiless tropic sun" (p. 159).

In a statement that splendidly amplifies the quotation from Whitman that he used as one of the epigraphs to *Black Power,* Wright expressed a conception of human oneness through the metaphor of Africa. Africa is one's self, one's life, "one's ultimate sense of things" (p. 158). A Western man might be repelled by what he saw in Africa and wish to destroy or to exploit it as something alien to his nature, but in truth it is himself he sees. If he sees it as horrible, it is still the "image of himself which his own soul projects out upon this Africa" (p. 158). Unlike the corrupted cultures of Europe and America—corrupted by the very rationalism and industrialism that Wright is supposed to champion—Africa, Wright found, held an attitude toward life that sprang from "a natural and poetic grasp of existence and all the emotional implications that such an attitude carries" (p. 226). He took exception to the inverted cultural values that disparaged African rites as regrettable "survivals," maintaining that such survivals are a retention of basic and primal attitudes toward life. Obliquely including himself in this African life, Wright pointed out that the social scientist would discover that the same primal attitudes exist among other people: "after all, what are the basic promptings of artists, poets, and actors but primal attitudes consciously held?" (p. 267).

Primal attitudes extended yet further. The man who came to Africa to study and preach a rational modernism insisted that "there is no reason why an African or a person of African descent—in America, England, or France—should abandon his primal outlook upon life if he finds that no other way of life is available, or if he is intimidated in his attempt to grasp the new way" (p. 266). This was a striking concession for Wright to make, and it measures how far he had gone toward accepting his own nature, the racial aspect of his identity, and the role of irrational factors in determining the forms of human culture. Transvaluing his values as he went along, Wright embraced the poetry and mystery of African life and its superb acceptance of its human nature, as distinct from Western life, which sought so strenuously to deny primal qualities, to destroy those who could not adjust to its frantic patterns, and, in particular, sought to rob black Americans of their history by depicting Africa as a dark continent peopled by savages. Africans had not known race consciousness, Wright pointed out. It was brought "into our lives. It came from without" (p. 199). Wright's profound discovery, as it emerged in his book, was the nature of black power: its acceptance of the world as spirit.

The Color Curtain, based on Wright's visit to the conference of African and Asian nations held at Bandung, Indonesia, in 1955, carried further his understanding of the emotional factor in national politics. Logic, he noted, could not solve problems "whose solutions come not by thinking but by living."[23] The ex-Communist Richard Wright, who still considered himself a Marxist dedicated to rational plans for organizing society without regard for such outmoded concepts as race and religion, had to accommodate himself to the Richard Wright who had to admit that the theoretical political factors that prevailed in Western government were not at all what held the minds of the Asians and Africans meeting at Bandung. The nonfiction books *Black Power, The Color Curtain,* and *Pagan Spain* demonstrate clearly that, despite the uninspired novels he was turning out in the 1950s, Wright was still possessed of a gifted imagination and talent. Settings are often given with great effectiveness, but above all he repeatedly gives his information and insights through skillfully arranged dialogues or through some dramatic encounter. Wright conveys his sense of revelation, as, for example, on the occasion of Sukarno's address at the opening of the conference. It came as a revelation to Wright that Sukarno was appealing to race and religion. These factors, so disdained in the intellectual politics Wright had absorbed in America and so cried down by the existentialist *monde* of Paris were the only realities understood by the representatives at Bandung.

"And, as I sat listening," Wright records, "I began to sense a deep and organic relation here in Bandung between race and religion, *two of the most powerful and irrational forces in human nature.*"[24] The fundamental reversal of perspective that was taking place in Wright's understanding of human consciousness made the old concepts by which he had controlled his fiction obsolete.

The final proof of his new way of perceiving and responding to experience came with his study of Spain. Early in *Pagan Spain,* Wright contrives a scene with a Spanish girl wherein he produces a *non serviam* worthy of Stephen Daedalus: " 'I have no religion in the formal sense of the word. . . . I have no race except that which is forced upon me. I have no country except that to which I'm obliged to belong. I have no traditions. I'm free. I have only the future.' "[25] It is appropriate that a young man's book should end with such a declaration; it is equally appropriate that a mature man's book should begin with it, and the rest of *Pagan Spain* will demonstrate Wright's responsiveness to the deep degree to which his perceptions are affected by his religious nature, his sense of race, his being an American, and the tensions or harmonies he feels as a man conditioned by the traditions of Western culture.

Using a technique similar to that he had employed in his novel *Lawd Today,* Wright inserted throughout *Pagan Spain* selections from the Falangist political catechism in order to dramatize the ridiculous discrepancy between the Falangist concept of the world and the actual concepts upon which life was lived in Spain. Perhaps there was an unintended irony in that much of the Falangist catechism was premised upon the kind of logic and authoritarianism that had characterized Wright's advice to Nkrumah, and his method of catechizing and theorizing in parts of *White Man, Listen!* The profound difference that Wright saw between Spain and the rest of the Western world forced him to turn again to the examination of what being Western meant. He finally decided that the difference was "the area of the *secular* that Western man, through the centuries and at tragic cost, had won and wrung from his own religious and irrational consciousness."[26] This would seem to be a positive achievement; but the fact is that man's "religious and irrational" drives continue to force their way through whatever rational structures are grafted upon them. Day by day as the three months of his first visit to Spain passed, Wright observed how the organs of official life, the Falange, the State, the Army, the Church, all "were drawing their vitality from some deep irrational core that made up the heart of Spanish reality."[27] As Wright progresses through Spain, the implications gather that what is true of Spain is true of the "Western" world, and especially of America.

As the title of his book indicates, Wright found Spain to be a pagan country, its primitive nature thinly concealed by modern dress. The statue of the Virgin at Montserrat was, to Wright, as much a fetish as any he had seen in the Gold Coast. Reliquaries in the cathedrals appalled him; it was the sacred ancestral bones of the Ashanti dead all over again. Aristocratic Spaniards and peasants both communicated to Wright their sense of Spain as a mystical entity that transcended distinctions of province, or wealth, or class. Like Hemingway, Wright saw primitive religious forces emerging in strange guises. The bullfight moved him as a religious ceremony, as a kind of primitive ritual with the matador as priest: "*Death must serve as a secular baptism of emotion to wash the heart clean of its illegal dirt.* . . . And the matador in his bright suit of lights was a kind of lay priest offering up the mass for thirty thousand guilty penitents."[28] The hooded penitents in the Seville Easter procession radiated the *juju* of Africa. With the persecuted Protestant minority, he felt an immediate identification.

As with *Black Power,* bit by bit the meaning of his experiences seeped into his record, and Wright betrayed how far he was from having escaped the nets of his American culture. A bullfight that he witnessed in a small town outside Madrid brought an image of an American lynching searingly to his mind. After the bull had been killed, the crowd rushed into the bullring and tore pieces from the slain animal, seizing first its testicles. "They went straight to the real object on that dead bull's body that the bull had symbolized for them and poured out the hate and frustration and bewilderment of their troubled and confused consciousnesses."[29] It must have been the image in Wright's mind of his childhood friend, Bob Robinson, who had been sexually mutilated and lynched.[30] A photograph of a lynched Negro in *Black Voices* showed bits of the body torn away; the image had appeared several times in Wright's fiction and was to appear again in *The Long Dream.* The hooded penitents in Seville brought an image of the Ku Kluxers horribly before his eyes: "Those hooded penitents had been protecting the Virgin, and in the Old American South hooded Ku Kluxers had been protecting 'the purity of white womanhood.' "[31] The persecution of the Protestants led Wright to reflect that he had been born a Protestant, and that he had felt toward the Protestants as the Protestants in Spain felt towards the Catholics. "What I felt most keenly in Spain was the needless, unnatural, and utterly barbarous nature of the psychological suffering that the Spanish Protestant was doomed to undergo at the hands of the Church and State officials and his Catholic neighbors. For that exquisite suffering and emotional torture, I have a spontaneous and profound sympathy." Then Wright brought forth his deepest response:

> I am an American Negro with a background of psychological suffering stemming from my previous position as a member of a persecuted racial minority. What drew my attention to the emotional plight of the Protestants in Spain was the undeniable and uncanny psychological affinities that they held in common with American Negroes, Jews, and other oppressed minorities. It is another proof, if any is needed today, that the main and decisive aspects of human reactions are conditioned and are not inborn.
>
> Indeed the quickest and simplest way to introduce this subject to the reader would be to tell him that I shall describe some of the facets of psychological problems and the emotional sufferings of a group of *white Negroes* whom I met in Spain, the assumption being that Negroes are Negroes because they are *treated* as Negroes.[32]

This was the very passion and idea that had created *Black Boy* and *Native Son.* The perspective alone was different, in that Wright's vision had been enlarged to include all oppressed minorities in the category *Negro,* and "America's Metaphor" had become the metaphor of humanity itself.

Plato, in designing his ideal republic, decided that he had to exclude the poets, for these men would bring their myths and their myth-making power with them and set men to dreaming of how the republic might be changed. Such a decision must have been difficult for Plato, the poet and myth-maker. Wright had always had a similar difficulty. His intelligence demanded societies designed on rational lines and a modern, industrial state. But when his felt perceptions of life took over, he became the spokesman of the oppressed minority of dreamers —as when Sarah, in his early story, "Long Black Song," while awaiting the arrival of the white men who are to destroy her husband, muses—"Somehow, men, black men and white men, land and houses, green cornfields and grey skies, gladness and dreams, were all a part of that which made life good. Yes, somehow, they were linked, like the spokes in a spinning wheel."

11
James Baldwin: The View from Another Country

I

When he was twenty-eight years old, James Baldwin made the desperate decision to take practically all of his money, the remains of a Rosenwald grant, and buy a plane ticket to Paris, afraid that if he waited for the next ship he would not have enough money to buy a ticket. Leaving America, as he saw it, was his only hope for survival as a writer, as distinct from a "Negro writer," and as a person, as distinct from an "American Negro." He was convinced that America would not only destroy his potentiality as a creative artist, but that it would destroy him with hatred and self-hatred, and he intended to leave it for good. Paris seemed a logical destination, but to go to Paris was not in itself the point. " 'If I'd been born in Mississippi, I might have *come* to New York. But, being born in New York, there's no place that you can *go*. You have to go *out*. *Out* of the country. And I went out of the country and I never intended to come back here. Ever. *Ever.*' "[1]

Paris became his home for eight years, and in those expatriate years Baldwin found the freedom and the opportunity to explore his personal history, to have those varied experiences that would reveal himself to himself, and to write as an artist responsible to his own sense of the truth of his experience. He was able "to step out of history," in his own phrase, and to assay what it meant to be an American and what the concept "Negro American" signified in

American culture. As other American novelists had discovered in the past, he found that the experience of expatriation enabled him to delve deeper into the truth of what it means to be an American and to bear witness against those divisive, degrading influences that act to pervert that meaning.

Although he had grown up in Harlem—or perhaps *because* he had grown up in Harlem—Baldwin had taken a certain measure of racial discrimination for granted. It seemed to be of the nature of life, and not until he left New York briefly to work in New Jersey did he encounter flagrant Jim Crow treatment and feel personally inflamed by racial hatred. Like the Richard Wright of *Black Boy*, Baldwin as an adolescent seems to have pursued his interest in literature without any concern that to the practical eye his literary interests had no relevance to the life he would be forced to lead. Unlike Wright, whose literary interests were soon channeled into social protest, Baldwin developed an enthusiasm for those masters of modern fiction who excelled in craftsmanship and whose criticism of society was implicit in their study of the modern mind. Since he was maturing in the depression and World War II years, Baldwin did engage in socio-political activities; he wrote about Harlem's storefront churches, often reviewed the "Negro novel," and, like any young Negro of the period who aspired to become a writer, made a study of Wright's work. In addition, Baldwin sought out Wright for advice about writing. But Baldwin's creative imagination was wholly unsympathetic to Wright's approach to literature; in fact, Wright and the black community's concept of literature as social protest became for Baldwin a snare he particularly wished to escape by leaving the country.

In his effort to explore and to understand his individual consciousness, Baldwin tried to reconstruct the emotional landscape of his parents' lives. He wished to comprehend how his natural desire for love and the natural bond between father and son had become twisted and broken; he wished to lay bare and to master the terrifying sexual guilt that accompanied his adolescence and to recreate a sense of his dilemma at being driven to choose between the saints of his father's church and the sinners of the Avenue with their insidious question, "Whose little boy are you?" He had been working on this autobiographical study for several years before he left New York, and he worked on it for almost four years in Europe before it was published as *Go Tell It On the Mountain* in 1953. Almost the first person Baldwin encountered in Paris was Richard Wright, and the pull he must have felt to come around to Wright's side of the literary question was answered once and for all in June, 1949, when he published "Everybody's Protest Novel." With this article, Baldwin made it clear that he was his own little boy and that he had no intention of becoming yet another American Negro writer treating The Problem.

It might well have been from Henry James that Baldwin learned the lesson, which James dispensed in "The Art of Fiction," that the moral sense and the artistic sense are not separable qualities, and that "the deepest quality of a work of art will always be the quality of the mind of the producer." Instead of trying for the effects of social realism, Baldwin placed most of his first novel in the South, a region he had never seen, and at a time when he was yet unborn. He was searching for the roots of the intense love-hate relationship he had held for David Baldwin, the man he believed for most of his early life to be his father. He wished to place in the perspective of his creative imagination what went into the making of such a profoundly embittered man, and to understand the parts played by his mother and his aunt in his childhood world, and to examine the central function of the church in his family life. Seemingly the white world played no part in this personal drama.

When *Go Tell It On the Mountain* was published, it should have been clear to Wright and his followers that Baldwin had written a novel of social protest after all. For, the deepest quality of a work of art being the quality of the mind of the producer, the novel communicated in every line a sense of a culture as perceived by a sensitive, rapidly maturing boy who is driven by a need to love and to be loved, and who must deal with a father whose pride was so broken by racial shame that he retreated into the bitter isolation of self-hatred; in addition, as the eldest child in a large family, his psychic agony must smolder beneath the desperate daily battle to secure food and shelter and to survive at the despised bottom of the social heap. John, whose life closely parallels Baldwin's own, "was not much interested in his people and still less in leading them anywhere." His one overriding need was love. As Baldwin describes the critical passages in the lives of the men and women who led up to and included John, he communicates as an inseparable quality of the drama a devastating analysis of the culture that destroys a man by holding always before him the image of himself as little better than a beast, which thereby corrupts the natural love between parent and child, and which, through its moral prejudices added to its racial prejudices, converts a child's sense of his natural desires into a process of self-loathing. In this first work Baldwin discovered his essential theme: the struggle of the individual for love in a culture that will tolerate love only under conditions that are always highly arbitrary and frequently impossible for a given individual to meet. The most telling quality of the novel is its indictment of American culture for the cruel battle it wages against man's essential nature, and for such a disastrous effect of this battle as racial antagonism.

In his subsequent fiction, Baldwin was to be more explicit in suggesting the effect upon his characters of the synthesis of sexual and racial phobias in American life. During his first years in Paris, however, his work on this novel must have been markedly influenced toward a cultural indictment by the kind of liberating experience he was undergoing. As he put it, "I found myself, willy-nilly, alchemized into an American the moment I touched French soil."[2] He also must have found himself to be, culturally, a highly specialized American, since his direct knowledge of America was limited almost entirely to New York City and to those social areas available to an impoverished young Negro. Once in Paris, however, as his essay "The Discovery of What It Means to be an American" demonstrates, he rapidly acquired a sense of his Americanness, and the sense of being the product of a unique culture, unmistakably different from the product of a European or an African culture.

A world opened up for him in Paris that, in its richness and variety, he could not have imagined in America. He lived in the bohemian squalor traditional with the fledgling artist, a squalor not greatly different from what he had known for years in Greenwich Village. The great difference resulted from being free of America's racial and moral conventions. He rapidly acquired friends of an astonishing variety—Arab vendors, an Egyptian banker, artists of various nationalities, famous intellectuals, prostitutes, and clochards. He deliberately set about opening himself to the widest possible range of experience, to " 'whole *areas* of life—which I would never have *dared* to deal with in America.' "[3] His sense of himself as American was consciously defined in discussion with other artists and intellectuals, American and European and African, and especially through such an illuminating experience as "The Conference of Negro-African Writers and Artists," which met in September, 1956, at the Sorbonne. In his report on the conference for *Encounter,* Baldwin made a special point of the fact that the African writers and artists were all, whether they wished to acknowledge the fact or not, deeply influenced by European culture. Much of the thrust of Baldwin's report was directed toward American participants and students of the conference who were concerned with affirming their African roots and with deemphasizing or even disowning their relationship with Europe and America. Baldwin insisted that the Negro in America was almost wholly an American cultural product and, as such, was derived far more from Europe than from Africa.

Unlike many literary expatriates, Baldwin did not indulge in extravagent praise of France as a land of freedom. He did find that the artist enjoyed a highly respected status in Europe as compared with the United States, but he found also that the American enjoyed unusual privileges and liberties solely because he was a foreigner. He observed that "The meaning of Europe for an American Negro was one of the things about which Richard Wright and I disagreed most vehemently. He was fond of referring to Paris as the 'city of refuge' —which it certainly was, God knows, for the likes of us. But it was not a city of refuge for the French, still less for anyone belonging to France; and it would not have been a city of refuge for us if we had not been armed with American passports."[4] Through association, for example, with the Algerians who comprised a large unemployed class in Paris, Baldwin observed how someone "belonging to France" could suffer from vicious discrimination. A lesson in the potential savagery of French justice was brought home to him when he was imprisoned over the Christmas holidays for being the receiver of stolen goods—a bed sheet. The conditions of his arrest and imprisonment were as brutal and terrifying as any he might have anticipated from police in a Southern state, and in the prison he saw and suffered with men who were facing a life of hideous imprisonment because, given the nature of society and their personal inadequacies, crime was the only possible career for them.

When Baldwin's case appeared in court, the charge of receiving a stolen sheet was read amidst "great merriment in the courtroom," and the case dismissed. Baldwin, however, had learned an important lesson. "This laughter is the laughter of those who consider themselves to be at a safe remove from all the wretched, for whom the pain of the living is not real. I had heard it so often in my native land that I had resolved to find a place where I would never hear it any more. In some deep, black, strong, and liberating way, my life, in my own eyes, began during that first year in Paris, when it was borne in on me that this laughter is universal and never can be stilled."[5]

When Baldwin went to stay for a few weeks in a remote Swiss village, he was made conscious as never before in his life of his distinctive racial characteristics. Having passed his childhood and youth in Harlem and the greater New York City area, he had never been made to feel his racial characteristics as "exotic" or "strange." In the Swiss village where a Negro was regarded as a human curiosity, a freak of nature, Baldwin suddenly realized that for Europeans black men were no real part of their society; black men were an abstract quantity belonging to colonies and continents across the seas. Yet as a black man born and raised in America he had no relationship, beyond the physical characteristics of his body, to the black people of colonies and countries beyond the seas. America had produced his consciousness; and America, as a culture, was to a large degree derived from this white European culture within which he seemed so thoroughly foreign. White Americans took from Europe, among their other traditions, the belief in white supremacy; and thus, by the irony of history, black men who had been part of America since before the founding of the Republic—antedating the arrival of most white Americans—were made continually to feel that they existed outside the mainstream of American culture. Indeed, they had been made to feel, as Wright forcefully pointed out, that they had no heritage at all except that of the auction block and primitive tribalism in African jungles. James Fenimore Cooper's novel *The Headsman* (1833) had pleaded for a comprehension of a "race" that was excluded from humanity in a Swiss canton because of its heritage, a "race" that he named significantly after Balthazar, the black Magus. Well over a century later Baldwin again used the example of a man of the race of Balthazar (traditionally a descendant of Ham) excluded from the Swiss community and made to feel separate from their culture because of the physical characteristics of his body. When the Swiss children followed Baldwin with innocent cries of "*Neger! Neger!*" he remembered American children and their knowing taunts of "Nigger! Nigger!", proclaiming him alien from the very culture within which he had his being.

Many of the Negroes whom Baldwin encountered in Paris were involved in political action designed to promote African nationalism and to correct abuses inflicted by white governments. While such men had suffered a great deal, it seemed to Baldwin that they had not endured the special suffering of the Negro in America—"the utter alienation of himself from his people and his past."[6] A tragic result of this alienation was the vulnerability of the Negro in America to the image of him projected by the whites. As a result of this image, generations of black men endured a profound, almost ineradicable self-hatred. Richard Wright had worked with the concept that Americans had created an artificial horror, "the American Negro," and this myth had for generations exerted its hideous power upon black Americans. Wright would have wiped out the whole of the Negro's American history, and his character "Bigger Thomas" was created as a violent expression of the destructive racial myth. Baldwin agreed to a point with Wright; he acknowledged that his father had been destroyed by believing what white people said about him, and in "My Dungeon Shook" he admonishes his nephew, "You can only be destroyed by believing that you really are what the white world calls a *nigger.*'"[7]

Baldwin differs significantly from Wright, however, in his insistence that the Negro, as American, is intrinsically related to the whole American cultural heritage; that it is essential for the Negro to recover as much as possible of his past and however bitter that past might be, to acknowledge and understand and accept it; and, finally, to see the unity of his humanity with all humanity. The myth of the "American Negro" has a powerful hold on the American mind, and Baldwin's writings affirm that the regenerative source of the myth is the American concept of Christianity—that bizarre amalgam of sexual repression, social divisions, and dedication to materialism and security which underwrites the national self-image. For Baldwin, the God of white Americans is a symptom of their cultural neurosis. And the compensating neurosis it breeds in black Americans can produce the kind of self-destructive behavior that Baldwin dramatized through the conduct of such characters as Rufus *(Another Country),* Richard *(Blues for Mister Charlie),* and Christopher *(Tell Me How Long the Train's Been Gone).* In an address at Kalamazoo College, Baldwin offered his own idea of God: "To be with God is really to be involved with some enormous, overwhelming desire, and joy, and power which you cannot control, which controls you. I conceive of my own life as a journey towards something I do not understand, which in the going toward, makes me better. I conceive of God, in fact, as a means of liberation and not a means to control others."[8] In proposing such a conception of God as part of a destructive attack upon the God of the white establishment, Baldwin placed himself squarely within the American tradition best exemplified by Emerson's Divinity School *Address.*

II

Baldwin's European experience, in teaching him how he was an American, taught him that the process of discovering his individual identity was no surface affair of losing illusions about America or about the relation of white to black American. Self-recognition began in accepting the fact that for centuries he had been shaped in the image of those qualities of human nature which influential white Americans wished to refuse to acknowledge as part of their own.

Despite the barbarism of this history, black Americans had to accept it and the country as their own. "The paradox—and a fearful paradox it is—is that the American Negro can have no future anywhere, on any continent, as long as he is unwilling to accept his past."[9] A major effect of the fearsome "American Negro" myth, however, had been to drive black Americans into two camps: the sinners and the saints. From his early childhood Baldwin had been aware of these two categories, and in *Go Tell It On the Mountain* it is, in large part, the need to choose between them that produces a hysterical conversion experience in John. He is "saved"; but when the hysteria passes, the grim realization comes that to remain with the saints is to be locked within oneself in a frigid hypocrisy. The histories of the characters Gabriel, Elizabeth, and Florence show the working of the iron law in the black community: nigger or saint.

If the Negro is to come into his rightful place as a fully integrated participant in American cultural life, it is Baldwin's contention that the white majority must first be healed of its neurotic conception of its human nature. It must learn to accept itself and cease to live in terms of the denials enshrined in its perverted version of Christianity —denials of death as well as of life. And it is in the life of the Negro that white discontents can find the life and the love missing from their civilization. "If the Negro doesn't save this country," Baldwin wrote, "then nobody else can. And if I can find another word than Negro it might be closer to what I mean. I don't mean the Negro as a person; I mean the Negro as an experience—a level of experience Americans always deny."[10] As a result of being systematically excluded for generations from the culture of the white majority, the Negro in America has suffered great psychological damage, but in general he has been spared the burden of the elaborate pattern of repression and sublimation by means of which the whites affirmed their "Christian" ideal. If there were a providential design, it might well be, from Baldwin's point of view, that black Americans had been excluded only in order that they might in the course of time redeem the culture from its destructive self-hatred, from its need for the scapegoat "American Negro."

Paris has traditionally been the city for the unleashing of the

American libido, and Baldwin's experience there, including most of all his close observation of his countrymen, was a revelation as to how much there was in common between white Americans and sinners on Harlem's Lennox Avenue. What was truly sinful was the American's concept of sin—the derogation of the natural impulses of the body, the denial of the heart for the sake of a social status that was contrived and manipulated for the basest reasons. It was on the basis of this perception that Baldwin constructed *Giovanni's Room.* As an epigraph to the novel Baldwin chose Whitman's line, "I am the man, I suffered, I was there." The line attests to the source of the novel in his own experience. It also attests to the fact that Baldwin was continuing Whitman's tradition of insisting upon the universality of human experience. And in this respect Baldwin was at one with other novelists in America's transcendentalist tradition: with Hawthorne, whose most brilliant fiction depicted the need of man to accept his human nature and his mortality; with Melville, whose imagination was fascinated by the possibilities of art for placing in a unifying perspective partial and antagonistic concepts of human experience; with James, whose major phase explored the spiritual attrition of Anglo-American culture because of its disregard for love; and with the explosive affirmations of Cummings's *The Enormous Room* and Henry Miller's *Tropic of Cancer.*

Giovanni's Room brings together two characters, each of whom represents an essentially different way of looking at life. The American, David, is aware of the demands of his sexual nature and is driven to satisfy them. Because of his conventional attitudes toward sexual behavior, however, he cannot tolerate his desires and plots relentlessly to betray them. In his effort to preserve an idea of himself created by conventional morality, he destroys the relationship that had enabled him to exist in a new relatedness to everything about him. Giovanni, Baldwin's counterpoise to David, feels that love is what essentially matters. He lives in the present, not in the possibilities of the future; values the truth of his emotional life, not conventional appearances; is concerned with persons, not with social categories of behavior. Time's winged chariot is always at David's back, bearing his fiancée and the baggage of economic questions, the job, and "settling down."

Giovanni's room, which is a symbol that gathers to itself a superb indifference to the passage of time and the worth of material things, occupies the full space of David's imagination as he narrates the story with the sense of gradual, belated, tragic recognitions and of final loss that echoes the narrative tone and similar meanings in Hemingway's *Farewell to Arms* and *The Snows of Kilimanjaro.*

Far from engaging in a special plea for any form of sexual behavior, Baldwin's novel suggests that the culture that produced David—with its rigid definition of male and female roles, its primary emphasis upon societal conventions and its disregard of the individual, and the tyranny of its warped religious ideas—places the American constantly in conflict with himself. The American resorts to "the Negro," in Baldwin's terminology someone excluded from the white moral orbit, to empty into a void the passion that should be the basis for enduring human connections.

The title of Baldwin's third novel, *Another Country,* echoes Marlowe's lines,

> Thou hast committed—
> Fornication: but that was in another country,
> And besides, the wench is dead.

and T. S. Eliot's use of the lines as an epigraph to the images of opulence and sterility in his poem "Portrait of a Lady." The vitality of the characters in Baldwin's novel is always sapped and is sometimes destroyed by the cultural configurations that rule their lives. All too often the love that brings them together is made cheap and contemptible by racial, or economic, or behavioral patterns. The narrator of the short story "This Morning, This Evening, So Soon," a black American singer returning to America after four years in Paris, is asked to sing by the white passengers aboard ship. His reflections state one of the central themes of *Another Country*: "Nothing was more familiar to them than the sight of a dark boy, singing, and there were few things on earth more necessary. It was under cover of darkness, my own darkness, that I could sing for them of the joys, passions, and terrors they smuggled about with them like steadily depreciating contraband. Under cover of the midnight fiction that I was unlike them because I was black, they could stealthily gaze at those treasures which they had been mysteriously forbidden to possess and were never permitted to declare."[11]

The title story of *Going To Meet the Man* includes a description of a lynching that seems pure Grand Guignol unless one bears in mind that it occurs in the nightmare of a Southern sheriff. Baldwin's intention is to communicate the idea that for the Southern white the Negro (and the symbolic function of this term must be borne in mind) has become the repository of sexual vitality and that the lynching enacted in Southern sleep is a subconscious effort to recover the power that has been repressed. The ritual murder of the black and the seizure of the genitals and phallic substitutes function for the community as a kind of primitive religious ceremony, the psychological equivalent of the Spanish bullfight. And the religion of the Negro is shaped by his role as victim. *Go Tell It On the Mountain* suggests, in part, that the Negro church is a refuge for black men who can no longer bear their degraded status. Here and in *The Fire Next Time* Baldwin presents the Negro church as premised upon blindness, loneliness, and terror. The Lord is a mighty fortress thrown up by the black man's fear and hatred to shield him from the whites. Church services become a means of disguising the sexuality that is, to him, clear proof that the whites are right and he is a filthy beast. Aside from its being a money-racket, Baldwin affirmed that the black church—created in the image of the white church—has no love in it. "It was a mask for hatred and self-hatred and despair." In "The Harlem Ghetto" he suggested that the churches operated as "a complete and exquisite fantasy revenge: white people own the earth and commit all manner of abomination and injustice on it; the bad will be punished and the good rewarded, for God is not sleeping, the judgment is not far off."[13]

III

In his fiction Baldwin has practiced a ruthless candor, insisting, for example, upon the publication of *Giovanni's Room* despite assurances that such a book would not be accepted by the public and might mean the end of his career. In hewing to the truth of his experience, he defied the societal convention of which Henry James had complained, that where art is concerned there is a part of ourselves that we agree not to know. Since the general reading public is steeped in the very attitudes that he would radically alter, it is no marvel that the ethical dimension of Baldwin's fiction has received less attention than those physical relationships in terms of which cultural values are explored. There is an irony in a writer's creating for the public the story of a man's gradual discovery of how their culture is destructive of the individual, only to have the public slap its racial or sexual labels on the result. It is of a piece with the irony of the fact that *The Fire Next Time,* a devastating attack upon a culture that most vividly demonstrates its perverted values in its extremes of black poverty and white opulence, should first appear in *The New Yorker,* sandwiched between advertisements for goods intended to assure the most pretentious status. As Baldwin and the editors of the magazine know, the sorrows of the Negro are one of the most prized consumer goods of the affluent white liberal.

The subject matter of Baldwin's fiction is determined by his conviction that only through accepting the ever-present burden of our common humanity can we achieve identity as individuals and as a people. Only through the agonizing changes that will bring about that acceptance will such a basic social relationship as the family endure and a church approximating the doctrines of Christ be possible. Seen in this light, Baldwin's views are not essentially different from those of Bronislaw Malinowski, who wrote in *Sex, Culture, and Myth*:

> I see forces in the modern world which will demand an independent and just treatment of unmarried love and perhaps even of homosexual love side by side with the standardized institutions. When they receive this just and fair treatment the now rebellious classes may, I hope, become less aggressive and less destructive to what is to me most valuable in human society: reproduction, marriage, the family and the home.[14]

Under America's present cultural dispensation, Baldwin sees the individual as necessarily engaged in telling himself a lie about the nature of human life and clinging to definitions that apply to nobody's life. In the world of Mister Charlie, "The plague is race, the plague is our concept of Christianity: and this raging plague has the power to destroy every human relationship."[15]

This attack upon the basis of the white American's concept of himself as Christian is as old as the nation itself. The concept that each man should be equal before the law follows from the concept that each man, without intermediaries, stands alone and equal before his God. Truth came primarily not from human institutions, but from each individual's search of his spirit, his private dialogue with God. "Any honest examination of the national life proves," Baldwin observed, "how far we are from the standard of human freedom with which we began. The recovery of this standard demands of everyone who loves this country a hard look at himself, for the greatest achievements must begin somewhere, and they always begin with the person."[16] On this Emersonian principle is based the whole of Baldwin's belief in the possibility of change. He does not place his faith in organizations, or causes, or even in other individuals; his motto might well be "Trust thyself!"

When he was first in Paris Baldwin met many Americans busily searching for their "identity" on the terraces of the Café Flore and the Café Deux Magots. It seemed to Baldwin a peculiarly American assumption that merely by declaring it so one might be free of all the forces that have produced him. And yet, as his essay "A Question of Identity" pointed out, the nature of American history lent itself to such an assumption, since America was composed largely of people who had willingly separated themselves from their forebears and sought to begin a new kind of life in America. Yet the new kind of life tended with time to become one kind of life, and the American who went to Europe had it made plain to him that he was part of a distinct culture, part of a people "with a unique and individual past." "From the vantage point of Europe he discovers his own country. And this is a discovery which not only brings to an end the alienation of the American from himself, but which also makes clear to him, for the first time, the extent of his involvement in the life of Europe."[17]

Baldwin's long stay in Europe, his independent stance, and such a work as *Giovanni's Room,* which seemingly had no relation to the black struggle in America, subjected him to criticism as an escapist, not merely from black political activists but from white liberals. To insist upon one's independence was unquestionably to invite misunderstanding, but it was out of such individualism that great social change originated: "From this void—ourselves—it is the function of society to protect us; but it is only this void, our unknown selves, demanding, forever, a new act of creation, which can save us—'from the evil that is in the world.' "[18] At the heart of Baldwin's position is a concept that is of the very essence of revolution, not in an immediate political sense but in the sense of ontological change, which results from referring one's experience of life to the intimate scrutiny of one's intuitional response; from the unrelenting effort to disentangle the self from the idols of den, cave, tribe, and marketplace; and from responding to the world with a sense of its continual fresh creation. On this ground Baldwin has close affinities with the great transcendentalists, who did not want to tinker with society but to alter mankind's way of conceiving of itself. In a speech to Harlem teachers in 1963, when he was asked what was the role of the white liberal, he replied "there is *no* role for the white liberal. He is one of our *afflictions.*"[19]

Such an attitude springs from a perception of human nature similar to that which led to the harsh treatment of reformers by Hawthorne in *The Blithedale Romance* and by James in *The Bostonians.* Like Hawthorne and James, Baldwin felt that the reformer was evading some essential relation with himself. He was familiar with black men whose blackness was used as a crutch and with black leaders whose profession was protest. But he found the white liberals to be acting on the very motivational basis that required to be changed. They were possessed of "a will to power that has nothing whatever to do with the principle they think they are upholding . . . their status in their own eyes is much more important than any real change. . . . Their pronouncements have nothing to do with reality, that's what I object to. Reality is involved with their relationship to themselves, their wives, their children; but this they have abdicated entirely, and use, then me, the Negro, as an opportunity to live safely."[20] But inconsistency is no hobgoblin of the transcendentalist, and, caught up in the excitement of the 1960s, Baldwin found himself transformed overnight into one of the foremost leaders of the black protest movement. In order to save himself as an artist and person, he had to flee once again to Europe.

It is a familiar paradox that just beneath the transcendentalist's belief in the uniqueness and primacy of the individual life lies his belief that all individuals are united by the divine principle that animates all. Sure of what is deep and constant within himself, he takes a point of view from which the world is after all a stage and the men and women merely players. Baldwin's expatriation had set him upon the road of self-discovery, comparing one culture with another, observing the manifold ways in which a person acts out the parts determined by his culture, and marveling at the number and variety of potential roles a man might play. Beginning with *Another Country*, Baldwin communicated something of this sense of life by making most of his principal characters writers, artists, singers, actors—people accustomed to play parts and to adapt themselves to different perspectives of value. *Tell Me How Long the Train's Been Gone* is narrated through the mind of an actor, Leo Proudhammer, whose consciousness makes dazzling leaps in American time and space, assuming the role of child and adult, poor and rich, black and white, and varied sexual, racial, and social roles. He is a man who might play almost any part, and at one point he "had a sudden, frightening apprehension of the possibilities every human being contains, a sense of life as an arbitrary series of groupings and regroupings, like the figures—if one can call them figures—in a kaleidoscope."[21] The novel depicts the various stages through which Leo has passed in arriving at the point where he can reflect over his past with control and comprehension. He may yet, one feels, play many roles, but with his deep self-knowledge he can never become, in Melville's and Thomas Mann's sense of the term, merely a confidence man. Because of his certain hold on his identity, he will be able to adapt to the parts demanded by the cultural drama without losing touch with himself.

In *The Fire Next Time* Baldwin spoke of the need for free men "to trust and to celebrate what is constant—birth, struggle, and death are constant, and so is love, though we may not always think so—and to apprehend the nature of change, to be able and willing to change. I speak of change not on the surface but in the depths—change in the sense of renewal."[22] Rufus *(Another Country)* was not able to change. He was locked into the role of "American Negro," and the hatred that he felt for whites accomplished his own destruction quite as much as it accomplished the destruction of the white girl who loved him. He was a victim of the culture, a suicide from the George Washington Bridge. His sister, Ida, continues the character of Rufus in the novel, but this time the character is capable of transcending the cultural incubus to arrive at the condition of love—a condition that Baldwin defined as one of being and grace. Giving up hatred and bitterness can be more difficult than giving up a tradition or a privilege; but such are the sacrifices Baldwin demands of his characters if they are to be set free. And both black and white characters had to make the same sacrifices, for "white men in this country and American Negroes in this country are really the same people. I only discovered this in Europe; perhaps it was always very obvious, but it never occurred to me before."[23] Baldwin found a metaphor for this oneness in a speech delivered at Kalamazoo College when he described the union of black and white America as a wedding—the two bound to each other as one flesh for all time.

James Baldwin continues the long line of American novelists, beginning with James Fenimore Cooper, who discovered through their experience of Europe the way in which American culture had shaped their minds and the unique quality of the American experience. Out of their reassessment of themselves and their reassessment of their country they have, like The Reverend Meridian Henry of *Blues for Mister Charlie,* mounted the platform that is at one and the same time the church pulpit and the courtroom witness stand. Armed with their sense of what is deepest and most constant in the spirit and the law, they have spoken as a witness to the truth. They have spoken to the nation as to a greater individual who might be helped through their fresh perspective to recover, as in the play, the meanings of the ever-present cross and the flag and the illusive stage.

Notes

Chapter 1. James Fenimore Cooper: The European Novels

1. James Fenimore Cooper, *Recollections of Europe* (Paris: Baudry, 1837), p. 307. Published in America as *Gleanings in Europe.*
2. *The Letters and Journals of James Fenimore Cooper,* ed. James Franklin Beard. 2 vols. (Cambridge, Mass.: Belknap Press of Harvard University Press, 1960), (2:11 to Peter Augustus Jay, Paris, 8 September 1830).
3. James Fenimore Cooper (anonymous), *Notions of the Americans Picked up by a Travelling Bachelor.* 2 vols. (London: H. Colburn, 1828), 1: 361.
4. James Fenimore Cooper, *The Bravo, The Works of James Fenimore Cooper,* Mohawk Edition. 33 vols. (New York: Putnam's, 1895–1900), pp. 384–85. Numbers in parenthesis following a quotation from one of Cooper's novels refer to page numbers in the Mohawk Edition.
5. *Letters,* 2: 106–7 (to Mrs. Peter Augustus Jay, Paris, 16 June 1831). The political section of the letter is addressed to Mr. Jay.
6. *Letters,* 2: 199 (to Armand Carrel, editor of *Le National,* where it was published 26(?) February 1832. My translation. The original text is as follows:

> "M. Saulnier ne compte pas les esclaves dans ses calculs sur la population. Pourquoi? Ne sont-ce pas des producteurs? Qui produit le coton, le tabac, le riz, le sucre des états meridionaux? Est-ce parce qu'ils n'ont pas les même droits politiques que les laboureurs français? Mais le laboureur français a-t-il les mêmes droits politiques que le laboureur blanc d'Amérique?"

Chapter 2. Melville's Redburn and the City

1. *The Letters of Herman Melville,* ed. Merrell R. Davis and William H. Gilman (New Haven: Yale University Press, 1960), p. 95.
2. *Journal of a Visit to London and the Continent by Herman Melville,* ed. Eleanor Melville Metcalf (Cambridge, Mass.: Harvard University Press, 1948), p. 23.

3. Herman Melville, *Redburn: His First Voyage* (New York: Russell & Russell, Inc.; reissued 1963, The Standard Edition). Page references to Melville's novels are to this edition.
4. *Letters,* p. 132 (to Nathaniel Hawthorne, 29 June 1851).
5. *Journal,* p. 25.
6. *Letters,* p. 125.
7. Edwin C. Guillet, *The Great Migration* (New York and Toronto: T. Nelson and Sons, 1937), pp. 84, p. 91. See also Marcus Lee Hansen, *The Atlantic Migration 1607–1860* (Cambridge: Harvard University Press, 1940), chap. 11, "The Flight from Hunger."
8. Oscar Handlin, *The Uprooted* (Boston: Little, Brown and Co., 1951), p. 51.
9. *Letters,* p. 93 (to Evert A. Duyckinck, 10 October 1849).

Chapter 3. Hawthorne's Dialogue with Rome

1. George Parsons Lathrop, "Biographical Sketch of Nathaniel Hawthorne," *The Complete Works of Nathaniel Hawthorne* (The Riverside Edition), ed. George Parsons Lathrop. 13 vols. (Boston and New York: Houghton, Mifflin & Co., 1882–83), 12: 533.
2. Nathaniel Hawthorne, *Our Old Home: A Series of English Sketches, The Centenary Edition of the Works of Nathaniel Hawthorne,* ed. William Charvat *et al.* (Columbus, Ohio: Ohio State University Press, 1962–), 5: 10.
3. Lathrop, "Biog. Sketch," 12: 517.
4. Caroline Ticknor, *Hawthorne and His Publisher* (1913; reissued Port Washington, N.Y.: Kennikat Press, Inc., 1969), p. 179.
5. Nathaniel Hawthorne, *Doctor Grimshawe's Secret,* Riverside Edition, 11: 470.
6. Lathrop, "Biog. Sketch," 12: 543.
7. Nathaniel Hawthorne, *The Ancestral Footstep,* Riverside Edition, 11: 470
8. Nathaniel Hawthorne, *The Marble Faun, Centenary Edition,* 4: 326. Subsequent page references to *The Marble Faun* are to this edition and volume.
9. Mrs. Hawthorne, *Notes in England and Italy* (New York: G. P. Putnam and Son, 1869), pp. 480, 493.

Chapter 4. Henry James and the American Aristocracy

1. Henry James, *A Small Boy and Others* (New York: Charles Scribner's Sons, 1913), pp. 56–57.
2. Henry James, *Notes of a Son and Brother* (New York: Charles Scribner's Sons, 1914), p. 67.
3. *Ibid.,* p. 315.
4. *Ibid.,* p. 316.
5. *Ibid.*

6. *Ibid.*
7. Walt Whitman, *Complete Poetry and Selected Prose,* ed. James E. Miller, Jr. (Boston: Houghton Mifflin Co., 1959), pp. 456–57.
8. *Ibid.,* p. 484.
9. Henry James, *Roderick Hudson* (New York: Charles Scribner's Sons, 1907), 1: 302. The New York Edition. Numbers in parenthesis following a quotation from a novel by James indicate page numbers of the novel in this edition.
10. James extended and altered the list of elements of European life absent from American life in a notebook entry for 1879 and in his *Hawthorne.* W. D. Howells's review of the *Hawthorne* produced a memorable exchange of letters on the subject, and in *The Portrait of a Lady* James introduced the topic again, giving a version of Howells's words to Isabel and of his own to Osmond.
11. *Quest for America 1810–1824,* ed. Charles L. Sanford (Garden City, N.Y.: Doubleday & Company, Inc., 1964), p. 280.
12. *The Letters of Henry James,* ed. Percy Lubbock. 2 vols. (New York: Charles Scribner's Sons, 1920), 2: 25 (to Edmund Gosse, 16 February 1905).

Chapter 5. Mark Twain's Pilgrim's Progress

1. Mark Twain, *The Innocents Abroad* (New York: Harper & Brothers, 1899), 1: 144. The "Uniform Edition." Numbers in parenthesis following a quotation from *Innocents* refer to the text (vols. 1 and 2) in this edition.
2. Twain's letters are included in *Traveling with the Innocents Abroad: Mark Twain's Original Reports from Europe and the Holy Land,* ed. Daniel Morley McKeithan (Norman: University of Oklahoma Press, 1958). Numbers in parenthesis following a quotation from Twain's letters in this text are preceded by an "L."
3. Walter Blair, *Mark Twain & Huck Finn* (Berkeley and Los Angeles: University of California Press, 1960), p. 275.
4. Albert Bigelow Paine, *Mark Twain A Biography.* 3 vols. (New York and London: Harper & Brothers, 1912), p. 1281.
5. See *Mark Twain of the Enterprise: Newspaper Articles and Other Documents 1862–1864,* ed. Henry Nash Smith with the assistance of Frederick Anderson (Berkeley and Los Angeles: University of California Press, 1957).
6. E. E. Branch, *The Literary Apprenticeship of Mark Twain* (Urbana: University of Illinois Press, 1950), pp. 143, 146.
7. See *Mark Twain's Letters from Hawaii,* ed. A. Grove Day (New York: Appleton and Century, 1966).
8. *Ibid.,* p. 129. Twain's sense of what the missionaries had accomplished had been unfortunately influenced by his reading of James Jackson Jarves's *History of the Sandwich Islands*; he censured the missionaries privately in his notebooks for "insincerity and hypocrisy," according to Philip S. Foner, *Mark Twain: Social Critic* (New York: International Publishers Co., 1958), p. 279.

9. *Mark Twain's Letters,* ed. A. B. Paine. 2 vols. (New York: Harper & Brothers, 1917), 1: 96.
10. Smith, *Enterprise.* Letter from Carson City dated 13 February 1864.
11. Notebook 34, p. 289, Mark Twain Papers. Cited in Roger B. Salomon, *Twain and the Image of History* (New Haven: Yale University Press, 1961), pp. 78–79.
12. James, *Letters,* 1: 22.
13. Twain, *Letters,* 1: 325 (29 March 1878).

Chapter 6. Henry James: Love in an Anglo-Saxon World

1. *The Letters of Henry James,* ed. Percy Lubbock. 2 vols. (New York: Charles Scribner's Sons, 1920), 1: 418 (To William James, 24 May 1903).
2. *Ibid.,* 1: 141–42.
3. *Ibid.,* 1: 375 (to W. D. Howells, 10 August 1901). See also 1: 166 (to Howells, 17 May 1890) and 1: 295 (to Miss Frances R. Morse, 19 Oct. 1898).
4. *The Notebooks of Henry James,* ed. F. O. Matthiessen and K. B. Murdock (New York: Oxford University Press, 1947), p. 226 (entry dated 31 Oct. 1895).
5. *Ibid.,* p. 174 (entry dated 7 Nov. 1894).
6. *Ibid.,* p. 372.
7. *Ibid.,* p. 227.
8. *The Ambassadors* (New York Edition 21 and 22), 1: 41.
9. See *Letters,* 1: 72 (to W. D. Howells, 31 Jan. 1880). See also chap. 4, n. 10 above. Under a changing format the dispute continued with James's brother William and, much later, with H. G. Wells.
10. Henry James, *The Middle Years* (London: W. Collins Sons & Co., 1917), p. 14.
11. *Ambassadors,* 1: 131.
12. *Ibid.,* 2: 323.
13. Henry James, *Notes of a Son and Brother,* (New York: Charles Scribner's Sons, 1914), p. 316.
14. *Letters,* 1: 114 (to Miss Grace Norton, 24 Jan. 1885).
15. *Ibid.,* 1: 280–81 (20 April 1898).
16. See *Notes of a Son and Brother,* pp. 475–83.
17. *Middle Years,* p. 75.
18. *Letters,* 1: 125 (to Charles Eliot Norton, 6 Dec. 1886).
19. *Middle Years,* p. 116.
20. *The Golden Bowl* (New York Edition 23 and 24), 2: 303–4.
21. *Ibid.,* 2: 357.
22. *Ibid.,* 2: 287, 331.
23. *Ibid.,* 1: 128.
24. *Ibid.,* 1: 9.
25. *Ibid.,* 1: 293.

26. *Ibid.*, 1: 31.
27. *Ibid.*, 1: 322.
28. *Ibid.*, 1: 307. Charlotte informs the Prince that she and Adam cannot have a child and that, " 'It's not, at any rate, . . . my fault. There it is.' " Through the combination of wealth and sexual impotence here and elsewhere in his fiction, James suggests how the commercialism of the culture alienates man from his natural self.
29. *Letters*, 1: 128 (to Miss Grace Norton, 23 July 1887).
30. *Ibid.*, 1: 420 (to William James, 24 May 1903).

Chapter 7. E. E. Cummings: Eros and Cambridge, Mass.

1. E. E. Cummings, *i: six non-lectures* (1953; reprinted New York: Atheneum, 1962), p. 31.
2. "The New Art," *Harvard Advocate* (June, 1915), reprinted in *E. E. Cummings: A Miscellany Revised*, ed. George J. Firmage (New York: October House, Inc., n.d.).
3. E. E. Cummings, "Burlesque, I love It!" *Stage* (March 1936), reprinted in *Miscellany Revised*, p. 292.
4. *i: six non-lectures*, p. 53.
5. *Ibid.*
6. *Ibid.*
7. E. E. Cummings, *The Enormous Room* (New York: The Modern Library, 1934), p. 65. Numbers in parenthesis following a quotation refer to pages in this edition.
8. For W. Slater Brown's letters, see Part One, 5, "The Poet at War," in Charles Norman, *The Magic-Maker E. E. Cummings* (New York: Duell, Sloan, and Pearce, 1958).
9. "T. S. Eliot," *The Dial* (June, 1920), reprinted in *Miscellany Revised*, p. 27.
10. E. E. Cummings, *Poems 1923–1954* (New York: Harcourt, Brace and World, 1954), p. 435.
11. "Gaston Lachaise," *The Dial* (February 1920), reprinted in *Miscellany Revised*, p. 20.
12. *Ibid.*
13. *Poems 1923–1954*, p. 58.
14. "The Adult, the Artist and the Circus," *Vanity Fair* (March 1927), reprinted in *Miscellany Revised*, p. 175.
15. "The Secret of the Zoo Exposed," *Vanity Fair* (March 1927), reprinted in *Miscellany Revised*, p. 175.
16. *Ibid.*
17. "A Foreword to Krazy Kat," *Sewanee Review* (Spring 1946), reprinted in *Miscellany Revised*, p. 327.

Chapter 8. Hemingway and Life as Play

1. In the light of what is now known of Hemingway's parents, Philip Young writes, "Their Victorianism was so preposterous—so, too, their lack of understanding—that as a context for his general rebellion the family now looks bigger than the war." *Ernest Hemingway: A Reconsideration* (University Park and London: Penn. State University Press, 1966), pp. 273–74. John Peale Bishop described the environment of Hemingway's youth as "monstrous and monotonous regimentation of mediocrity" in "The Missing All" (1948, reprinted in *Ernest Hemingway: The Man and His Work,* ed. John K. M. McCaffery [New York: The World Publishing Co., 1950], p. 269).
2. Leicester Hemingway, *My Brother; Ernest Hemingway* (New York: The World Publishing Co., 1961), p. 16.
3. See Constance Cappel Montgomery, *Hemingway in Michigan* (New York: Fleet, 1966), p. 32.
4. See Charles A. Fenton, *The Apprenticeship of Ernest Hemingway* (New York: Farrar, Straus & Cudahy, 1954), p. 72.
5. Ernest Hemingway, *The Fifth Column and the First Forty-nine Stories* (New York: Charles Scribner's Sons, 1939), p. 591.
6. See Carlos Baker, *Ernest Hemingway: A Life Story* (New York: Charles Scribner's Sons, 1969), p. 50.
7. See, especially, "Now I Lay Me" *(Stories,* pp. 463–64), "The Doctor and the Doctor's Wife" (*Stories,* pp. 199–201), "Soldier's Home" (*Stories,* pp. 247–50), and "Fathers and Sons" (*Stories,* pp. 587–89 and 594–97).
8. The parents' letters are cited in Baker, *Hemingway,* pp. 72–73.
9. See Montgomery, *Hemingway in Michigan,* pp. 142–43.
10. Malcolm Cowley, ed., *The Portable Hemingway* (New York: The Viking Press, 1944), "Introduction," p. xix.
11. Sigmund Freud, *Reflections on War and Death,* from *Imago* 5: 1915.
12. A significant critical protest was made by Edmund Wilson in 1939: "Going back over Hemingway's books today, we can see clearly what an error of the politicos it was to accuse him of an indifference to society. His whole work is a criticism of society: he has responded to every pressure of the moral atmosphere of the time, as it is felt at the roots of human relations, with a sensitivity almost unrivaled." "Hemingway: Gauge of Morale," reprinted in McCaffrey, *Hemingway: The Man and His Work,* p. 230.
13. Cited in Baker, *Hemingway,* p. 160.
14. Ernest Hemingway, *A Farewell to Arms* (New York: Charles Scribner's Sons, 1929), p. 350.
15. Baker, *Hemingway,* p. 241.
16. Hemingway, *Stories,* p. 131.
17. The concept of life as play is to some degree implicit in the concept of a "code"

or "rituals" for dealing with experience. See Malcolm Cowley, "Nightmare and Ritual in Hemingway," in *Hemingway: A Collection of Critical Essays,* ed. Robert P. Weeks (Englewood Cliffs, N.J.: Prentice-Hall, 1962), p. 48. Jackson J. Benson, in *Hemingway: The Writer's Art of Self-Defence* (Minneapolis: University of Minnesota Press, 1969), sees the center of Hemingway's concept of tragedy in the conflict between the game man creates for himself and the game he is forced to play. Benson sees the concept of game, for Hemingway, as "A Structure for Emotional Control."

18. Emerson may have also intended an allusion to Schiller's celebrated statement, a touchstone of German Romanticism: "Man plays only when he is human, and he is truly human only when he is at play."
19. Like these contemporary European writers, Hemingway found European peasants and workers to have strong religious impulses but no confidence in their official church. Jake Barnes *(The Sun Also Rises),* the older waiter in "A Clean Well-Lighted Place," Anselmo *(For Whom the Bell Tolls),* and Santiago *(The Old Man and the Sea)* all want to pray and do pray even though they feel that the *words* of their prayers are meaningless. Hemingway repeatedly chose the titles of his works from a familiar religious text in order to convert the words of the text into an ironic social criticism.
20. Cf. Erik H. Erikson's observation, in *Insight and Responsibility* (New York: Norton, 1964), p. 99, "To fathom the limits of human existence, you must have fully experienced, at some concrete time and space, the 'rules of the game.'"
21. Johan Huizinger, *Homo Ludens: A Study in the Play-Element in Culture* (Boston: Beacon Press, Humanitas reprints), p. 27. The passage from Plato's *Laws,* VII, 803, is given by Huizinger (*Homo Ludens,* pp. 18–19) as follows: "I say that a man must be serious with the serious. God alone is worthy of supreme seriousness, but man is made God's plaything, and that is the best part of him. Therefore every man and woman should live life accordingly, and play the noblest games and be of another mind from what they are at present. . . . For they deem war a serious thing, though in war there is neither play nor culture worthy the name, which are the things *we* deem most serious. Hence all must live in peace as well as they possibly can. What, then, is the right way of living? Life must be lived as play, playing certain games, making sacrifices, singing and dancing, and then a man will be able to propitiate the gods, and defend himself against his enemies, and win the contest."
22. Reprinted as "Tuna Fishing in Spain" in *By-Line: Ernest Hemingway,* ed. William White (New York: Charles Scribner's Sons, 1967).
23. Ernest Hemingway, *Green Hills of Africa* (New York: Charles Scribner's Sons, 1935), pp. 148–50; Robert W. Lewis, Jr., in *Hemingway on Love* (Austin and London: University of Texas Press, 1965), finds that the "Gulf Stream Feeling" in *Green Hills of Africa* is a form of *agape.* In fact, Hemingway's "love" extended not only to the Masai hunters, but to their culture and their land. He writes: "I loved this country and felt at home . . ." (p. 191); "I would come back to where

it pleased me to live; to really live. Not just to let life pass. Our people went to America because that was the good place to go then. It had been a good country and we had made a bloody mess of it . . ." (p. 192).

Chapter 9. Henry Miller's Democratic Vistas

1. Henry Miller, *Black Spring* (New York: Grove Press, 1963), p. 52.
2. *The Michael Fraenkel—Henry Miller Correspondence called Hamlet,* 2 vols. (Paris-New York: Carrefour, 1939–41), pp. 264–65 (Apr. 1, 1937).
3. *Hamlet,* p. 265 (Apr. 1, 1937).
4. *Ibid.,* p. 383 (Oct. 17, 1938).
5. *Black Spring,* p. 113.
6. Henry James, *The American Scene* (London: Chapman and Hall, 1907), pp. 136–37.
7. *Black Spring,* pp. 115–16.
8. *Ibid.,* 114.
9. *Ibid.,* pp. 126–27.
10. Henry Miller, *The Colossus of Maroussi* (New York: New Directions, 1941), p. 51. See also *idem, Tropic of Capricorn* (New York: Grove Press, 1961), pp. 217–18; "A Bodhisattva Artist," in *Henry Miller Selected Prose,* 2 vols. (London: MacGibbon and Kee, 1965), 2: 322; *idem, Nexus* (New York: Grove Press, 1965), p. 214; *idem, Tropic of Cancer* (New York: Grove Press, 1961), p. 67; *idem, Plexus* (New York: Grove Press, 1965), p. 313; *Black Spring,* pp. 28–29, 192; *Hamlet,* p. 264.
11. *Black Spring,* p. 192.
12. *Plexus,* p. 563. Miller states that it was Du Bois who accepted and published his first article to appear in print (*Plexus,* p. 560).
13. William A. Gordon, *Writer & Critic* (Baton Rouge: Louisiana State University Press, 1968), pp. 43–44 (letter from Miller dated Aug. 27, 1966).
14. "The Absolute Collective," *Selected Prose,* 2: 279.
15. Annette Kar Baxter, *Henry Miller Expatriate* (Pittsburgh: University of Pittsburgh Press, 1961), pp. 103–4 (letter, Miller to Keyserling, Feb. 17, 1936).
16. Henry Miller, *The Time of Assassins* (New York: New Directions, 1956), p. 143.
17. See *Hamlet,* p. 170 (June 19, 1936).
18. *Capricorn,* p. 289.
19. *Cancer,* p. 68.
20. *Black Spring,* p. 189.
21. Henry Miller, "Glittering Pie," in *The Cosmological Eye* (New York: New Directions, 1939), p. 339.
22. "Good News! God is Love!" *Selected Prose,* 1: 108.
23. "Murder the Murderer," *Selected Prose,* 2: 425. See also *Plexus,* pp. 349–50.
24. *Nexus,* p. 304.
25. *Capricorn,* p. 43.

26. Henry Miller, "Raimu," in *The Wisdom of the Heart* (London: Editions Poetry London, 1947), p. 66.
27. Henry Miller, *Sexus* (New York: Grove Press, 1965), p. 161.
28. "Bufano, the Man of Hard Materials," in *Selected Prose,* 2: 361.
29. "A Bodhisattva Artist," in *Selected Prose,* 1: 321.
30. "Reunion in Barcelona," in *The Intimate Henry Miller,* ed. Alfred Perlès (New York: New Directions, 1939), p. 13.
31. *Nexus,* p. 272.
32. *Henry Miller Letters to Anaïs Nin,* ed. Gunther Stuhlman (New York: Putnam, 1965) (letter of Aug. 24, 1938).
33. *Hamlet,* p. 266 (Apr. 1, 1937); p. 130 (Feb. 15, 1936).
34. *Cancer,* pp. 93–94.
35. *Plexus,* p. 87.
36. *Sexus,* p. 265.
37. *Capricorn,* p. 120.
38. *Ibid.,* p. 145.
39. *Ibid.,* p. 285.
40. *Cancer,* p. 243.
41. Henry Miller, *The World of Sex* (New York: Grove Press, 1940), p. 86.
42. *The Intimate Henry Miller,* p. 135.
43. See, "When I Reach for My Revolver," in *Selected Prose,* 1: 377.
44. "Of Art and the Future," in *Sunday after the War, Selected Prose,* 1: 506.
45. "An Open Letter to Surrealists Everywhere," in *The Cosmological Eye,* p. 168.
46. Henry Miller, *Remember to Remember* (New York: New Directions, 1947), p. 28.
47. *Ibid.,* p. 156.
48. *Colossus of Maroussi,* p. 75.
49. *Cosmological Eye,* p. 160.
50. *Cancer,* p. 254.
51. "Stand Still Like a Humming-Bird," in *Selected Prose,* 1: 10.
52. *Hamlet,* p. 288 (Sept. 1937).
53. *Cosmological Eye,* p. 157.
54. *Ibid.,* pp. 151–52.
55. *Letters to Anaïs Nin,* pp. 336–37.
56. *Hamlet,* pp. 290–91 (Sept. 7, 1937).
57. *Remember to Remember,* p. 213.
58. *Ibid.,* esp. conclusion to the essay "Remember to Remember."
59. *Cosmological Eye,* p. 152.
60. *Sexus,* p. 260.
61. *Cosmological Eye,* p. 176.
62. See "Balzac and his Double," "Seraphita" and "Walt Whitman" in *Selected prose,* 2; see also *Lawrence Durrell and Henry Miller, A Private Correspondence,* ed. George Wickes (New York: Dutton, 1963), p. 153 (letter from Miller dated Apr. 1939).

63. Henry Miller, *The Books in My Life* (New York: New Directions, 1952), "Letter to Pierre Lesdain," p. 223.
64. *Ibid.,* p. 229.
65. *Ibid.,* "Jean Giono," p. 104.
66. *Cancer,* pp. 239–40.
67. *Books in My Life,* "Letter to Pierre Lesdain" (May 20, 1950), p. 253.

Chapter 10. Richard Wright: The Expatriate as Native Son

1. Richard Wright, *Black Boy* (New York: Harper and Brothers, 1945), p. 218.
2. *Ibid.,* p. 227.
3. Richard Wright, "I Tried To Be a Communist," *Atlantic Monthly* 184 (Aug.–Sept. 1944); reprinted in *The God That Failed,* ed. Richard Crossman (New York: Harper and Brothers, 1949), p. 121.
4. This statement formed part of the original *Black Boy* manuscript and is cited by Constance Webb in *Richard Wright* (New York: G. P. Putnam's Sons, 1968), p. 122.
5. Richard Wright, *12 Million Black Voices* (1941; reprinted New York: Arno Press and *The New York Times,* 1969), p. 30.
6. Richard Wright, "The Man Who Went to Chicago," in *Eight Men* (New York: Pyramid Books, 1969), p. 181.
7. *Black Voices,* p. 146.
8. See, for example, Saunders Redding, "The Alien Land of Richard Wright," in *Soon, One Morning,* ed. Herbert Hill (New York: Alfred A. Knopf, 1969).
9. *Black Boy,* p. 33.
10. *God That Failed,* p. 162.
11. *Eight Men,* pp. 192–93.
12. *Ibid.,* pp. 191–92.
13. Revised version published in *Cross-section 1944,* ed. Edwin Seaver; reprinted in *Eight Men.*
14. Richard Wright, "Introduction" to *Black Metropolis,* Horace Cayton and St. Clair Drake (New York: Harcourt, Brace, 1945).
15. See Webb, *Richard Wright,* p. 290.
16. Richard Wright, *The Outsider* (New York: Harper and Brothers, 1953), p. 123.
17. *Ibid.,* pp. 359–60.
18. *Ibid.,* p. 135.
19. *Ibid.,* p. 361.
20. *Ibid.,* p. 362.
21. Richard Wright, *Black Power* (New York: Harper and Brothers, 1954), p. 347. Numbers in parenthesis following a quotation refer to page numbers in this edition.
22. Cited in Webb, *Richard Wright,* p. 337.
23. Richard Wright, *The Color Curtain* (Cleveland: World, 1956), p. 55.

24. *Ibid.*, p. 140.
25. Richard Wright, *Pagan Spain* (New York: Harper and Brothers, 1957), p. 17.
26. *Ibid.*, p. 192.
27. *Ibid.*
28. *Ibid.*, p. 99.
29. *Ibid.*, p. 135.
30. Webb, *Richard Wright,* p. 64.
31. *Pagan Spain,* p. 237.
32. *Ibid.*, p. 138.

Chapter 11. James Baldwin: The View from Another Country

1. Quoted in Fern Marja Eckman, *The Furious Passage of James Baldwin* (New York: M. Evans & Co., 1966), p. 113.
2. James Baldwin, *Nobody Knows My Name* (New York: Dial Press, 1961), p. 75.
3. Eckman, *Baldwin,* p. 30.
4. *Nobody Knows My Name,* p. 149.
5. James Baldwin, *Notes of a Native Son* (Boston: Beacon Press, 1955), p. 158.
6. *Ibid.*, p. 122.
7. James Baldwin, *The Fire Next Time* (New York: Dial Press, 1963), p. 13.
8. *Nobody Knows My Name,* p. 113.
9. *Fire Next Time,* p. 71.
10. Quoted in "Disturber of the Peace: James Baldwin," *The Black American Writer,* ed. C. W. E. Bigsby (DeLand, Fla.: Everett/Edwards, 1969), p. 208.
11. James Baldwin, *Going To Meet the Man* (New York: Dial Press, 1965), p. 138.
12. *Fire Next Time,* p. 40.
13. *Notes of a Native Son,* p. 66.
14. Bronislaw Malinowski, *Sex, Culture, and Myth* (New York: Harcourt, Brace & World, 1962), pp. 112–13.
15. James Baldwin, "Notes for Blues," *Blues for Mister Charlie* (New York: Dial Press, 1964), p. 7.
16. *Nobody Knows My Name,* p. 99.
17. *Notes of a Native Son,* p. 137.
18. *Ibid.*, p. 21.
19. Eckman, *Baldwin,* p. 217.
20. Bigsby, *Black American Writer,* p. 200.
21. James Baldwin, *Tell Me How Long the Train's Been Gone* (New York: Dial Press, 1968), p. 144.
22. *Fire Next Time,* p. 79.
23. Bigsby, *Black American Writer,* p. 81.
24. Eckman, *Baldwin,* p. 154.

Selected Bibliography

Allen, Jerry. *The Adventures of Mark Twain.* Boston: Little, Brown, and Company, 1954.

Andrews, Kenneth R. *Nook Farm: Mark Twain's Hartford Circle.* Cambridge, Mass.: Harvard University Press, 1950.

Andrews, Wayne. *Architecture, Ambition, and Americans: A Social History of American Architecture.* New York: Free Press, 1964.

Baker, Carlos. *Hemingway: The Writer as Artist.* Princeton: Princeton University Press, 1963.

———. *Ernest Hemingway: A Life Story.* New York: Charles Scribner's Sons, 1969.

Baker, Paul R. *The Fortunate Pilgrims: Americans in Italy, 1800–1860.* Cambridge, Mass.: Harvard University Press, 1964.

Baldwin, James. *Go Tell It On the Mountain.* New York: Dial Press, 1954.

———. *Giovanni's Room.* New York: Dial Press, 1956.

———. *Another Country.* New York: Dial Press, 1960.

———. *Notes of a Native Son.* Boston: Beacon Press, 1955.

———. *Nobody Knows My Name.* New York: Dial Press, 1961.

———. *The Fire Next Time.* New York: Dial Press, 1963.

———. *Blues for Mister Charlie.* New York: Dial Press, 1964.

———. *Going To Meet the Man.* New York: Dial Press, 1965.

———. *Tell Me How Long the Train's Been Gone.* New York: Dial Press, 1968.

———. *The Amen Corner.* London: Michael Joseph, Ltd., 1969.

Baum, S. V., ed. *E. E. Cummings and the Critics.* East Lansing: Michigan State University Press, 1962.

Baxter, Annette Kar. *Henry Miller Expatriate.* Pittsburgh: University of Pittsburgh Press, 1961.

Beard, Charles A. and Beard, Mary R. *The American Spirit: A Study of the Idea of Civilization in the United States.* New York: Macmillan, 1942.

Beard, James Franklin, ed. *The Letters and Journals of James Fenimore Cooper.* 2 vols. Cambridge, Mass: The Belknap Press of Harvard University Press, 1960.

Bellamy, Gladys Carmen. *Mark Twain as a Literary Artist.* Norman: University of Oklahoma Press, 1950.

Benson, Jackson J. *Hemingway: The Writer's Art of Self-Defense.* Minneapolis: University of Minnesota Press, 1969.

Bewley, Marius. *The Complex Fate: Hawthorne, Henry James and Some Other American Writers,* 1952; New York: Gordian Press, 1967.

Bigsby, C. W. E., ed. *The Black American Writer.* vol. 1, Fiction. Deland, Fla.: Everett/Edwards, Inc., 1969.

Blackmur, Richard P. *A Primer of Ignorance.* New York: Harcourt, Brace, Jovanovich, 1967.

Blair, Walter. *Mark Twain & Huck Finn.* Berkeley and Los Angeles: University of California Press, 1960.

Bone, Robert. *Richard Wright.* Minneapolis: University of Minnesota Press, 1969.

Boorstin, Daniel J. *The Lost World of Thomas Jefferson.* New York: Henry Holt, 1948.

______. *America and the Image of Europe: Reflections on American Thought.* New York: Meridian Books, 1960.

______. *The Americans: The Colonial Experience.* New York: Random House, 1958.

______. *The Americans: The National Experience.* New York: Random House, 1965.

Branch, Edgar Marquess. *The Literary Apprenticeship of Mark Twain.* Urbana: University of Illinois Press, 1950.

Brignano, Russell Carl. *Richard Wright.* Pittsburgh: University of Pittsburgh Press, 1970.

Brogan, Denis W. *The American Character.* New York: Knopf, 1954.

Brooks, Van Wyck. *The Ordeal of Mark Twain.* New York, Dutton, 1920; rev. ed. Meridian Books, 1933.

———. *The Dream of Arcadia: American Writers and Artists in Italy, 1760–1915.* New York: Dutton, 1958.

Brown, Norman O. *Life Against Death: The Psychoanalytical Meaning of History.* Middletown, Conn.: Wesleyan University Press, 1959.

Bruckberger, R. L. *Image of America.* Paris: Librairie Gallimard, 1958; New York: Viking Press, 1964.

Canby, Henry Seidel. *Turn West, Turn East: Mark Twain and Henry James.* New York: Biblo and Tannen, 1951.

Cash, W. J. *The Mind of the South.* New York: Knopf, 1941.

Cayton, Horace and Drake, St. Clair. *Black Metropolis.* New York: Harcourt, Brace, 1945.

Chase, Richard. *Herman Melville.* New York: Macmillan, 1949.

———. *The American Novel and Its Tradition.* New York: Doubleday, 1957.

Commager, Henry Steele. *The American Mind: An Interpretation of American Thought and Character Since the 1880's.* New Haven: Yale University Press, 1950.

Cooper, James Fenimore. *The Works of James Fenimore Cooper.* 33 vols. Mohawk Edition. New York: Putnam's, 1895–1900.

———. (anonymous). *Notions of the Americans Picked up by a Travelling Bachelor.* 2 vols. London: H. Colburn, 1828.

———. *Recollections of Europe.* Paris: Baudry, 1837 [Published in America as *Gleanings in Europe*].

———. *The American Democrat.* New York: Vintage Books, 1956.

Cooper, James Fenimore [nephew], ed. *The Correspondence of James Fenimore Cooper.* 2 vols. New Haven: Yale University Press, 1929.

Cowley, Malcolm. *Exile's Return: A Literary Odyssey of the 1920's.* New York: Norton, 1934; new edition, Viking Press, 1951.

Cox, Harvey. *The Secular City.* New York: Macmillan, 1965.

Croly, Herbert. *The Promise of American Life.* New York: The Macmillan Company, 1909; E. P. Dutton, 1963.

Crossman, Richard, ed. *The God That Failed.* New York: Harper & Brothers, 1949.

Cummings, Edward Estlin. *The Enormous Room.* New York: The Modern Library, 1934.

______. *i: six non-lectures.* 1953; New York: Atheneum, 1962.

______. *Poems 1923–1954.* New York: Harcourt, Brace & World, 1954.

______. *Xaipe.* New York: Oxford University Press, 1950.

Curti, Merle E. *The Growth of American Thought.* New York: Harper & Row, 1943; 2nd. ed. 1951.

Davis, Merrell R. and Gilman, William H., eds. *The Letters of Herman Melville.* New Haven: Yale University Press, 1960.

Day, A. Grove, ed. *Mark Twain's Letters from Hawaii.* New York: Appleton & Century, 1966.

Degler, Carl N. *Out of Our Past: The Forces that Shaped Modern America.* rev. ed. New York: Harper & Row, 1959.

Denny, Margaret and Gilman, William H., eds. *The American Writer and the European Experience.* Minneapolis: University of Minnesota Press, 1950.

De Tocqueville, Alexis. *Democracy in America.* New York: Oxford University Press, 1947.

DeVoto, Bernard. *Mark Twain at Work.* Cambridge, Mass.: Harvard University Press, 1942.

Dickinson, Leon T. "Mark Twain's Revisions in Writing *The Innocents Abroad.*" *American Literature* 19 (May 1947): 139–57.

Dunbar, Ernest, ed. *The Black Expatriates.* New York: Dutton, 1968.

Earnest, Ernest. *Expatriates and Patriots: American Scholars, Artists and Writers in Europe.* Durham, N.C.: Duke University Press, 1968.

Eckman, Fern Marja. *The Furious Passage of James Baldwin.* New York: M. Evans, 1966.

Edel, Leon. *The Life of Henry James.* 5 vols. Philadelphia and New York: J. B. Lippincott, 1953–1971. *Henry James: The Untried Years (1843–1870).* 1953. *Henry James: The Conquest of London (1870–1881).* 1962. *Henry James: The Middle Years (1882–1895).* 1962. *Henry James: The Treacherous Years (1895–1901).* 1969. *Henry James: The Master (1901–1916).* 1971.

Ellison, Ralph. *Shadow and Act.* New York: Random House, 1964.

Erikson, Erik H. *Insight and Responsibility.* New York: Norton, 1964.

Fairbanks, Henry G. *The Lasting Loneliness of Nathaniel Hawthorne:*

A Study of the Sources of Alienation in Modern Man. Albany: Magi Books, Inc., 1965.

Fenton, Charles. *The Apprenticeship of Ernest Hemingway.* New York: Farrar, Straus & Cudahy, 1954.

Fiedler, Leslie A. *Love and Death in the American Novel.* New York: World, 1962.

Firmage, George J., ed. *E. E. Cummings: A Miscellany Revised.* New York: October House, Inc., n.d.

———. *E. E. Cummings: A Bibliography.* Middletown, Conn.: Wesleyan University Press, 1960.

Foner, Philip S. *Mark Twain: Social Critic.* New York: International Publishers, 1958.

Freud, Sigmund. *Civilization, War and Death.* New York: Hillary, 1953.

———. *Civilization and Its Discontents.* New York: Norton, 1962.

Friedman, Norman. *E. E. Cummings: The Growth of a Writer.* Carbondale, Ill.: Southern Illinois University Press, 1964.

Ganzel, Dewey. *Mark Twain Abroad: The Cruise of the Quaker City.* Chicago: University of Chicago Press, 1968.

Gaull, Marilyn. "Language and Identity: A Study of E. E. Cummings' *The Enormous Room.*" *American Quarterly* 19, no. 4 (Winter 1967): 645–62.

Gilman, William H. *Melville's Early Life and* Redburn. New York: New York University Press, 1951.

Gordon, William A. *The Mind and Art of Henry Miller.* Baton Rouge: Louisiana State University Press, 1967.

———. *Writer & Critic: A Correspondence with Henry Miller.* Baton Rouge: Louisiana State University Press, 1968.

Grossman, James. *James Fenimore Cooper.* New York: William Sloane Associates, 1949.

Grund, Francis. *Aristocracy in America.* New York: Harper Torch Books, 1959.

Guillet, Edwin C. *The Great Migration.* New York: T. Nelson, 1937.

Hall, Lawrence Sargent. *Hawthorne: Critic of Society.* New Haven: Yale University Press, 1944.

Handlin, Oscar. *The Uprooted.* Boston: Little, Brown, and Company, 1951.

______ and Burchard, John, eds. *The Historian and the City*. Cambridge, Mass.: M.I.T. Press, 1963.

Hansen, Marcus Lee. *The Atlantic Migration 1607–1860*. Cambridge, Mass.: Harvard University Press, 1940.

______. *The Immigrant in American History*. Cambridge, Mass.: Harvard University Press, 1942.

Hart, James D. "Hawthorne's Italian Diary." *American Literature* 34, no. 4 (Jan. 1963): 562–67.

Hartz, Louis. *The Liberal Tradition in America: An Interpretation of American Political Thought Since the Revolution*. New York: Harcourt, Brace & World, 1955.

Hassan, Ihab. *Radical Innocence: The Contemporary American Novel*. Princeton: Princeton University Press, 1961.

______. *The Literature of Silence: Henry Miller and Samuel Beckett*. New York: Random House, 1967.

Hawthorne, Mrs. *Notes in England and Italy*. New York: Putnam, 1869.

Hawthorne, Nathaniel. *The Complete Works of Nathaniel Hawthorne*. 13 vols. The Riverside Edition. George Parsons Lathrop, ed. Boston and New York: Houghton, Mifflin, 1882–1883.

______. *The Centenary Edition of the Works of Nathaniel Hawthorne*. William Charvat *et al.*, eds. Columbus, Ohio: Ohio State University Press, 1962–

______. *English Notebooks*. Randall Steward, ed. New York: Russell, 1962 (reprint of 1941).

Hemingway, Ernest. *The Torrents of Spring: A Romantic Novel in Honor of the Passing of a Great Race*. New York: Charles Scribner's Sons, 1926.

______. *The Fifth Column and the First Forty-nine Stories*. New York: Charles Scribner's Sons, 1939.

______. *The Sun Also Rises*. New York: Charles Scribner's Sons, 1926.

______. *Men Without Women*. New York: Charles Scribner's Sons, 1927.

______. *A Farewell to Arms*. New York: Charles Scribner's Sons, 1929.

______. *Death in the Afternoon*. New York: Charles Scribner's Sons, 1932.

———. *Winner Take Nothing.* New York: Charles Scribner's Sons, 1933.

———. *To Have and Have Not.* New York: Charles Scribner's Sons, 1937.

———. *Green Hills of Africa.* New York: Charles Scribner's Sons, 1935.

———. *For Whom the Bell Tolls.* New York: Charles Scribner's Sons, 1940.

———. *Across the River and Into the Trees.* New York: Charles Scribner's Sons, 1950.

———. *The Old Man and the Sea.* New York: Charles Scribner's Sons, 1952.

———. *A Moveable Feast.* New York: Charles Scribner's Sons, 1964.

———. *Islands in the Stream.* New York: Charles Scribner's Sons, 1970.

Hemingway, Leicester. *My Brother, Ernest Hemingway.* New York: World, 1961.

Hill, Herbert, ed. *Soon, One Morning: New Writing by American Negroes, 1940–1962.* New York: Knopf, 1963.

Hoffman, Frederick J. *The Mortal No: Death and the Modern Imagination.* Princeton: Princeton University Press, 1964.

———. *The Twenties: American Writing in the Postwar Decade.* rev. ed. New York: The Free Press, 1965.

Hofstadter, Richard. *The American Political Tradition and the Men Who Made It.* New York: Knopf, 1948.

House, Kay Seymour. *Cooper's Americans.* Columbus, Ohio: Ohio State University Press, 1965.

Hovey, Richard B. *Hemingway: The Inward Terrain.* Seattle: University of Washington Press, 1968.

Howard, Leon. *Herman Melville: A Biography.* Berkeley and Los Angeles: University of California Press, 1951.

Howells, William Dean. *My Mark Twain.* New York: 1910.

Huizinga, Johan. *Homo Ludens: A Study of the Play-Element in Culture.* Boston: Beacon Press, Humanitas reprints, 1950.

James, Henry. *The Novels and Tales of Henry James.* The New York Edition. 26 vols. New York: Charles Scribner's Sons, 1907–1917.

———. *A Small Boy and Others.* New York: Charles Scribner's Sons, 1913.

______. *Notes of a Son and Brother.* New York: Charles Scribner's Sons, 1914.

______. *The Middle Years.* London: W. Collins, 1917.

______. *The American Scene.* London: Chapman and Hall, 1907.

Jones, Howard Mumford. *Ideas in America.* Cambridge, Mass.: Harvard University Press, 1945.

______. *Jeffersonianism and the American Novel.* New York: Teachers College Press, Teachers College, Columbia University, 1966.

Kaplan, Justin. *Mr. Clemens and Mark Twain: A Biography.* New York: Simon and Schuster, 1966.

Killinger, John. *Hemingway and the Dead Gods: A Study in Existentialism.* Lexington: University Press of Kentucky, 1960.

Levy, Leo B. "*The Marble Faun:* Hawthorne's Landscape of the Fall." *American Literature* 42, no. 2 (May 1970): 139–56.

Lewis, Richard W. B. *The American Adam: Innocence, Tragedy, and Tradition in the Nineteenth Century.* Chicago: University of Chicago Press, 1955.

Lewis, Robert W. Jr. *Hemingway On Love.* Austin: University of Texas Press, 1965.

Leyda, Jay. *The Melville Log.* New York: Harcourt & Brace, 1951.

Lowenfels, Walter. "Unpublished Preface to *Tropic of Cancer.*" *Massachusetts Review* 5 (Spring 1964): 481–91.

Lubbock, Percy, ed. *The Letters of Henry James.* New York: Charles Scribner's Sons, 1920.

Lynd, Staughton. *Intellectual Origins of American Radicalism.* New York: Random House, Pantheon, 1968.

MacShane, Frank, ed. *The American in Europe: A Collection of Impressions by Americans Written from the 17th Century to the Present.* New York: Dutton, 1965.

Marcuse, Herbert. *One Dimensional Man.* Boston: Beacon Press, 1964.

______. *Eros and Civilization: A Philosophical Inquiry into Freud.* Boston: Beacon Press, 1955.

Marks, Barry A. *E. E. Cummings.* New York: Twayne, 1964.

Martin, Jay. *Harvests of Change: American Literature 1865–1914.* Englewood Cliffs, N.J.: Prentice-Hall, 1967.

Matthiessen, F. O. and Murdoch, K. B., eds. *The Notebooks of Henry James.* New York: Oxford University Press, 1947.

May, Henry T. *The End of American Innocence: A Study of the First Years of Our Own Time 1912–1917.* New York: Knopf, 1959.

McCaffery, John K. M., ed. *Ernest Hemingway The Man and His Work.* New York: World, 1950.

McCall, Dan. *The Example of Richard Wright.* New York: Harcourt, Brace, Jovanovich, 1969.

McCarthy, Harold T. *Henry James: The Creative Process.* New York: Fairleigh-Dickinson University Press, 1968.

McCloskey, John C. "Mark Twain as Critic in *The Innocents Abroad.*" *American Literature* 25, no. 2 (May 1953).

McKeithan, Daniel Morley, ed. *Traveling with the Innocents Abroad: Mark Twain's Original Reports from Europe and the Holy Land.* Norman: University of Oklahoma Press, 1958.

Melville, Herman. *The Complete Writings of Herman Melville.* The Northwestern-Newberry edition. Hayford, Harrison *et al.,* eds. Chicago and Evanston: Northwestern University Press and the Newberry Library, 1968–

———. *The Works of Herman Melville* 16 vols. The Standard Edition. Raymond M. Weaver, ed. London, 1922–1924. Reissued, New York: Russell and Russell, Inc., 1963.

Metcalf, Eleanor Melville, ed. *Journal of a Visit to London and the Continent by Herman Melville.* Cambridge, Mass.: Harvard University Press, 1948.

Meyers, Marvin. *The Jacksonian Persuasion: Politics and Belief.* New York: Random House, 1960.

Miller, Henry. *Black Spring.* New York: Grove Press, 1963.

———. *The Michael Fraenkel-Henry Miller Correspondence Called Hamlet.* 2 vols. New York and Paris: Carrefour, 1939–1941.

———. *The Colossus of Maroussi.* New York: New Directions, 1941.

———. *Tropic of Cancer.* New York: Grove Press, 1961.

———. *Tropic of Capricorn.* New York: Grove Press, 1961.

———. *The Time of Assassins: A Study of Rimbaud.* New York: New Directions, 1956.

———. *Henry Miller: Selected Prose.* 2 vols. London: MacGibbon and Kee, 1965.

———. *Quiet Days in Clichy.* New York: Grove Press, 1965.

———. *Sexus.* New York: Grove Press, 1965.

———. *Plexus.* New York: Grove Press, 1965.

———. *Nexus.* New York: Grove Press, 1965.

———. *The Air-Conditioned Nightmare.* New York: New Directions, 1970.

———. *The Cosmological Eye.* New York: New Directions, 1939.

———. *The Wisdom of the Heart.* London: Editions Poetry London, 1947.

———. *The World of Sex.* New York: Grove Press, 1940.

———. *Remember to Remember.* New York: New Directions, 1947.

———. *The Books in My Life.* New York: New Directions, 1952.

———. *Big Sur and the Oranges of Hieronymous Bosch.* New York: New Directions, 1964.

Montgomery, Constance Cappel. *Hemingway in Michigan.* New York: Fleet, 1966.

Neider, Charles, ed. *The Autobiography of Mark Twain.* New York: Harper & Row, 1959.

Norman, Charles. *The Magic-Maker: E. E. Cummings.* New York: Duell, Sloan, and Pearce, 1958.

Nuhn, Ferner. *The Wind Blew From the East: A Study in the Orientation of American Culture.* Port Washington, N.Y.: Kennikat, 1942.

Olmstead, Clifton E. *Religion in America: Past and Present.* Englewood Cliffs, N.J.: Prentice-Hall, 1961.

Paine, Albert Bigelow, ed. *Mark Twain's Letters.* 2 vols. New York: Harper & Brothers, 1917.

———. *Mark Twain: A Biography.* 3 vols. New York: Harper & Brothers, 1912.

Parkes, Henry Bamford. *The American Experience: An Interpretation of the History and Civilization of the American People.* New York: Knopf, 1947.

Perlès, Alfred, ed. *The Intimate Henry Miller.* New York: New Directions, 1939.

Persons, Stow. *American Minds: A History of Ideas.* New York: Holt, Rinehart, Winston, 1958.

Rossiter, Clinton L. *Seedtime of the Republic.* 3 vols. New York: Harcourt, Brace, and Jovanovich, 1953.

Salomon, Roger B. *Twain and the Image of History.* New Haven: Yale University Press, 1961.

Sanford, Charles L. ed. *Quest for America 1810–1824.* Garden City, N. Y.: Doubleday, 1964.

Schlesinger, Arthur M. Jr. *The Age of Jackson.* Boston: Little, Brown, 1945.

Scott, Arthur L. "*The Innocents Abroad* Revalued." *Western Humanities Review* 7 (Summer 1953): 215–23.

———. "Mark Twain Looks at Europe," *South Atlantic Quarterly,* vol. 52 (July, 1953), 399–413.

———. "Mark Twain's Revisions of *The Innocents Abroad* for the British Edition of 1872." *American Literature,* vol. 25 (March, 1953), 43–61.

———, ed. *Mark Twain: Selected Criticism.* Dallas: Southern Methodist University Press, 1955.

Scrimgeour, Gary J. "*The Marble Faun:* Hawthorne's Faery Land." *American Literature* 36, no. 3 (November 1964): 271–87.

Shain, Charles E. "The Journal of the *Quaker City* Captain." *New England Quarterly* 28, no. 3 (Sept. 1955): 388–97.

Smith, David E. "*The Enormous Room* and *The Pilgrim's Progress.*" *Twentieth Century Literature* 11, no. 2 (July 1965): 67–75.

Smith, Henry Nash. *Mark Twain's Fable of Progress: Political and Economic Ideas in* A Connecticut Yankee. New Brunswick, N.J.: Rutgers University Press, 1964.

———. *Mark Twain: The Development of a Writer.* Cambridge, Mass.: Harvard University Press, 1962.

———, ed. *Mark Twain of the Enterprise: Newspaper Articles and Other Documents 1862–1864.* Berkeley and Los Angeles: University of California Press, 1957.

Smith, Julian. "Christ Times Four: Hemingway's Unknown Spanish Civil War Stories." *Arizona Quarterly* 25, no. 1 (Spring 1969): 5–17.

Smith, James Ward and Jamison, A. Leland, eds. *The Shaping of American Religion.* Princeton: Princeton University Press, 1961.

Sperry, Willard L. *Religion in America.* New York: Macmillan, 1946.

Spiller, Robert E. *Fenimore Cooper, Critic of His Times.* New York: Minton, Balch, 1931.

Stein, William Bysshe. "Ritual in Hemingway's 'Big Two-Hearted River.'" *Texas Studies in Lit. and Lang.* 1, no. 4 (Winter 1960): 555–61.

Stewart, Randall. *The English Notebooks of Nathaniel Hawthorne.* New York: Russell and Russell, 1941; reprinted 1962.

______. *Nathaniel Hawthorne: A Biography.* New Haven: Yale University Press, 1948.

Stone, Albert E. Jr. *The Innocent Eye: Childhood in Mark Twain's Imagination.* New Haven: Yale University Press, 1961.

Strout, Cushing. *The American Image of the Old World.* New York: Harper & Row, 1963.

Stuhlman, Gunther, ed. *Henry Miller's Letters to Anaïs Nin.* New York: Putnam, 1965.

Taylor, William R. *Cavalier and Yankee: The Old South and American National Character.* New York: Braziller, 1961.

Ticknor, Caroline. *Hawthorne and His Publisher.* Port Washington, N.Y.: Kennikat Press, 1969.

Tillich, Paul. *The Religious Situation.* New York: Henry Holt, 1932.

Trollope, Mrs. Frances. *Domestic Manners of the Americans.* New York: Knopf, 1949.

Twain, Mark. *Letters from the Sandwich Islands.* San Francisco: Grabhorn Press, 1937.

______. *The Writings of Mark Twain.* 25 vols. The Uniform Authorized Edition. New York: Harper and Brothers, 1899–1910.

Waggoner, Hyatt H. *Hawthorne: A Critical Study.* Cambridge, Mass: Harvard University Press, 1955.

Walker, Warren S. *James Fenimore Cooper: An Introduction and Interpretation.* New York: Barnes and Noble, 1962.

Warner, W. Lloyd. *American Life: Dream and Reality.* rev. ed. Chicago: University of Chicago Press, 1962.

Webb, Constance. *Richard Wright: A Biography.* New York: Putnam's, 1968.

Wecter, Dixon. *Sam Clemens of Hannibal.* Boston: Houghton, Mifflin, 1952.

______, ed. *Mark Twain to Mrs. Fairbanks.* San Marino, Calif.: Huntington Library, 1949.

______, ed. *The Love Letters of Mark Twain.* New York: Harper & Brothers, 1949.

Weeks, Robert P., ed. *Hemingway: A Collection of Critical Essays.* New York: Prentice-Hall, 1962.

Wegelin, Christof. *The Image of Europe in Henry James.* Dallas: Southern Methodist University Press, 1958.

Wegner, Robert E. *The Poetry and Prose of E. E. Cummings.* New York: Harcourt, Brace and World, 1965.

Weimer, David R. *The City as Metaphor.* New York: Random House, 1966.

White, William, ed. *By-Line: Ernest Hemingway.* New York: Scribner, 1967.

———, ed. *Studies in* The Sun Also Rises. Columbus, Ohio: Merrill, 1969.

Whitman, Walt. *Complete Poetry and Selected Prose,* James E. Miller, Jr., ed. Boston: Houghton, Mifflin, 1959.

Wickes, George. *Lawrence Durrell and Henry Miller, A Private Correspondence.* New York: Dutton, 1963.

———, ed. *Henry Miller and the Critics.* Carbondale: Southern Illinois University Press, 1963.

Wright, Richard. *Uncle Tom's Children.* New York: Harper & Brothers, 1940.

———. *Native Son.* New York: Harper & Brothers, 1940.

———. *12 Million Black Voices.* 1941; reprinted, New York: Arno Press and *The New York Times,* 1969.

———. *Black Boy.* New York: Harper & Brothers, 1945.

———. *The Outsider.* New York: Harper & Brothers, 1953.

———. *Black Power: A Record of Reactions in a Land of Pathos.* New York: Harper & Brothers, 1954.

———. *The Color Curtain: A Report on the Bandung Conference.* New York: World, 1956.

———. *Pagan Spain.* New York: Harper & Brothers, 1957.

———. *White Man, Listen!.* New York: Doubleday, 1957.

———. *The Long Dream.* Garden City, N.Y.: Doubleday, 1958.

———. *Eight Men.* New York: World, 1961.

———. *Lawd Today.* New York: Walker, 1963.

Young, Philip. *Ernest Hemingway: A Reconsideration.* University Park: Pennsylvania State University Press, 1966.

Index